SWĀ'

(Bliss of the Self)

A commentary on
Bhagavan Sri Ramana Maharshi's
Uḷḷadu Nārpadu

By

Sri Ramanacharanatirtha
Nochur Venkataraman

Sri Ramanasramam
Tiruvannamalai - 606603, INDIA
2016

SWĀTMASUKHI (Bliss of the Self) - English
Commentary by
Sri Ramanacharanatirtha Nochur Venkataraman
on
Bhagavan Sri Ramana Maharshi's Uḷḷadu Nārpadu

CC No. 1170

ISBN: 978-81-8288-248-5

First Edition: 2016 - 2000 Copies

Price: ₹ 120/-

Published by
V.S. Ramanan
President
Sri Ramanasramam
Tiruvannamalai - 606603
Tamil Nadu, INDIA

Email: ashram@gururamana.org
Website: www.sriramanamaharshi.org

Printed by
sri bharathi printers
Bengaluru - 560079

Preface

Uḷḷadu Nārpadu contains the essence of Sri Bhagavan Ramana Maharshi's teaching. It is indeed the most comprehensive guide for a seeker to do *Atmavichara.* This one book is enough for a Sadhaka to absorb Sri Bhagavan's teaching. This indeed can be called as *'Ramanopanishad'.* Upanishad means *jnana* or *Brahma-vidya.* In that sense this is the Upanishad of Sri Ramana. It shines as the Sun amongst the stars of many Vedantic works in its presentation of perfect knowledge of the Atman. Sri Bhagavan wrote many works while living in the caves and Skandasramam on the hill before he descended to the valley of Arunachala. Most of these works were written by Bhagavan compelled by the prayers of devotees. Uḷḷadu Nārpadu is the fruit of Muruganar Swami's prayer. This work Uḷḷadu Nārpadu was written by Bhagavan in 1928 and was first published in 1931. The Tamil metre used in these forty verses is venba. The tongalor piece of sentence connecting one verse with the other makes it kali venba which makes the 42 verses as one single whole. When chanted in chorus it very much resembles the Vedic chanting.

'Swatmasukhi' means 'the bliss of Self'. This is an elaborate commentary on Uḷḷadu Nārpadu. The supplement to Uḷḷadu Nārpadu which consists mostly of translations done by Bhagavan from Sanskrit are not included in this work, Swatmasukhi. This commentary has already been published in Malayalam and Tamil. Now we are releasing this classic work in English.

Our thanks to Smt. Vasanthi Murali, Smt. Jayasri Sukumaran, Smt. Meera Karthik and Sri Chandra Bhasi for the help rendered by them in editing this work. Our thanks and pranams to respected Sri KVS who wrote the foreword to the book.

Publishers
Sri Ramanasramam

Foreword

At the end of his spellbinding first sermon at Sarnath near Kasi, Bhagavan Buddha was asked by some of the astounded listeners if he was an Avatar (incarnation). He said 'No'. To other such queries, he replied 'I don't know'. They then asked the noble one: 'Then, Sir, who are you?'. He said 'Buddhoham' (I am Awakened).

Of Bhagavan Ramana too, we can only say that he was Buddha, the Awakened One. All we have to do is to wake up like him and be free from all that we have conjured up in our sleep of ignorance. Indeed, there was not a single moment when Bhagavan was not in the perfect jnani's state of jagrat sushupti, the super wakeful-sleep state. This book Swatmasukhi, is a commentary on Sri Bhagavan's 'Ulladu Naarpadu' (Forty Verses on Reality) which is the perfect Science of Awakening, of Self-knowledge, of realizing one's true identity as the Self.

Bhagavan Ramana is unique in being everyone's swaroopa. He ever shines as the pure, non-dual essence, the egoless, the otherless One Reality which is our own true nature. Poet-devotee Sri Muruganar, in the thirtieth concluding verse which he added to Sri Bhagavan's Upadesa Undiyaar (Spiritual Instructions) aptly refers to Bhagavan as 'Taanaam Ramanesan', Ramana the Self.

Sri Bhagavan Ramana was essentially a silent Master. However, for our sake, he has graced us with some written works of which 'Naan Yaar?' (Who Am I?)

in prose and 'Ulladu Naarpadu' in verse occupy a special place as seminal works as the complete science of Self-knowledge.'Ulladu Naarpadu' is a mirror in which we can see our own true form. Each word of the Forty Verses has the power to awaken us to Reality if studied with total attention and assimilated.

One look of Bhagavan made the ripe fruit, that Mastan Saheb, the Muslim weaver of Desur, was, in Bhagavan's own words, fall fulfilled. Out of Bhagavan's few hundreds of words flowed many thousands of words of praise and exegesis from the inspired pen of Poet Muruganar. One word 'Iru' (Be, stay) changed the life of Ramaswamy who became Thinnai Swami. Sri Bhagavan made garrulous people reticent, mute people eloquent. It was all the alchemy of his Grace and their total devotion. The River of his Grace is a perennial one and it is for us to get into it and join those blessed devotees. This book is a great help in enabling us to do that.

Clear, elaborate, very helpful commentaries have been written on 'Ulladu Naarpadu' and its Sanskrit rendering 'Sat Darsanam' by fortunate devotees like Muruganar, Sadhu Om, Lakshmana Sarma and Kanakammal who spent their days in the sacred presence of Bhagavan and by scholarly devotees like T.M.P. Mahadevan who often came for Bhagavan's darsan. Besides, as Dr Mees (Sadhu Ekarasa), the Dutch philosopher-devotee wrote, Bhagavan does not need interpreters; his own words are enough. Hence, those, who have not yet had a chance to listen to the discourses of Nochur Venkataraman, might naturally ask what significant new insights can be offered, especially by such a young man. Though the best answer to this query is 'Read the book and see for yourself', the following observations may be of help.

Venkataraman is one of those blessed ones who were caught young in Bhagavan's net of grace. He was barely thirteen when he heard of Bhagavan and the Name cast a spell on him, and from the age of eighteen he started discoursing on Bhagavan's teachings, first in Malayalam, then in his mother-tongue Tamil and then in English. He is an unusually brilliant young man and lightning-quick on the uptake. His memory is incredible and he is endowed with an extraordinarily clear vision of the Vedantic truth, deeply read in almost every Vedantic work in Sanskrit and many in Tamil and Malayalam and has a great capacity to communicate to large audiences in three languages with astonishing lucidity. He is totally devoted to Bhagavan whose life and teachings have proved to be the jnaanaanjana (the ointment of knowledge) which have opened his eyes of wisdom. He treats every word of Bhagavan as a taaraka mantra (liberating mantra) and seems to have done a great deal of nididhyaasana (deep contemplation) on his words. Often, he devotes a whole discourse to the explanation of a single word, phrase or line of Bhagavan. Above all, he is totally mindful in living by the words of Bhagavan. Even when he scintillates on the dais, he seems impersonal and at other times he is silent to a fault. He is blissfully bereft of even legitimate pride. He speaks and writes much more from actual experience than from his prodigious erudition and memory.

Venkataraman's credentials for writing this very important book, therefore, are impeccable. Anyway, the proof of the pudding is in the eating. So, eat and be thrilled. Better still, be eaten and be blessed for, as Bhagavan says in verse 21 of Ulladu Naarpadu: "How may one see God? To see Him is to be consumed by Him."

KVS
Sri Ramanasramam

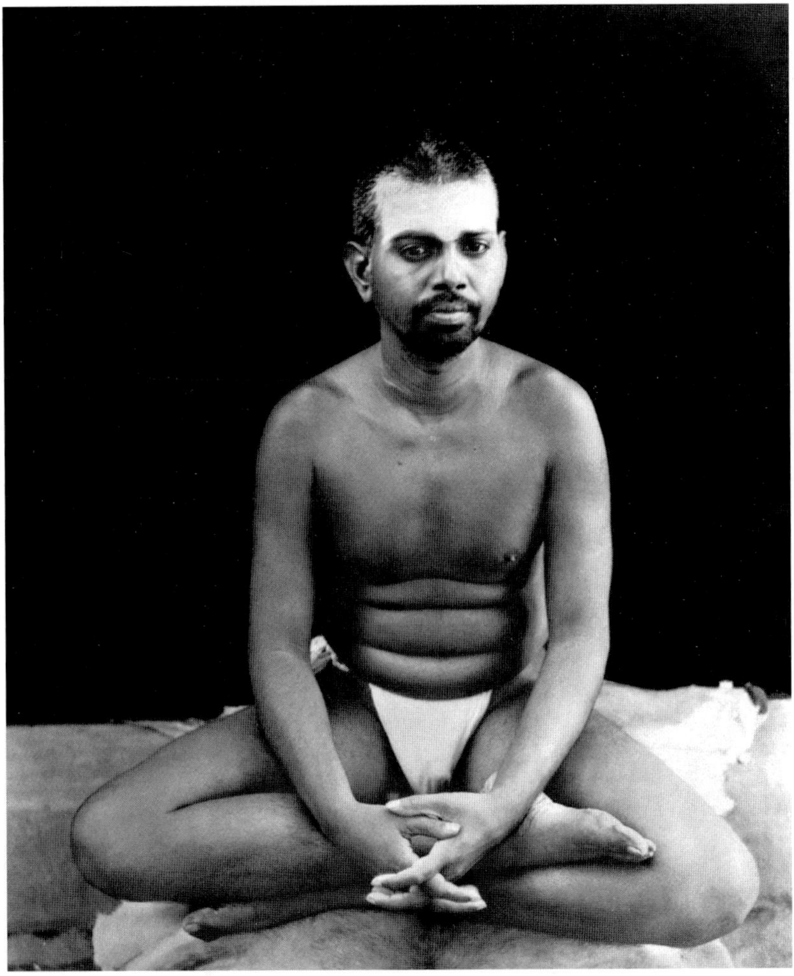

MAṄGAḶĀCHARAṆA--VEṆBĀ *

uḷḷa-dala duḷḷa-vuṇar vuḷḷadō vuḷḷa-poru
ḷuḷḷa-laṛa vuḷḷattē yuḷḷa-dā—luḷḷa-menu
muḷḷa-poru ḷuḷḷaleva nuḷḷattē yuḷḷa-paḍi
yuḷḷadē yuḷḷa luṇar-vāyē

uḷḷadu aladu uḷḷa uṇarvu uḷḷadō!	Can there be an experience of existence as 'I AM' without the existence of 'That which is', the beingness?
uḷḷa poruḷ	that reality, the *sat*, 'That which is'
uḷḷattē uḷḷal aṛa uḷḷadāl	is in the heart devoid of thoughts - beyond the current of becoming
uḷḷam enum uḷḷaporuḷ uḷḷal evan?	Who is the one that can limit that reality - which is called the 'heart' - with the mind and meditate?
uḷḷattē uḷḷa-paḍi	as it is in the heart
uḷḷadē uḷḷal	to abide thus is realization
uṇarvāyē	know this

* Invocatory Verse

Paraphrase:

Can there be an experience of existence as 'I AM' without the existence of 'That which is', the beingness? That reality, the *sat*, 'That which is' is in the heart devoid of thoughts (beyond the current of becoming) is known as heart. Who is the one that can limit 'That' with the mind and meditate? Know that to abide as 'That' in the heart is realization.

Commentary

The word *uḷḷadu* means 'That which Is' - the *sat* in Sanskrit. Sri Bhagavan has composed this *maṅgaḷa veṇba* using the single word, *uḷḷadu*. This work which contains forty two verses is an Upanishad that starts with the most auspicious word *uḷḷadu* and ends in the last verse with the word *uṇar* (be aware). Thus this scripture, in essence, gives us the message: 'Be aware of the truth'. *Ātmānubhūti* is the fruit of listening *(śravaṇa)* to this teaching from a realized Master. Some devotees like Muruganar and Lakshmana Sarma were blessed to listen to this directly from Bhagavan Ramana himself.

Everyone experiences one's own existence as 'I am'. 'I am' itself is the very centre of all experiences. It is of the nature of pure awareness. This awareness alone can be referred to as 'experience' - *anubhava*. In Vedanta, 'I' is another name for *anubhava* (experience) and all sensory perceptions are *pratibhāsa* (appearance). *Aham* (I am) is 'experience' and *idam* (this) is 'perception'. *Uḷḷa-daladu uḷḷa-uṇarvu uḷḷadō!* - What else other than the Self *(sad-vastu)* can have the awareness 'I am'? This one statement can put the mind into the state of realization. 'I is realization', 'Existence is realization' are other such 'Words made of light' that Bhagavan has given to devotees in the Talks.

The mind or the senses are not needed for one to be conscious of one's own existence as 'I am'. The awareness that shines forth as 'I' 'I' is self-effulgent – *swayamprakāśa*. The experience of 'I am' is self-evident to anyone even in a dark room. To know whether there are others around, it is necessary to use the sense organs such as the eyes and ears. The one and only experience that can be had directly, without using the senses, is the awareness 'I am'. This immediate experience or awareness is itself Brahman - this is the revelation of the Upanishads - *yassākṣād aparōkṣād Brahma* (Br. Up.) (*Parōkṣam* - that which is hidden; which is beyond the reach of the senses. *Aparōkṣam* - that which is never hidden; that which exists here and now as the truth. It is too subtle to be grasped by the senses, though nearer than all things.)

Uḷḷattē uḷḷa-laṛa uḷḷa-dāl - Darkness cannot exist in the Sun. Similarly the mind cannot exist in the Atman. Mind is the *uḷḷal,* the shadow that is born as a result of inattention or unawareness of the Self. When attention is focused on the Self, the mind vanishes; when attention is directed outward, the mind becomes activated. This force alternating between the centre and the circumference is the mind. This strange play of *śakti* (*vidyā-avidyā swarūpiṇī*) reveals the Self when centered in the heart and projects the world when estranged from the heart. Centre is another name for the Self. To be centered is to experience the Self. When someone questioned Bhagavan about his central teaching he replied "Centre itself is my central teaching". Here *uḷḷam* means centre. In the centre the mind cannot survive; hence *uḷḷal aṛa.*

How can one grasp by means of the mind, this immeasurable reality which is simple existence or beingness? Who is the knower? *Uḷḷal evan?* 'How can one know the knower?' - *vijñātāram arē kēna vijānīyāt* - remarks the Brihadaranyaka Upanishad. 'To be That' is to realize it. To simply stay in the 'I am' or pure existence is itself the path as well as the goal. Bhagavan addresses Arunachala as *irundoḷir*[1] in Arunachala Ashtakam. *Irundu* (*iruppu*) in Tamil means 'beingness' or existence (i.e. the *'sat'* in Sanskrit), *oḷir* (*oḷi*) means 'to shine forth' or 'effulgence' (i.e. the *'chit'* in Sanskrit). *Satvabhāsikā chit kvavētarā?* - Where is another light that can illumine existence? Existence itself is light says Bhagavan in Upadesa Saram.

Just as it is impossible to acquire knowledge about external objects without employing the mind, it is equally impossible to realize one's own Self, the *swarūpa,* with the operation of the mind. Still we do need to use the mind. Knowingly it has to subside in the Self. Convinced beyond all doubt that one's own Self is Existence-Consciousness-Bliss, one must simply abide in the Self. Such conscious abidance alone will release one from all contact-born sufferings. Let the

---

[1] *irundu-oḷir; iruppu—sat* or Existence; *oḷir—chit* or Consciousness.

thought waves that rise in the mind move like clouds in the sky. 'I am not the clouds but their substratum, the space is I am' - firmly abide in this conviction[2]. Abide in this state effortlessly. The more effort you make, the more the ego is activated. As long as there is this movement of the ego, there will also be contact with *prakṛti,* the field of suffering. Bhagavan says *uḷḷal aṛa. Uḷḷal* means the movement of the ego that shines with the borrowed light of the *sat-chit,* the Atman and thereby appears to be 'real'. Its constant character is "I am this, I am that, I will become this, I will become that" and so on. When this *uḷḷal* subsides (see v. 27, *nān udiyāduḷḷa nilai)* the Self shines forth. It is true that even when *uḷḷal* - the ego - is there, the Self which is existence, consciousness and peace, shines as its *adhiṣṭhāna* (substratum). Since the attention is devoured by this *uḷḷal* (the becoming), *uḷḷadu* (the being) is not experienced as it is.

Know that none of the perceived objects ranging from the ego to the body is the real 'I'. Leave aside even this knowledge and just be aware 'I am'. Hold on to the simple existence which is the substratum of everything. Be absolutely still, just 'Be'. In that silence the intuitive experience of the Self will arise from the depth. Sri Bhagavan's oft-repeated teaching to many of his devotees was *chumma iru* - Be still. In Aksharamanamalai Bhagavan reveals that Arunachala

---

[2] "A strong conviction is necessary that I am the Self, transcending the mind and the phenomena.... Hold the Self even during mental activities..... All that is necessary is the stern belief that you are the Self." – Talks - 406

transmitted this teaching directly to him. In stillness alone will you come to know that, which is beyond mind. Such effortless awareness is known as *asparśayōga,* the *samādhi* untouched by the mind. This is a state where the *tripuṭi* - threefold knot - meditation, meditator and object of meditation - is silent. *Pratyabhijña* - the intuitive recognition of the Self - alone prevails here. Peace here is the very nature of the Self. Peace that is touched by the ego is fleeting. It comes and goes. It is a temporary state of yoga that occurs when the mind is stilled through some practice. It comes, stays and leaves - *yōgōhi prabhavāpyayau* - says Kathopanishad; but *jnana,* the awareness of the Self, remains constant.

In *jnana*, the mind is not just controlled; it is completely abandoned. An illusion can be destroyed only by ignoring it. You ignore it by knowing its illusory nature. The water in the mirage need not be dried out; it can only be ignored as unreal. One should turn the attention away from the *upādhi* (body-mind equipment) and firmly fix it in the pure awareness 'I am'. One needs to reject the characteristics of the body-mind, knowing them as dream-like and rest in the heart. This is what is meant by *uḷḷattē uḷḷapaḍi uḷḷal* (to abide in the heart as it is).

When Sri Muruganar Swami prayed to Bhagavan Ramana to bless him by granting the experience of the Self, Bhagavan's *upadēśa* was *irundapaḍikkē iru*– 'Be as you are'.

porunda viḷaṅgumānmānubhūti yenakku pugalenḍrēn
irundapaḍikkē iruvenḍrān endai ramaṇaviṛayōnē

Sri Ramana Sannidhi Murai; Irai Pani Nitral - 10

When he then asked, how one is to conduct worldly affairs - *iṛaivan aruḷ seluttum vazhikkē sel* – 'Move as the grace of God leads you' was the *upadēśa* of Bhagavan. These two sentences sum up the entire teaching of the Vedas.

Hṛdayam or heart is indeed the centre of Self-experience - *Ātmānubhūti. Hṛdi ayam tasmāt hṛdayam* (He abides in the heart; hence, *hṛdayam*) - this is the etymology of the term *hṛdayam* (spiritual heart). *Hṛdayam vastu nāmam* is the Malayalam version. But in this verse Bhagavan says that the heart itself is the Lord. If the heart is the seat of Brahman, it implies that it is more pervasive than Brahman. The gist is that, heart itself is Brahman.

Sri Bhagavan has told that the only way one can locate the heart-centre is by tracing the I-thought to its source. This process of Self-enquiry we will see elucidated in these forty verses. *Uḷḷam* in Tamil means the heart. The term *uḷḷōm* which means 'I am here' has been transformed or rather 'transworded' to become the word *uḷḷam*. As the Lord shines there, He is also known as *kaḍa-uḷ,* i.e. the extreme end within, the terminus of the inner-path. *Uḷ* means 'within'; *uḷḷam* means 'that which is within' - the 'I am'. In this centre there is no touch of duality at all. All that is outside this is akin to a magic show conjured up by the mind and the senses.

In this first verse, Bhagavan has explained the nature *(swarūpalakṣaṇam)* of Brahman. This *maṅgaḷa śloka* of the text contains the entire meaning of Vedanta. All the remaining verses are mostly an elucidation of this *maṅgaḷa śloka. Uḷḷadu* means truth. *Yat tisṛbhi: avasthābhi: na vyabhicarati tat satyam* - that which remains constant in all the three states is truth. This is the definition of *satyam* (truth). *Uḷḷadu* is that which remains changeless during waking, dream and deep sleep states. It is the ever-present, ever-attained awarenes.

ādou antēca yannāsti vartamānēpi tat tathā - (Mandukya Karika)

'That which was not there in the beginning and will not be there in the end, is not real even if it appears to exist in the present,' is the law. Let us examine the three states.

1 – In the waking state *(jāgrat),* the body exists, the mind exists; I am.

2 – In the dream state *(swapna),* the body does not exist, the mind exists; I am.

3 – In the deep sleep state *(suṣupti),* neither the body nor the mind exists; but I, the reality persist there too.

When the body and mind are present, I exist; when the body and mind are not present, then too, I exist. This is the *anvaya-vyatirēka* method of reasoning which is helpful in exploring the inner most experience. In the deep-sleep state, even though the individual 'I' is not, existence or reality is there as *sukharūpam* (of the nature of happiness). In deep sleep, when the body and mind are not there, that which remains as the import of 'I', that essence, that existence in the form of happiness - that is the reality - I am That.

ahampadārtthastvahamādisākṣī
nityam suṣuptāvapi bhāva darśanāt

– Vivekachudamani 294

'The reality which is the implied meaning of the term 'I' *(aham)* is a witness to all the objects beginning with the ego to the body. That Self is seen to persist in deep-sleep as well.'

How can we know this? Every day, when the *upādhīs* (adjuncts) - beginning from the ego to the body - disappear in deep sleep, *sad-vastu* - the pure ever-present existence - alone remains. This can be intuited by those who contemplate deeply on the deep sleep state. One who has recognized the consciousness that exists in *suṣupti* (deep sleep), has indeed comprehended the experiential-meaning (*ānubhavikārttha*) of the *mahāvākya 'Prajñānam Brahma'* (Brahman is pure consciousness). Deep contemplation on the *suṣupti* state will reveal the hitherto ignored value of that bodiless, mindless state. That is the only state where all have an intimation of the Self. In the traditional *śravaṇa-manana-nididhyāsana* path of the Upanishads, there are methods of contemplation that make one glide into the realm where one is able to experience the wakeful-sleep state or *jāgratsuṣupti*. The interval moments between sleep and waking called *swāpa-prabōdhasandhyā* should be meditated upon. As soon as one wakes up, one has to enquire: 'Where was I just a while ago? What was my nature in dreamless-sleep?' For those who reflect deeply on these lines, the veil between the waking and sleep states will be slowly lifted and the sacred wholeness of *suṣupti* will reveal itself in the waking state. This is indeed the *nirvikalpa samādhi.* Sri Chandrasekhara Bharathi Mahaswami has mentioned about this contemplation in his profound commentary on Vivekachudamani.

vichārāt tīkṣṇatāmētya dhī: paśyati param padam

– Yoga Vasishtam

'The intellect that has become single-pointed by enquiry clearly perceives the supreme state of the Self'.

With the insight born of such plumbing within, we will directly perceive that the pure consciousness that we are, is unaffected by the activities of the body or the thoughts of the mind and that we are the *nitya-siddha* (ever-attained), *nityamukta* (ever-free), *nityaśuddha* (ever-pure) and *nitya-buddha* (ever-known) *swarūpa* by nature. We will see very clearly that, like the serpent in a rope or like water in a mirage, the *upādhīs* like the body, and the states like waking and dream, are all mere appearances in the Self. Then the imaginary appearances *(uḷḷal)* will no more cast their spell on us and abidance in the Self becomes effortless. This is the 'natural state' or *sahaja nirvikalpa.*

MAṄGAḶĀCHARAṆA--VEṆBĀ II

...yuḷḷe
maraṇa-bhaya mikkuḷavam makkaḷara ṇāga
maraṇa-bhava millā mahēśan—chara-ṇamē
sārvar-tañ sārvoḍu-tāñ sāvuṭṭṛār sāveṇṇañ
sārvarō sāvā davar-nittar

uḷḷē	Within
maraṇa bhayam mikkuḷa	with intense fear of death
am makkaḷ	those spiritually mature beings
maraṇa bhavam illā	devoid of both birth and death
araṇ āga	shining as fortress of protection
mahēśan charaṇamē sārvar	the feet of Mahesha, the supreme Lord of all, will seek as refuge
tam sārvoḍu	along with their vāsanās (latent tendencies) and attachments
tām sāvuṭṭṛār	the jīva-bhāva (individuality, the ego-sense) the effect of ignorance removed and annihilated
sāvā davar	the deathless ones,
sāveṇṇam sārvarō	will they ever again entertain the thought of death?
nittar	they live forever

Paraphrase:

Those spiritually mature beings with intense fear of death, find the birthless and deathless Lord Mahesha alone as a fortress of protection and they take sole refuge at His feet. Such surrendered devotees behold their own death and wake up to the deathless nature of their Self. Along with their *jīva-bhāva* (individual-sense) all their *vāsanās* also get destroyed. Will such *jīvanmuktās* (the liberated souls) who have transcended death, ever again entertain the thought of death?

Commentary

Death is another name for the body. "When you walk, death walks; when you sit, death sits; when you move about, it is death that moves about. Dear one! Wake up! Death is more intimate to you than your own self" Rama teaches his brother Bharata in Ramayana. Body and death are not different. Death occurs continually in the body. Hence the fear of death will vanish only when body-identification ceases. Only if there is clarity regarding the illusory nature of the body, will there be an end to the fear of death that is born of body-identification. Fear of death possesses and torments even those who have discriminative intelligence. But the wise will not submit to it easily. They embark on an intense search for a way out. A divine restlessness sets in, forcing them to find out how death may be transcended. To such people there is only one refuge, the feet of the Lord. The Lord's feet mean the Lord Himself.

In Patanjali's Yoga sutras we find a *sūtra* – *'īśwara praṇidānāt'* which means the experience of yoga comes by complete surrender to *Īśwara*. There Patanjali gives a unique definition for *Īśwara*. *Klēśa karma vipākāsair aparāmṛṣṭa: puruṣa viśēṣa:* – invoked by the seeker, *Īśwara* or God manifests as a special person who lives as an ideal amidst all outer karmic problems and inner mental problems and demonstrates to the devotee how to remain totally unaffected by them. Seeing such a form and unconsciously surrendering to it, the devotee glides into another realm. Such a solid manifestation is known as *nirmāṇa kāyā* or *swēchhōpātta pṛthak vapu:* (a form assumed out of His own free will for rescuing the devotee). This is also the Guru-principle which forces the ego to submit. Such sport of grace we see depicted in the life of many devotees in Periya Puranam. This demonstration of grace is known as *taḍuttu āṭkoḷḷal*. Without such a devouring power of grace it is indeed impossible for a seeker to surrender and do away with the ego. We frequently see this mentioned in the Tamil hymns written by Bhagavan. This state of surrender alone is fearlessness and that is realization.

martyō mṛtyuvyāḷabhīta: palāyan
lōkān sarvānnirbhayam nādhyagacchat
tvatpādābjam prāpya yadṛcchayādya
swastha: śētē mṛtyurasmādapaiti –Srimad Bhagavatam 10-3-27

'To escape from the all-devouring serpent called death, man flees to all corners of the world. However, he never finds a place where he is free from fear. Finally, he surrenders at the Feet of the Lord and rests there in peace; death flees from him then.'

The celebrated story of an encounter with death is there in the Kathopanishad, where the wise boy Nachiketa enters the portal of death and dares to ask the god of death - Yama - about the secret of death. Here Yama himself declares - 'to the knower of the Self, Death is a delicious side dish' - *mṛtyur yasya upasēchanam*. In the puranic story of Markhandeya, when the boy came to know that his death was imminent, he began worshipping Siva with intense devotion. When the god of death arrived to take his life, Siva manifested there and the boy clung tightly to the Lord's feet. Siva dealt a death-blow to death itself. Thus the boy gained life eternal.

It is the ego-'I' which is overtaken by the fear of dying. When this ego *(ahaṅkāra)* dissolves and disappears into its source, the heart, the most auspicious, fearless abode of *Īśwara* shines forth as the haven of protection. Surrendering to the Lord implies that the 'I' gets absorbed in the Lord. When the individual-sense gets dissolved in the infinite, unbroken consciousness - *satyam-śivam* - the eternal reality which is birthless and deathless shines by itself. This alone is truth.

To overcome the fear of death, first of all, the idea of death that lies hidden deep within needs to be awakened. Siva's initiation or bestowal of grace on the devotee is the awakening of the fear of death in him. This latent fear, when invoked, burns like fire in the consciousness of a man of discrimination: "I am bound to die one day, how terrible is that fact! Is there any way to escape this fate?" He then restlessly begins to search for a remedy. Self realization of Bhagavan Sri Ramana Maharshi is itself an illustration of this deep urge to solve the mystery of death. It was indeed the death-experience that turned out to be the grace of

Arunachala which bestowed the highest realization on him. Here are Bhagavan's own words:

"It was about six weeks before I left Madurai for good, that the great change in my life took place. It was quite sudden. I was sitting in a room on the first floor of my uncle's house. I seldom had any sickness and on that day, there was nothing wrong with my health, but a sudden violent fear of death overtook me. There was nothing in my state of health to account for it and I did not try to account for it or to find out whether there was any reason for the fear. I just felt 'I am going to die' and began thinking what to do about it. It did not occur to me to consult a doctor or my elders or friends. I felt that I had to solve the problem myself, then and there."

This was the fear of death as experienced by the Maharshi. The following words describe how this brave boy, hardly seventeen years old then, confronted death. It was this confrontation that brought about Self-realization.

"The shock of the fear of death drove my mind inwards and I said to myself mentally, without actually framing the words - 'now death has come; what does it mean? What is it that is dying? This body dies.' And I at once dramatized the occurrence of death. I lay with my limbs stretched out stiff as though *rigor-mortis* had set in and imitated a corpse so as to give greater reality to the enquiry. I held my breath and kept my lips tightly closed so that no sound could escape so that neither the word 'I' nor any other word could be uttered! 'Well then', I said to myself, 'this body is dead. It will be carried stiff to the burning ground and there burnt and reduced to ashes. But with the death of this body, am 'I' dead? Is the body 'I'? It is silent and inert but I feel the full force of my personality and even the voice of the 'I' within me, apart from it. So I am the spirit transcending the body. The body dies, but the spirit that transcends it cannot be touched by death. This means I am the deathless spirit.' All this was not dull thought; it flashed through me vividly as living truth, which I perceived directly, almost without thought process. 'I' was something very real, the only real thing about my present state and all the conscious activity connected with my body was centered on that 'I'. From that moment onwards the 'I' or 'Self' focused attention on itself by a powerful fascination. Fear of death had vanished once and for all. The absorption in the Self continued unbroken from that time on. Other thoughts might come and go like the various notes of music, but the 'I' continued like the fundamental *śruti* note, that underlies and blends with all the other notes. Whether the body was engaged in talking, reading or anything else, I was still centered on 'I'."

It was this profound wisdom of Self-enquiry born of the death experience that transformed the young Venkataraman into Ramana Maharshi! It is in the light of this experience that Bhagavan composed the above *śloka— Maraṇabhayam mikkuḷavam makkaḷ...* In order to be aware of the Self as existence, we must have the dispassionate insight that the body and the world perceived by the sense organs are perishable and illusory. Even this is not sufficient; bodily attachments and desire for pleasure must cease. If bodily attachments are not removed, suffering will continue even if there is *vivēka*. Actually speaking, desire will come to an end only when pleasure-seeking turns insipid and unbearable. If the pot is hot, one naturally drops it. So if you intensely contemplate the pain of separation, fear, disease, death and so on and develop a sense of dispassion *(vairāgya),* then that *vivēka* born of *vichāra* will give you enough passion to renounce emotional attachment to the body. Death - one's own and that of near and dear ones - is a matter of fear. See what Lord Buddha says:

yadi janma jarā maraṇam na bhavēt
yadi chēṣṭaviyōgabhayam na bhavēt
yadi sarvamanityamidam na bhavēt
iha janmani kasya ratir na bhavēt

'Had there been no birth, old age or death, had there been no fear of separation from the near and dear, had everything here not been perishable, then who would not find joy in this worldly life?'

The fear of death that arises out of *vivēka* ignites the hidden fire of *jnana*. First of all it brings about the knowledge that the body-mind (which is ever a limitation) is distinct from the real Self. There cannot be any factual or illusory relationship between the body-mind and the Self, ever - whether in the past, present or in the future. The *śruti* declares: *asaṅgō hyayam puruṣa:* (Br. Up.) - 'This Self is ever unattached'. This *mantra* is indeed a *mahāvākya* that can put a listener into the state of instant realization. When a devotee asked Bhagavan how to renounce attachments, the reply was "the Self has already renounced all attachments". Once a seeker knows the Self, it puts him instantly in the state of effortless detachment, *nisarga-vairāgya*. Self-knowledge is renunciation - *sanyāsō nirmalam jñānam* - declares the Ramana Gita.

The moment you know this, you experience freedom. Freedom is the nature of the Self. If the power of *śraddha* is withdrawn from the body and directed towards the *chit* - the Self, that is felt as 'I'-'I', the mind comes in contact with the heart and the timeless, eternal being will reveal itself spontaneously. For those who have directly perceived the deathless nature of the Self, where is the fear of death? This is why Bhagavan asks - *sāvādavar nittar sāveṇṇam sārvarō?* – 'Will those deathless beings ever again fear death? Can there be death for those beings who are eternal?'

As a result of *vichāra*, a *mumukṣu* endowed with discrimination, begins to understand with increasing clarity that the world, its people and the things, and even his own body and intellect that he so much depends upon, are all caught in the grip of inevitable destruction. This insight leads him to a temporary state of fear. His fear is similar to that of a mariner who, in the middle of his voyage, suddenly realizes that his ship has many holes in it! This state is called *nirvēdam* in the Upanishads (Literally this means transcending the ritualistic portion of the Vedas); it is also called *paravairāgyam* - intense dispassion. Such a detached seeker enquires and finds that, for him, the only safe and reliable fortress of security is the feet of Mahesha, the supreme Lord. Who exactly is Mahesha?

na draṣṭuranya: paramō hi tasya
vīkṣā svamūlē pravilīya niṣṭhā - Sat-darsanam – 22

'There is no supreme being apart from the seer, the awareness within. To behold Him is to trace back to the source and abide there.'

This place of refuge is the heart-centre, the source of the 'I'-thought, where one experiences the reality. Even if one surrenders oneself to an external God, due to the destruction of the ego, this internal protective centre of fearlessness shines forth on its own. This is what is meant by *maraṇa-bhavamillā mahēśan charaṇam* (to take refuge at the feet of Mahesha who is deathless and birthless).

Once a devotee prostrated before Bhagavan Ramana and tightly holding His feet, said: "I take refuge at the feet of my Guru". Bhagavan replied, "Are these the feet of the Guru? The Guru's feet are ever shining within you as 'I-I'. Hold on to them unceasingly!" This is the sole, eternal place of refuge. The fear of death will be eliminated only if one intuits this as one's own Self by *pratyabhijñā samādhi bōdha* (instantaneous intuitive recognition of one's Self).

In Srimad Bhagavatam, sage Sukabrahma gives this *jnana* to Pareekshit on the seventh day of his divine discourse; the day on which he had been cursed to die of the poisonous bite of serpent Takshaka. See their divine dialogue: "*Tvam tu rājan mariṣyēti paśubuddhimimām jahi* - O King! The feeling that you will die is due to your identification with the body. Give up this identification. *Na jāta: tvam* - You have never been born. You are the Atman. How can there be birth for the Atman, which by its very nature is eternal? Your nature is

Brahman. *Aham Brahma* - Brahman itself shines within you as *aham-aham,* as the 'I-I'. Consider this truth, *Brahmāham* (I am Brahman); hold on to this awareness, observe this with intense attention. Be absorbed. Remain as the Self by the Self, with total identification with the Self. The ignorance that 'I am this body' will vanish like a dream from your consciousness. The body is like a pot; the 'I' is like the space; let the pot stay or break to pieces - is there any loss for space within the pot?" On hearing these words that proclaim the essence of the *mahāvākyās,* the grateful king declared aloud ecstatically: *"siddhōsmi, anugṛhītōsmi* (I have realized the Self, I am blessed!) O Lord! I do not fear death; *praviṣṭō brahmanirvāṇam* (I have entered *Brahma nirvāṇa!)".* This is the *śuddham vimalam viśōkam amṛtam satyam* - the pure, unsullied, joyful nectar of truth, obtained by the grace of the satguru.

The sole refuge for a seeker who is overwhelmed by the fear of death is the presence of a Guru who is a *jīvanmukta.* The Guru makes the attention of a *mumukṣu* (a seeker endowed with perfect *vairāgya),* turn inward, and directs it towards the real Self untouched by death. As the Guru points towards the Self he is called *dēśika*. The mind illumined by the Guru flows towards and merges with the *chit* or pure awareness. To know the *tatva* is to recognize and abide in the *chit. Chitva darśanam tatva darśanam* — (Upadesa Saram)

veḷi viḍayaṅgaḷai viṭṭu manam-tan
oḷi uru ōrdale undī paṛa
uṇmai uṇarcchiyām undī-paṛa (Upadesa Undiyar)

'It is true wisdom for the mind to turn away from outer objects and behold its own effulgent form.'

Thus by bestowing *jnana*, God in the form of the Guru becomes the birthless, deathless fortress of refuge for the seeker. "O Lord Vittala! All these days I mistook the 'I' to be me; now by the Guru's grace, I have come to know that it is You. I have seen my own death and O Lord, now death is no more for me!" sings Namadeva, the saint of Maharashtra. "The Lord descended as my Guru and bestowed his grace on me. That state dawned and swallowed the 'I' which was me and shone forth as 'I' - the pristine state of deathlessness!" These are the words of another saint of Arunachala, Arunagirinathar. As it is said in Dakshinamurty stotra, 'God, Guru and the Self are nothing but different forms of the same, boundless being'.

The insight that one's individuality is an illusion is truly the destruction of the *jīvabhāva*. Hence Bhagavan declares *tam sārvoḍu tām sāvuṭṭrār*. The source of all attachments is the ego-'I'. Its destruction in a way is death itself. However, along with its destruction, the real-'I' shines forth; the unshakable conviction that one is the birthless, deathless, eternal reality simultaneously arises. Hence this profound transformation is referred to as, *sāvāmal sāvu* or experiencing one's own death without dying. This experience is called variously as *pratyabhijña*, *jnana* or *mukti*. He, who passes through this experience, transcends death and attains immortality. *Sāveṇṇam sārvarō* - for such a one, there will never again arise the thought of death.

'For whom is the thought of death?' 'For me'. 'Who is this 'I'?' When one enquires in this manner, the individual

-'I' dissolves in the source and eternity is experienced; consciousness, that is the immortal Self, reveals itself. This is *sadyōmukti* – freedom, here and now. By constant Self-enquiry, he who merges his individuality in the infinite consciousness becomes bodiless.

aśarīram vāvasantam

na priyāpriyē spṛśata: – Chandogya Upanishad 8-12-1

'The duality of likes and dislikes does not touch one who lives without body'.

aśarīram śarīrēṣu anavasthēṣvavasthitam

mahāntam vibhumātmānam matvā dhīrō na śōchati

–Kathopanishad 2-22

'He who knows the Self, the 'I' within the mortal body as the bodiless-being, as all-pervading, as the supreme principle, transcends suffering. Or he who knows his own Self, the 'I' within as bodiless, or as that which has never at any time been associated with the body, is a *dhīra* (a brave one).'

"Bodilessness is a foregone conclusion" asserts Bhagavan. Even though he remains in a body, he is without the body. An intelligent man, who knows that there is no water in the mirage, will not be deluded by seeing the water. Similarly the liberated one who has known that there is no body in the Self will not be deluded by the body, though he perceives it. Will such a person then become insensitive to bodily heat and cold, pleasure and pain? These will continue to be experienced. Yet, one may ask, for whom is the experience? Are these experiences for consciousness or for the inert body? They are not experienced by consciousness which is of the nature of eternal bliss; and they are not experienced by the body, as the inert body by itself cannot experience anything. Between these two, it is the reflected consciousness, the spurious-'I' or the ego or the *chit-jaḍa granthi* that arrogates to itself the pain and sorrow. Even while experiencing intense pain, if one enquires carefully: 'For whom is this pain?', then the ego or the primary thought will disappear, and the bliss of *samādhi* will reveal itself. That is why the Lord proclaims in the Bhagavad Gita that the *sthita-prajña* (man of steady wisdom) has the awareness of the Self *(paramātmā samāhitā)* even in the midst of the dualities of pain and pleasure. Other than this state of yoga which releases one from *du:khasamyōga* (contact with suffering) there is no refuge for those who are caught in the whirlpool of *samsāra.*

The above two verses are the *maṅgaḷācharaṇa ślokas*. The first one refers to truth *(uḷḷadu)* as the Self, the *nirguṇa* Brahman. When Kavyakanta Ganapati Muni prayed that a *śloka* about *Īśwara* might be included, the Maharshi composed a second *maṅgaḷācharaṇa śloka* with the words *maraṇa-bhavamillā mahēśan*. The first *śloka* highlights *jnana* through Self-enquiry *(vichārajñāna),* and the second one, surrender *(śaraṇāgati).* The first is the path of *vichārā* - enquiry; the second that of *bhakti* - devotion.

The source of the 'I'-thought is the heart, the *svaswarūpā*. The natural state when the 'I'-thought does not arise, is described by Bhagavan as *uḷḷattē uḷḷapaḍi uḷḷal.* When the 'I'-thought arises and intermingles with the bodily-limitation, the fear of birth and death arises. Then one surrenders to that which is birthless and deathless, Mahesha. This is the path of devotion. Through Self-enquiry, truth is directly experienced. Through devotion, one surrenders to the Lord as one's fortress of refuge and protection. By directly perceiving the truth with the help of Self-enquiry or by devotionally taking refuge in 'That', either way, the assumed contact with the body and the objects will vanish. When one realizes that the unreal has no existence, reality will shine forth brilliantly. One is the path of intuitive-attention or *śraddha*; the other is the path of faith or surrender to a higher power. Some seekers have the *samskāra* to do *vichārā* - they recognize the Self first through enquiry and then their whole being gets absorbed in it with *bhāva* (divine fervor). Others who have the *bhāva samskāra* of *bhakti* surrender first to the Lord and then know Him as the Self. Even a great *jnani* like Bhagavan Ramana Maharshi, being overwhelmed by devotion surrendered to Mahesha in the form of Arunachala. *Un iṣṭam en iṣṭam* – 'Thy will is my will' said Bhagavan. This is a journey through *bhakti* to *jnana* (from devotion to knowledge). Some travel through *jnana* and reach *bhakti*. To recognize the Self is *jnana* and to delightfully get absorbed in it is *bhakti*. Either way, *jnana* and *bhakti* are indispensable. When the Guru points to the truth, attention falls on the Self. Some emotionally accept this experience as the Lord, and renouncing everything else, surrender to Him.

vadanti tattatvavida: tatvam yajjñānamadvayam
brahmēti paramātmēti bhagavān iti śabdyatē

–Srimad Bhagavatam 1-2-11

'This very same non-dual awareness is called 'Bhagavan' by *bhaktās*, 'Brahman' by *jñānīs* and 'Paramatma' by *yōgīs*.'

Some know it as the Self and by enquiry abide in it. While enquiry traces the ego to its source, in surrender, the ego merges in the same source by faith in God. There is absolutely no difference between the two. Enquiry happens with the help of the subtle intellect; surrender happens with the ego itself. By enquiry one recognizes the Self and *pratyabhijña* occurs. Through devotion, one surrenders to the higher being and merges in Him. In a way grace is the final word in spirituality. "You need not eliminate the wrong 'I'. How can 'I' eliminate itself? ..... All that you need do is to find out its origin and abide there. Your efforts can extend only thus far. Then the beyond will take care of itself. You are helpless there. No effort can reach it." (Talks - 197)

THE HOLY WAR

When the battle was over the war was lost
And in that defeat was my victory
I fought and fought only to perish
On the ashes of my dead self
Was the resurrection of the Divine
The fight was indeed a noble one
In which the warrior was crucified to death
And that death was another
Name for God, Truth or Love.

(From the collection of poems - 'On the Wings of Ecstasy')

Note: The deep import of these two *maṅgaḷācharaṇa ślokas* will become very clear if read again after going through the entire commentary.

VERSE ONE

...pārvai-sēr
nāmulakaṅ kāṇḍalā nānāvāñ śatti-yuḷa
vōrmudalai yoppa loru-talaiyē—nāma-vuru
chittira-mum pārp-pānuñ sērpaḍa-mu māroḷi-yu
mattanai-yun tānā mavan

pārvai-sēr	With the senses turned outward
nām ulakam kāṇḍalāl	since we directly perceive the physical world
nānāvām śakti uḷa	possessing the inscrutable power of appearing as many
ōrmudalai oppal	acceptance of a primordial (causal) principle
oru-talaiyē	is beyond dispute
nāma uru chittiramum	the world-picture of names and forms
pārppānum sērpaḍamum	the perceiver of that, namely, the jīva, the screen on which the pictures of names and forms appear
ār oḷiyum	the light of awareness that illumines them
attanaiyum tān	all these are nothing
ām avan	but He, the Atman, who shines as 'I-I' (in the heart)

Paraphrase:

With the senses turned outward - since we directly perceive the world, acceptance of a supreme source possessing the inscrutable power of appearing as many, is indisputable. The world-picture of names and forms, the perceiver of it, namely the *jīva,* the screen on which the pictures of names and forms appear, the light of awareness that illumines them, all these are nothing but He, the Atman, who shines as 'I - I' (in the heart).

Commentary

The process of going from what is perceived by the senses, to the direct and immediate awareness of the Self is called as *taṭastha* in the *śāstrās*. This *śloka* begins with the three words 'we', 'the world' and 'seeing'. Among these, 'we', that is the 'I' *(aham)* or consciousness alone is real experience. This can be called direct experience *(aparōkṣam)*. The 'world' is what we perceive through the senses; it is *pratīti.* This may also be called *pratyakṣam* or that which is only sensory perception. The direct and immediate experience of 'I' is the reality. It is in this awareness that the world is perceived. An immeasurable power arising from this reality and expanding as the mind and the senses and manifesting itself as the world is called 'creation' *(sarga)*. It is inevitable that we need to acknowledge a power which is the cause for this manifestation. Bhagavan Ramana Himself says in Arunachala Ashtakam: *uḷadunil aladilā adiśaya śakti* – 'There exists hidden in Thee an inscrutable power which is not separate from Thee'. But this same power turns into *avidyā* and veils the reality and gives rise to the division of the seer and the seen. It is this *āvaraṇa* that veils the truth. How can this veil be removed?

In faint light, one mistakes a garland for a snake and is frightened. This fear is based on an illusion. Yet, this illusion veils our intellect, and without affecting the garland in any way, projects it as a snake. This veiling does not affect the Self. This veiling is the defect of the intellect. Once light comes, the garland is seen as it is and the illusion of the snake disappears. In the same way when one wakes up to the grace of the Guru, non-dual awareness shines forth and the *tripuṭi* caused by ignorance vanishes. The individual-'I', the world and the light that illumines them - all these are nothing but the Atman, the substratum. It is this same idea that is expressed in this Malayala *kīrtanam:*

ōmkāramāya poruḷ mūnnāy piriñjuḍane āṅkāramāyi

– Harināmakīrtanam

'The primordial Word - Om - splits into three and becomes the ego'.

Vivekachudamani expresses this idea too:

tvam aham idam itīyam kalpanā buddhidōṣāt
prabhavati paramātmanyadvayē nirviśēṣē Sloka 355

It is because of *avidyā* (ignorance) that the *vikalpās* (images and concepts that veil the nature of the Self) such as 'I', 'you' and 'this' are fancied in Brahman, which is unconditioned, indivisible awareness. It is the everyday experience of all, that, in deep sleep these images don't arise. That which remains even there is the *adhiṣṭhana, the* Atman. When through enquiry the *adhiṣṭhāna* (substratum) is beheld in awareness, then there will arise the intuition 'I am that' and all - the names and forms, the seer, the seen, the screen and the light that illumines them - is only He, the Self: *Nāma uru chittiramum pārppānum sērpaḍamum āroḷiyum attanaiyum tānām avan.* Although waves, bubbles, froth and icebergs appear in the ocean, the sole constituent for all these is water. He who understands this is a seer of Oneness. *Salila ēkō draṣṭā advaitō bhavati,* says the Upanishad.

One who has seen his own Self, has seen God. For such a person, this world is merely a moving picture on the screen that is God. This world is perceived as an illusory appearance *(vivarta)* on the unchanging, eternal and self-effulgent supreme Self. Seeing a snake in a rope is an example of *vivarta* (illusory appearance); milk changing into curd, is an example of *pariṇāma* (evolution). According to the authentic experiences of the sages the world is a *vivarta,* it is not an evolution. That is, the appearance of the world has not brought about any change in Brahman. The movie on the screen is an apt example. For, the movie which appears on the screen causes no change whatsoever to the screen. In a movie, however, the seer remains separate from the picture and the screen. Here the one who sees, that which is seen, the light and the screen - all this, is the supreme Brahman which is Existence-Consciousness-Bliss.

This verse reveals the meaning of the *mahāvākya - sarvaṁ khalvidam Brahma* - **All this here is indeed Brahman***;* or *ātmaivēdam sarvam* - **Everything here is the Atman** - *Attanayum tān ām avan.* Here, *avan* or 'He', the third person singular, is the

Lord Himself who is the supreme first person: *uttama puruṣa*. *Tānē tānē tattuvam* – 'Indeed 'I am' is the truth; reveal it Yourself, O Arunachala!' sings Bhagavan in Aksharamanamalai.

THE VISION

The dawn came in the horizon
And unveiled were all forms!
When the veil was lifted
All the names too vanished;
Everyone was He; He alone!
The joy of THE VISION!
It was a perception, divine
Unknown hitherto to the mind
All the dualistic castles fell down
All frightening creatures of darkness
Vanished anon from sight
Who beheld the vision? - It's a mystery!
No seer and the seen; no he or she or 'I'
One solidified mass of peace.
The great release, eternal relaxation; *nirvāṇa*!

(Poem from 'On the Wings of Ecstasy')

VERSE TWO

...ulagu—karttanuyir

mummu-dalai yemma-tamu muṛkoḷḷu mōrmu-dalē

mummu-dalāi niṛku-menḍṛu mummu-dalu—mum-mudalē

yennal-ahaṅ kāra mirukku-maṭṭē yān-keṭṭu

tannilai-yi niṭṭṛa ṭṛalai-yāguṅ

ulagu kartan uyir	world, God and jīva
em matamum	all religions, at the very outset postulate and
mum mudalai mun koḷḷum	accept the three principles.
ōr mudalē mum mudalāi niṛkum	only one principle itself appears as three
enḍṛum mum mudalum	that the three, forever
mummudalē ennal	remain as three distinct principles, to say so
ahaṅkāram irukkum maṭṭē	is just as long as the ego remains
yān keṭṭu	with the cessation of the ego, the 'I'
tannilaiyil niṭṭral talai āgum	abiding in one's swarūpa, the Self, is the most auspicious

Paraphrase:

All religions accept the three postulates - the world, the *jīva* (soul) and God. However, the one principle alone appears as three. The argument 'the three ever remain as three independent entities', is possible only as long as the ego remains. The best and the highest state is to abide in one's own *swarūpa,* the Self, after the cessation of the ego-I.

Commentary

A notable incident occurred once. A person, who had met Bhagavan Ramana in Virupaksha cave or elsewhere earlier, visited Bhagavan again in the present ashram. Earlier, Bhagavan was seen leading a severely austere life - there was no ashram and he had no possessions whatsoever. He was a *mouni* (in silence) and was leading a mendicant's life begging for his sustenance. But in the ashram, along with moderate conveniences, the Maharshi sat on a couch, ate in the dining hall and conversed with devotees when required. On seeing this, the visitor who was quite ignorant about the inner state of Bhagavan, and thinking that external renunciation was greater, said to Bhagavan: "Swami! You were so great while you were on the hill. What austerity you had! See, now possessions, people and comforts have all gathered around you. Alas! You have become spoilt Swami!" When Bhagavan heard the words: "*nee keṭṭuṭṭe sāmi* - You have become spoilt," he smiled and said, "Hum, um...." (yes, yes....) Hearing this, the other devotees protested, "Bhagavan, you are agreeing with what he says!" Bhagavan replied: "Of course! What he says is correct. *Yān keṭṭu tannilayil niṭṭral talai* - only when the

'I' is destroyed (spoilt) one abides in peace. He voices the truth!" Bhagavan was punning on the Tamil word *'keṭṭuppōdal'* which means both 'to be lost' and 'to be spoilt'.

The underlying note behind all of Bhagavan's teachings is that the destruction of the ego itself is liberation. No experience that retains the ego will be enduring. According to Bhagavan, accepting the individual-'I' and trying to seek Brahman, God or liberation as an external objective goal, is like the thief assuming the guise of a policeman to search for the thief which is he himself.

Disregarding the ego or dismissing it as unreal, one must abide in the Self. Once the ego is burnt to ashes by sheer disregard, the bliss of liberation will be experienced in its fullness. If the ego is regarded as real, it will project limitations, dualities, triads, the gods, and other worlds. It will make us imagine the existence of various types of bondage and limitations and compel us to struggle needlessly to overcome them. This is the complex power of delusion. The heart of Bhagavan's teaching is that first and foremost, one must reject the individuality. "Without stirring the consciousness by any thought or imagination, remain still and abide in the *swaswarūpa,* the Self" - this is Bhagavan's teaching.

kanmādi siṛidindṛi chummā amarndirukka ammā ahattil-
ānma jyōtiyē nidānu bhūtiyē; irādu bhītiyē; inba-vam bōdhiyē
ayyē! ati sulabham—ānma viddhai
ayyē ati sulabham! – Atmavidya Keertanam - 4

'Abide in stillness, without any movement of tongue, mind or body. And behold the effulgence of the Self within; absence of all fear; the vast ocean of bliss. Ha, that simple is *ātma-vidyā!*' So sings Bhagavan Sri Ramana Maharshi. In fact there is only one method involved - refusal to accept the reality of the ego. The individuality or the *jīvabhāva* is itself the seed of ignorance. This is called the primal ignorance *(mūla-avidyā)*. Any *sādhana* or spiritual practice that is undertaken with the presumption that the individuality is real, cannot destroy the ego-sense at all.

jīvam kalpayatē pūrvam tatō bhāvān pṛthak vidhān

– Gaudapadakarika

'First of all we assume an individual self - *jīva* - in the undivided consciousness and from this, a series of thoughts and images continue to emerge.'

How can we eliminate this individual ego? Great sages (mahatmas) who have understood its mystery declare that the one and only way this can happen is through the grace and *upadēśa* of the Guru. The words of a satguru will bring about the awareness that the sense of individuality the - *jīvabhāva* - is unreal, and that the infinite reality, Brahman alone exists. With the well-aimed arrow of a single Word - *oupaniṣadam mahāstram* - the satguru at one stroke destroys the *tripuṭi* and that very instant the lamp of Self-knowledge is lit. 'He who fancies to claim the treasure hidden in the Upanishadic words without experiencing his own death is a fake - *kapaṭayati* - and not a knower of Brahman. To him, there is not the effulgence of *chit* that shines when the *tripuṭi* is erased' says sage Narayana Guru in his Atmopadesa Satakam.

The poet Sri Arunagirinadar sings:

chumma iru sollaṛa enḍṛadumē; ammā poruḷonḍṛum aṛindilanē

– Kandar Anubhuti

'The moment Lord Muruga appeared as my satguru and told me, 'Be word-less and remain silent' *(sollaṛa, chummā iru),* the three entities, *īśwara, jīva and jagat* vanished without any trace and instantly the unceasing experience of bliss was born'.

Let us pay attention to Bhagavan's words:

"Truly there is no cause for you to be miserable and unhappy. You yourself impose limitations on your true nature of infinite being and then weep that you are but a finite creature. Then you take up this or that *sādhana* to transcend the non-existent limitations. But if your *sādhana* itself assumes the existence of the limitations, how can it help you to transcend them? Hence I say, know that you are really the infinite, pure being, the Self absolute. You are always that Self and nothing but that Self. Know then that true knowledge does not create a new being for you, it only removes your 'ignorant ignorance'. Bliss is not added to your nature, it is merely revealed as your true and natural state, eternal and imperishable. The only way to be rid of your grief is to know and be the Self. How can this be unattainable?" (Maharshi's Gospel – Self-enquiry)

What an emphatic declaration of the *mahāvākya*! Are these words not the shower of sheer grace? Can there ever be sorrow for one who has listened to these words with *śraddha*? Is it possible that he ever falls back into ignorance?

When the whole world continually hypnotises us by constantly asserting that we are the body, we are a man or woman, we have such and such obligations, we are limited and so on, there is no other way to wake up from this awful dream than by hearing the thunderous roar of the satguru's voice which declares: *Tat Tvam Asi* (You Are That!).

Namō nama: satgurubhya:! - One's heart dances in pure ecstasy! The whole universe is trivial before the glory of the Guru! *Sādhana,* scriptural scholarship or dignity of birth or status — none of these are helpful to one without the grace of a satguru. The moment one hears the words of a satguru, all adversities get transformed into prosperity, emptiness becomes fullness, the desert turns into a beautiful garden; the individual becomes the Supreme Self! Even the *upagurus* impose discipleship on us and prescribe dos and don'ts. It is the satguru alone who dismisses all conceptions including discipleship and bathes us in the cool, celestial waters of the Self. At the very moment of hearing his words, the disciple is released; he prostrates shedding tears of joy, '*Namō nama: satgurubhya:* (prostrations to my satguru). The glory of the satguru is indeed beyond description! Oh! I am being carried away. Let us get back to the topic on hand. Self-realization is complete release from the sense of doership and enjoyership. If the individual ego is accepted as real *(yān irukkum maṭṭē),* innumerable triads such as 'God, the individual, the world' and 'the seer, the seen, seeing', will arise in the mind. It is based on this basic error that all creeds through the ages have affirmed the existence of these triads! When, by enquiring

'Who am I?' one traces the ego to its source, instantly, all these triads will vanish just as a dream vanishes on waking up. The absolute, non-dual, pure Self alone will shine forth as 'I - I' in the heart.

For the cessation of the ego, the bold pursuance of the Self-enquiry 'Who am I?' is inevitable. One must not trouble oneself trying to research into the entities - the God, the *jīva* and the world. The solution for the miseries in a dream is in waking up and not in enquiring into that which is seen in the dream! Whether one is a follower of advaita, dvaita or visishtadvaita — one's mere faith alone in these doctrines will never lead to Liberation. Whatever be the doctrine that one follows, Self-knowledge is essential to attain peace, to attain liberation from *samsāra*. And this will not take place without the complete erasing of the ego. All doctrines rely upon the mind and the ego for their survival. Whatever be a man's religion, as long as the ego *(ahantai)* and mind born of *avidyā*, remain unaffected, he will continue to be in misery. The only herb that can erase *avidyā dōṣā* is *jnana.* Hence, *ātmavichāra* is indispensable for Self-knowledge.

The extinction of the ego will bring about supreme happiness to the follower of any faith. On the other hand, if the ego is not erased, there will not be any benefit derived from the nobility of one's faith or even from the divinity of one's Guru. Therefore Bhagavan says: *yān keṭṭu tan nilayil niṭṭral talai.* **To be ego-less and to abide in one's own glory is indeed supreme.** Whatever be his religion, one who knows this will attain peace and will have the qualities of *amānitva* (humility) and the like, described in the Gita as divine virtues. He will be untouched by feelings of pride in his faith or hatred towards other faiths but will remain a devoted follower of his own.

THE GREAT TEACHER

The great Teacher who was none other than God
Who walked the earth declared to me "You are Brahman".
Then and there I ceased to exist as a person.
He, the impersonal being, blazes forth as 'I', 'I'.
An awakening into the timeless, an awakening into the Infinity
An awakening which is but a rediscovery of the
Primordial teaching in the depth of one's awareness.
This vision of the Master filled the heart with gratefulness.
Tears rolled on and on expressing the inner fulfillment.
What else can be given in return to the Omnipotent being
Who was solidified nectarine ocean of compassion!

(Poem from 'On the Wings of Ecstasy')

VERSE THREE

...konnē

ulagu-meipoi tōṭṭram ulagaṛi-vām anḍren-ḍṛu

ulagu-sukham anḍren ḍṛurait-ten—ulagu viṭṭu

tannai-yōrn donḍṛi-ranḍu tānaṭṭṛu nānaṭṭṛa

annilai-yel lārkkum oppām

konnē	fruitless, it is
'ulagu mei' 'poi	to argue that the world is real; no, it is false
tōṭṭram'	it is an appearance only (illusory)
'ulagu aṛivu ām'	the world is chit (sentient)
'anḍṛu' enḍṛu	no; but it is jaḍa (insentient)
'ulagu sukham' 'anḍṛu'	the world is of the nature of happiness; no, it is of the nature of misery
enḍṛu uraittu en?	of what avail are these futile arguments?
ulagu viṭṭu tannai ōrndu	giving up the world, turning the attention towards one's own Self,
onḍṛu iranḍu	free of the notions of oneness or duality
tān aṭṭṛu nān aṭṭṛa annilai	the illumined state where the 'I' does not arise
ellārkkum oppu ām	is acceptable to all (discerning people)

Paraphrase:

Of what avail is it to indulge in verbal arguments saying 'the world is real'; 'no, it is an illusory appearance'; 'the world is *chit* (sentient)'; 'no it is but *jaḍa';* 'it is happiness'; 'no it is full of misery'? That illumined state, freed of the notions of oneness and duality, where the 'I' does not arise is indeed fulfilling and acceptable to all.

Commentary

Advaitam kēcidicchanti dvaitamicchanti chāparē
samam tattvam na vindanti dvaitādvaita vivarjitam

– Avadhuta Gita 1–36

'Some are attached to the doctrine of advaita; some others are attached to dvaita. Neither of them attains the supreme truth, that which is beyond dvaita and advaita; that which is beyond all doctrines."

Advaita is neither a religion nor a doctrine. Once when Bhagavan Ramana was speaking about Self-knowledge, a devotee asked: "Bhagavan, is this Vedanta or *Siddhānta*?" Bhagavan replied: "It is neither. It is *anubhava* - experience." The Self is the ever-attained experience of all, at all times. Hence Srimad Bhagavatam speaks of the Lord as *kēvala anubhavānanda swarūpa: Paramēśwara*: - 'Lord is of the nature of divisionless awareness and bliss'. That experience which glows by its own effulgence as 'I am', without the help of the sense organs and the mind is the Supreme Lord Himself. If one could stay focused on the throbbing of 'I' unhindered by the images of the mind, the awareness will glow more and more clear, cloudless. In the stillness will shine the Whole. When thinking ceases, when the pulsation *(sphūrti)* 'I' vanishes in the source, *nān aṭṭṛa annilai* – the illumined state is revealed where the limitation of ego is not.

Once, a devotee, Varanasi Subbulakshmi Amma arrived at Virupaksha Cave to meet Bhagavan Ramana. After the death of her husband, this lady had been leading a pious life studying advaitic texts, performing austerities and going on pilgrimages. It was at that time that she heard about the Maharshi. On meeting Bhagavan, she asked: "Swami, is Atman of the nature of consciousness or of the nature of light? How shall I meditate on it?" Sri Bhagavan replied: "Not imagining it to be this or that, of this form or that form is itself the nature of the Atman!" Hence the oft-repeated teaching - **"Be still, word-less"**

All theories about the Atman, that it is advaita or dvaita, pure or impure, are all imaginations of the mind. When the mind becomes still, then the seer remains in his own Self - *tadā draṣtu: swarūpē avastthānam*—(Yoga Sutra). 'Stillness is Self-realization' - *niścalatattvē jīvanmukti:* - says Acharya Sankara.

bhāvabalattināl bhāvanātīta
sadbhāvattiruttalē undīpaṛa
parabhakti tattuvam undīpaṛa – Upadesa Undiyar - 9

'Through intensity of devotion transcending all imaginations, making the mind abide in the Self unwaveringly is parabhakti'.

Neither the mind nor the senses are necessary to know that 'I exist'. 'I am' *(aham)* alone is *anubhava*-awareness or experience. All that is known through the senses is only a dream, an illusion. Self alone is experience. Illusion pertains to *prakṛti* or *māyā.* How does one recognize the 'I am' experience? One recognizes the 'I am' experience through the 'I am' experience itself; not by using the mind or the intellect. In fact, even the mind and intellect are activated only by the power of the I-consciousness. The discriminative faculty of the intellect is only a partial expression of this consciousness. The thoughts and imaginations of the mind are mere expressions of this consciousness.

If the seeker gives the fullest attention to the experience of 'I am', at that very moment he becomes the knower of truth. In the absolute reality, even 'I' is just a sprout. Yet, to experience the immeasurable, the 'I' is the door. The 'I' is an illusion in its gross form; however, in its real form it is the experience of Brahman. The ego 'I' is the *aham vṛtti;* whereas, the experience 'I am' in reality is the *aham bōdha.*

When the *aham vṛtti* ('I'-thought) ceases to operate and consciousness purged of all *vāsanās* shines forth clearly, the profound silence *(mounam)* reveals itself. This is internal stillness. So long as there is any movement of the 'I'-thought, even if the mouth is shut tight, there will not be the peace of stillness. That state of being without the 'I'-thought *(nān aṭṭra annilai),* is one of supreme peace. This is Self-realization. One can say very little about it. One who has experienced this truth will be the least concerned about theories whether the world is real or illusory, joyous or sorrowful. His attention would be drawn inward from the 'seen' to the 'seer' and established in it. All research about the world is merely an intellectual exercise.

Once a visitor asked Bhagavan: "How has *sṛṣṭi* (creation) come about? Some say it is due to *karma,* others say it is the Lord's *līlā* or sport. What is the truth?" Bhagavan: Various accounts are given in books. But is there creation? Only if there is creation we have to explain how it came about. We may not know all that. But that we exist is certain. Why not know the 'I' and the present and then see if there is creation? (Day by Day with Bhagavan, Devaraja Mudaliar, 1946)

What we need is peace. And that will be obtained only when the mind subsides. Therefore the intelligent person must focus his attention on quietening the mind, and not on adhering to any particular doctrine. *Parōhi yōga: manasa: samādhi:* (The highest yoga is equanimity of the mind) declares the Bhagavatam. That is why Bhagavan says that one must meditate on one's own Self without paying attention to the world - *ulagai viṭṭu tannai ōrndu.*

anātma chintanam tyaktvā kaśmalam du:kha kāraṇam
chintayātmānamānandarūpam yanmukti kāraṇam

— Vivekachudamani - Sloka 382

'Without dissipating one's thoughts on the non-self *(anātma-vastu)* which leads to sorrow, constantly meditate on the blissful Self'.

When thoughts are turned outward through the senses, the body and the world are born outwardly, and the *chitta* (mind) and the *ahaṅkāra* (the ego-'I') are born inwardly.

When thoughts become one-pointed and subside in the heart, the body and the world which are outside and the mind, intellect, ego and memory *(manō-buddhyahamkāra-chittāni)* which are inside - all these disappear and absolute consciousness shines. This consciousness is the supreme reality. All the rest are the lamentable modifications of an extroverted vision. A *mumukṣu,* who aims at liberation from the world *(samsāra-nivṛtti)* and perfect peace, must try only to get grounded in the *samādhi,* i.e. awareness of the Self, instead of attempting to gather worldly knowledge. Seeing the seer with the inner eye, one must abide in silence, free from all thoughts, in one's own Self, which is pure consciousness. This is *chittvadarśanam* (experience of the Self). This is also *tattvadarśanam* (absolute awareness).

Externalizing one's thoughts and setting them in motion is action or *pravṛtti. Nivṛtti* or the path of knowledge means directing one's thoughts inward - towards one's own Self. One who does this is a *sanyāsi.* Renouncing the world lies in the plane of one's inner awareness. Why must one ignore the world? It is in order to meditate on one's Self. Even if one assumes all the external signs of a *sanyāsi,* but does not direct his attention towards the Self, one is not a real *sanyāsi.* Self-knowledge and incessant meditation on the Self are the real and vital signs of a *sanyāsi.* In the Gita Bhashyam, Adi Sankara says: *jñānam sanyāsa lakṣaṇam.* In the Ramana Gita, Bhagavan declares: *Sanyāsō nirmalam jñānam na kāṣāyō na muṇḍanam.* In short, living in a manner in which one can ignore the world and absorb oneself in Self-awareness, is itself *sanyāsa*. This is purely subjective.

There are those who learn the *śāstrās* – possibly dvaita or advaita, become great scholars but get into quarrels and disputes, and waste their lives fighting each other. The question, '*enḍṛu uraittu en?*' (What is the point in such disputes?) - is the mighty blow that is meant to expose their foolishness. Even by knowing a little of the sacred teaching, one can understand that the goal is the quietening of the mind. So what is required is to get absorbed in *Ātmavichāra*. Everyone experiences happiness in the state of deep sleep devoid of dreams *(annilai ellārkkum oppām).* In that state, there is absolutely no thought-modification such as 'I', 'you' or 'he'; 'the individual', 'the world' and 'God' *(jīva, jagat, Īśwara*); advaita or dvaita. There, all enjoy happiness. That happiness is our real nature. In deep sleep, one experiences happiness, because the mind subsides. The bliss in realization is because of the mind abiding in the Self consciously.

How does *manōnāśa* happen? When the rope is seen with the light of a torch, the snake which was superimposed upon it due to ignorance vanishes. In the same way, when the Self is seen through the teachings of the Guru, one realizes that the *upādhīs* like mind and body, superimposed on the Self, do not have any existence apart from the Self. He who has understood that the mirage in the desert does not really have water in it, will not pay any attention to it, even if the illusion continues to persist. Likewise, a *jīvanmukta* - who has realized that the *upādhīs* like the body and mind are mere illusory appearances in the Self, and are all unreal - will never pay any attention to them even if they seem to appear before him till the end of his *prārabdha*. This may be called *bādhānāśa*. Making an object non-existent externally is known as *rūpanāśa*. *Bādhānāśa* means making it non-existent internally, i.e., simply by knowing that it is unreal and holding no attachment or aversion towards it. In the path of *jnana*, *bādhānāśa* is more important than *rūpanāśa*. Often, even when the form is destroyed, the attachment and aversion towards persons and objects stay within us and disturb us. On the other hand, although the form is not destroyed, but attachment and aversion towards it disappears, then, as far as we are concerned, it is destroyed for good. This is *bādhānāśa*. This is what is meant by *ulagai viḍal* and when Self-knowledge dawns, the luminous kingdom of the Self will shine within us.

Like the two wings of a bird, the wings of *vairāgya* (detachment) and *bōdha* (Self-knowledge) are indispensable for a person in order to soar in *chidākāśa*. The foundation for these is the power of discrimination *(vivēka)* that lies hidden within man - this is in fact the principle of Guru-*tattva.*

Vivēka functions in two ways - first, by awakening the mind to the fact that everything in the world is transient and that the world is full of sorrow; it makes the mind introverted. This introversion is *vairāgya*. Secondly, it separates the eternal Self or our own consciousness from the *upādhīs* like the body, and directs the mind's attention towards it. That is, it gives rise to the experience of eternal, pure, unalloyed consciousness. It makes us realize our eternal separation — non-attachment — from the transient objects of nature, like the body. It reveals our permanent existence in truth — that is, in the *nitya śuddha buddha mukta swarūpa* (Eternal-Pure-Aware-Free Self). The external Guru and *satsaṅga* are only a means to awaken this latent *vivēka.* The awakening of *vivēka* is indeed grace.

THE INNER JOURNEY

The news, 'truth is within' was heard.
Now, no more sleep, no more dreams,
Perception through the five turns insipid;
The doors of senses are shut, the inner door opens,
The lamp is lit within, the mind glides with awe
Into the realm of the unknowable,
Through uninterrupted '**innering**' she gets a glimpse!
Lo the sacred presence of the Ancient One!
The mind is withdrawn from the seen to the seer.
The seer swallows the seen and glows as sheer effulgence!!

VERSE FOUR

...ūnē—tunnum

uruvan-tā nāyin ulagupara maṭṭṛā

muruvan-tā nanḍṛē luvaṭṭṛin—uruvat-tai

kaṇṇuṛu-dal yāva-nevan kaṇṇalāṛ kāṭci-yuṇḍō

kaṇṇadu-tā nanta-milā kaṇṇāmē

ūnē tunnum	made up of flesh
uruvam tān āyin	if, one is the form of the body
ulagu param aṭṭru ām	the world, and God will also be, with form
uruvam tān anḍṛēl	if one is not the form of the body
uvaṭṭṛin uruvattai	the form of these (world and God)
kaṇṇuṛudal yāvan?	who is there who can see
evan!	how to see!
kaṇ adu tān	the eye, that perceives
antam ilā kaṇ	shines as the infinite (limitless) Eye of awareness
kaṇṇalāl kāṭci uṇḍō?	can the perception be different from the eye

Paraphrase:

If one considers oneself the form of this body of flesh, then the world and God will also be forms. If one realizes oneself to be formless, as awareness, then who remains to perceive the form of the world and God? And how is one to perceive? The mind-eye that hitherto perceived other forms, now shines (after being dissolved in the form of *jnana* - Atman) as Atman — the limitless eye of *jnana.* Can there be perception without the perceiver? Can perception be different from the perceiving eye?

Commentary

The individual-'I' arises in pure consciousness, and expands into subtle names and forms as thoughts. Gradually, it becomes the organs of the senses, and it is when the *chit-jyōti* (the Light of consciousness) flows outward through them that the picture of the visible world unfolds itself. By this time, it splits into the seer (the 'I'), the seen (the world), and the instruments of seeing (the mind and the senses). At this stage, the seer is with a body, his mind is tainted with thoughts about objects, and the visible world is filled with inert gross names and forms. This is the projection of the world by the mysterious divine energy - *atiśayaśakti.*

By the yoga of involution the same force re-enters the primordial-womb and merges into the effulgent being. If the seer turning inwards completely absorbs the body in the mind, and the mind in the heart (or the witness consciousness) there will be the vision of *prajñānētra*. In that state the vision will be free of all images *(padārtha abhāvani)* and brimming with pure intelligence - *ṛtambarā tatra prajñā (*Yoga sutra*).* Sat-darsanam conveys the same idea in the words - *sā dṛṣṭirēkā anavadhirhi pūrṇā* - **That vision is One, Boundless, Whole.** This is the third eye of Siva (His *jñānanētra*). This is the I-consciousness. The ultimate vision is the radiance of the I-consciousness as *śuddhasamvit* (pure awareness), unmixed with thoughts. It is that very consciousness which sees through the holes called the 'eyes'. See how beautifully Bhagavan expresses this in his song on Self-knowledge.

viṇṇā diya-viḷakkum kaṇṇā-diya poṛikkum
kaṇṇā manak-kaṇukkum kaṇṇāi mana-viṇukkum
viṇṇāi-oru poruḷ vēṛeṇṇā dirunda-paḍi
uḷnāḍuḷattoḷi-rum aṇṇā malai enānmā-
kāṇumē; aruḷum vēṇumē; anbu pūṇumē; inbu tōṇumē

- Atmavidya keertanam - Charanam 5

'The mind is that which gives light to the five senses of perception like the eyes, which in turn light up the entire material cosmos beginning from sky. The eye that gives light to the mind-space is that infinite space of awareness. Remaining steadfastly as that *chidākāśa* and without thinking of anything else and in perfect stillness, with the heart seeking oneself within oneself, Annamalai, (Arunachala Siva) my own Self shines forth in all splendor. For this, His grace is required. For that, abundant love must be there for that divine Self; then the love, the bliss of the Self, wells up from the heart.' Thus sings Bhagavan Ramana in Atmavidya Keertanam.

Kaṇṇalāl kāṭci uṇḍō? - *yādṛśī dṛṣṭi: tādṛśam dṛśyam* (As is the vision, so is the seen) - this is the law. As long as the mind-eye exists, the world *(prapañcha)* will be seen. When the mind subsides and the *chitswarūpa* blazes forth, the world transfigures as Brahman.

As long as we believe that we are the body, it is not wrong to worship the Lord with name and form. Also, one can observe that religions which do not accept the mystic traditions that worship forms, do not seem to advance spiritually. Thus Bhagavan Himself says in the Ramana Gita - *upāsanam vinā jñānam naivasyād iti niścaya:* - 'Without *upāsana* one cannot attain *jnana;* this is certain'. However, worship varies according to the imagination of the worshipper. For the same reason it cannot by itself be the absolute experience of truth. When the *mumukṣu*'s mind is made one-pointed by *upāsana*, the Upanishad guides him through a process of negation saying: *nēdam yadidam upāsatē* – **'what you meditate on is not Brahman but by which you meditate is Brahman'.** Thus a seeker's attention is slowly shifted from the seen to the seer. Hence *śāstrās* say: *vastutantrō bhavēt bōdha: kartṛtantram upāsanam* – 'Self-knowledge is based on absolute reality; while *upāsana* depends on the imagination or free will of the worshipper.'

One day, some followers of Islam came to see Sri Bhagavan. They started a dialogue with Bhagavan with the intention of proving that worshipping God in the form of an image was wrong.

V: Does God have a form?

B: Who says He has?

V: In that case, is it not wrong to worship Him in a form?

B: Let it be so, do you have a form?

V: Yes, as we can see.

B: Are you this form; about five and a half feet in height, dark complexioned, with a beard and moustache?

V: Yes.

B: While you were asleep, were you of the same form?

V: Since I woke up, I have remained in this form only.

B: After the body dies, will you be in the same form?

V: Yes.

B: If that is so, when your relatives take away the body for rites of burial, will the body cry out: 'This is my house. I will remain here only. You must not take me away and bury me'? It was then that wisdom dawned upon that person. He realized that he, who had started the discussion in ignorance, was arriving at the threshold of a new knowledge.

V: I am not the body, but the *jīva* within.

B: Till now you were thinking, 'I am the body'. All other ignorance arises out of this primal ignorance. Until this primal ignorance is destroyed, the sequence of ignorance will continue. When this ignorance is destroyed, all other ignorance will disappear. As long as one believes, 'I am the body' and 'I have a form', it is not wrong to worship God in a form. If the mind that is always thinking of one's own body and the bodies of others, is made one-pointed by focusing on the name and form of the Lord, *sarūpabhakti* results. Thus, when the mind gets purified and knowledge is attained, it becomes clear that one has no name and form but is the formless Self; all names and forms will disappear and consciousness alone will shine forth.

VERSE FIVE

...yeṇṇil

uḍalpañcha kōśa vuruvadanā laindu

muḍal-ennuñ solli loḍuṅgu—muḍalanḍṛi

yuṇḍō vulaga muḍalviṭ ṭulagattai

kaṇḍā ruḷarō kazhaṛu-vāi

yeṇṇil	if we think deeply
uḍal pañcha kōśa uru	body is a form consisting of five sheaths
adanāl uḍalennum sollil	therefore in the term 'body'
aindum oḍuṅgum	all five of them are included
uḍalanḍṛi ulagam uṇḍō	is there a visible world without the body?
uḍal viṭṭu ulagattai kaṇḍār uḷarō	without a body is there anyone who has seen the world
kazhaṛuvāi	think it over and tell me.

Paraphrase:

The body is a form made up of five sheaths. Hence, the single term 'body' includes all the five sheaths. In the state of absence of a body, can there be any perception of the world appearance? Is the world ever seen by anyone without identifying oneself with a body as 'I'?

Commentary

According to Vedanta there are five sheaths in the body - the *annamaya, prāṇamaya, manōmaya, vijñānamaya, and ānandamaya kōśās*. These five sheaths together form the body-adjunct. They are not like sheaths placed one behind the other. Each one is permeated by the remaining four. Only by their specific characteristics can one distinguish each of them. In this, *annamaya kōśa* is the gross body; the *prāṇamaya, manōmaya* and *vijñānamaya kōśās* combine to form the subtle body; and the *ānandamaya kōśa* is the causal body. All these distinctions are of course mental. To simplify matters, it would suffice to group these five together and call it the 'body'. All the three bodies containing these five sheaths pertain to *prakṛti* (nature) or *māyā* - the seen. But our real nature is the seer – Existence, Consciousness, i.e. *puruṣa,* the Atman.

The actions pertaining to the gross body, thoughts and images of the mind, the subtle body, sleep, with its 'not knowing' of the causal body - all these are in *prakṛti.* They have nothing to do with the Self, the pure existence. These three are associated with the world alone. The Self, the 'I', is not at all affected by the activities, emotions, sleep, meditation, *samādhi* and the like. All these are happening only in the *upādhi* - the realm of limitation. "If the 'I' is known, purged of the *upādhi,* then the immeasurable is known" says Bhagavan in his Upadesa Undiyar.

tannai upādhiviṭṭ ōrvadu tān īśan
tannai uṇarvadām undīpaṛa
tān āy oḷirvadāl undīpaṛa – Upadesa Undiyar - 25

The body-adjuncts are the means for perceiving the world. In the state of deep sleep the world disappears. If the world is real it ought to be available in sleep too. Even in that state where the world picture completely ceases the Self prevails as mere existence. This gives an intimation of the Self that is free of the body and the world.

In Srimad Bhagavad Gita, Bhagavan Sri Krishna talks of the two kinds of *prakṛti* - *parāprakṛti* and *aparāprakṛti* in the chapter 'Jnana Vijnana Yoga'. *Aparāprakṛti* consists of earth, water, fire, wind, space, mind, intellect and *ahaṅkāra*. All these eight put together are contained in the term 'body' which consists of the three *śarīrās*. The *parāprakṛti* is the indivisible consciousness and the substratum of all these which appears as the *jīva*, or the limited individual ego-'I'. The world is a reflection of *parā* (the consciousness), through the *aparāprakṛti* or the 'body'. According to Advaita Vedanta, this *aparāprakṛti* is an illusion in *parā* like the mirage in a desert. The world - *lōkā* - literally means 'that which is seen' *(ālōkyatē iti lōka:)*. The world is a visible phenomenon seen by pure *chit (parā)* through the kaleidoscope of an *upādhi*, from the ego to the body. If the *upādhi* or the kaleidoscope is removed, there is no world. The deep sleep state, devoid of the body and mind, is itself the evidence for this. In this state where is the body, where is the world? When the mind arises, the specific individual ego-'I' arises, and along with it the mind-intellect-ego complex recognized by the 'I' appears inside; and the world appears outside through the senses.

All these put together, which appear both inside and outside, are included within the term 'body'. The light that illumines this is *chit (parā,* consciousness). When attention is directed towards consciousness, the body, world and the like vanishes from the awareness. 'Anything which is seen is perishable' is the law. Hence whatever be the doctrine, it is not good for the attention to be trapped in the 'seen'. Therefore it is the *dṛṣṭi-sṛṣṭi vādā* - which states that the visible phenomena emerge only when the seer sees it - that is beneficial for a seeker as it totally ends the attachment to the world. If one believes that creation occurs as different from the seer (*sṛṣṭi dṛṣṭi vādā*), then inquisitiveness can never be quelled.

The Five *Kōśās*

Annamaya kōśa – is made up of flesh. It has got its name because it is formed by the food we eat. Modern science calls it 'matter'.

Prāṇamaya kōśa - Prāṇamaya kōśa is the realm of vital energy between *annamaya* and *manōmaya kōśās*. It connects the *annamaya* and *manōmaya kōśās*. It is the subtle form of *annamaya*, and the gross form of *manōmaya*. The organs of action are contained within this.

Manōmaya kōśa - This is of the nature of *saṅkalpa* and *vikalpa*. All desires reside in this.

Vijñānamaya kōśa - Intellect, ego and the organs of perception are within this fold.

Ānandamaya kōśa - This is experienced during deep sleep. All instruments within the other *kōśās* are included within the *ānandamaya kōśa*. As the destruction of *vāsanās* or the destruction of ignorance has not taken place in the waking state, reality that is pure bliss itself remains as *ānandamaya kōśa* in the deep sleep state. Therefore no one experiences the bliss of *mukti* by sleeping. In the waking state, if through

Self-enquiry, one restrains and completely annihilates the ego and the *vāsanās*, the bliss which is experienced during deep sleep will be consciously experienced during the waking state. This experience may be called *jāgrat-suṣupti, samādhi* or *brāhmī-sthiti.*

It is the *āvaraṇa* or the veiling power of ignorance that projects the limitation of a sheath, a *kōśa*, on the pure Self that is bliss itself. When this veiling gets removed, the yogi, with his clear, unveiled vision, recognizes that bliss as his real nature. Instantly, the spell of the five *kōśās,* the three bodies and the three states will disappear, and the unique *brāhmīśthiti* or supreme peace will bloom in the placid inner lake of the heart as a motionless sheet of water. This peace itself is the heart-centre. For such a liberated one, the heart which is of the nature of peace alone is real; the mind, senses, sheaths, states, *samādhi*, mental projections, *sādhana* and the *sādhaka* - all are unreal. (See Talks with Sri Ramana Maharshi 624, 4.2.1939)

THE RELEASE

To identify with the body is to shuttle
From death to birth, from pleasure to pain.
This body is indeed a product of nature's magic.
It is woven of the 'wool of mind'; mere dream stuff!
All miseries pester the form; the body.
Miseries touch not the formless.
Formless, bodiless is thy nature; claim it and Be.
Released for ever from disease, dread, death and all delusion.

VERSE SIX

...kaṇḍa
ulagaim pulanga ḷuru-vēṛan ḍṛav-vaim
pula-naim poṛik-kup pula-nā—mulagai-mana
monḍṛaim poṛi-vāyā lōrndiḍuda lānma-nattai
yanḍṛiyula guṇḍō vaṛai

kaṇḍa	what is seen
ulagu aim pulangaḷ uru	the world is but the appearance of the five sensory perceptions
vēṛu anḍṛu	it is not different from that
avvaim pulan	those five sense-objects (sound, touch, form, taste and smell)
aim poṛik-ku pulanām	are known by the five sense organs
manam onḍṛu ulagai	the mind alone, this world
aim poṛivāyāl	through the five sense organs
ōrndiḍudalāl	since, knows
manattai anḍṛi	other than the mind
ulaguṇḍō! aṛai?	is there a world? If so, tell me.

Paraphrase:

The world that is perceptible to the eyes is nothing other than the five sensory perceptions, namely, taste, form, touch, sound and smell, which are known through the five sense organs, namely, the tongue, eyes, skin, ears and nose. Since it is the mind alone that is aware of the world through the five sense organs, tell me is there a world other than mind?

Commentary

The notion that the world is real is the basis of all worldly life. What is meant by the universe? Seeing, hearing, smelling, touching, tasting - it is these five sensory perceptions that we call the world *(prapañcha).* Bhagavan says that the world is nothing but the form of the five senses.

As there are five sense organs, the experience of the world appears to be five-fold. If there had been one more sense organ, there might have been one more mode of perception. Certain creatures have only three or two or just one sense organ. Their world is not like that of ours. The nature of perception of the world varies in accordance with the sense organs. The sense organs are mere outlets. It is the mind that gets scattered through them. The mind expands itself as - form through the eyes, sound through the ears, smell through the nose, taste through the tongue and touch through the skin. This expansion is the world. Is this not just *manōmaya* - merely mental? Where indeed is the world without the mind? The declaration is: *manōmayam tad bhuvanam* (Sat-darsanam).

In the dream state, the mind sees, hears and performs other functions without the help of the sense organs. This implies that all sense organs are contained within the mind. Even for one who is asleep in a dark room, the dream-scenes appear in bright light. From this it is obvious that the light needed for the reflection of the universe is also within the mind. Even the body appears only when the mind arises.

In the earlier *śloka*, it was stated that the world is known with the help of the body. And the body appears only when the mind arises. From this, it can be deduced that the world is contained in the body, and the body in the mind.

na hyāstyavidyā manasōtiriktā
manōhyavidyā bhavabandhahētu:
tasmin vinaṣṭē sakalam vinaṣṭam
vijṛmbhitēsmin sakalam vijṛmbhatē - Vivekachudamani 169

'There is no ignorance apart from the mind. The mind itself is ignorance. The mind itself is the cause for bondage. If the mind is destroyed, everything will disappear. When the mind arises, everything appears.'

Daily in deep sleep, we experience this truth. When the mind dissolves, there is no world and no body. Neither is there the individual *jīva*, 'I'. When the mind arises, the sprout of the individual-'I' comes up. Along with it, the body and the world also arise. The waking state occurs when the mind blooms, and the deep sleep state occurs when it dissolves. Dreams are seen when the mind is at half-bloom. Everything is only of the mind. The real Self has absolutely no relation to this.

buddhēr jāgaraṇam swapna: suṣuptiriti vṛttaya:

– Srimad Bhagavatam 7-7-25

'The waking, dream and deep sleep states are all of the intellect.'

The awareness or the consciousness that stands as a witness to all these is the substratum, the *kūṭastha. 'Kūṭastha'* means 'the immovable'. In that *kūṭastha chaitanya,* the three states that pertain solely to the intellect do not exist at all. If one's real nature is established in that substratum or *kūṭastha,* then one will be able to see that the world - which is purely mental - is only an appearance that rises and sets in one's own Self; and that one's Self is the real experiential consciousness, and the substratum of all experiences. If one carefully watches the experience of 'I-I', the *kēvalānubhūtisattā* (the non-dual consciousness) will shine forth. The mind is an indefinable power that springs up like a mirage in the desert. From the mind, the other manifestations emerge. The mind is not separate from thoughts. If all the thoughts are removed, there will be no object called the mind. All the mind-modifications arise from the heart. When all these modifications subside in the heart, the world and the body will disappear, and the supreme Self will radiate - Arunachala Siva will blaze forth.

The two world-wars took place during Bhagavan Sri Ramana's lifetime. In the Ashram, even in Bhagavan's presence, war-news would come in from time to time. There would also be discussions on them. Hearing the commotion raised by people who had read in the newspapers about Hitler, Mussolini, Britain, Germany, etc., Bhagavan would remain still without batting an eye-lid. At times, Bhagavan would be seen reading the newspaper. But not a single word about the war would come from his lips. Seeing this, a devotee, asked: "Bhagavan! How are you able to sit as if nothing has happened, when the war is raging in all its fury?" In response, Bhagavan remarked in a calm but serious tone: "Where is the war taking place? In my world, I do not see any war. The war is staged only in the thoughts of your mind. You have given the name war to certain specific imaginations of the mind. If the thoughts are subdued, creation is not there; even the world is not there. Then where is war?" This is the state of a *jnani*. Right here, even when the *jnani* appears to have a body, he has transcended it. *Ihaiva tairjita: sarga:* - 'Here itself creation has been transcended by them'. By whom? *Ēṣām sāmyē sthitam mana:* - i.e., 'By those whose minds rest in equanimity' says the Bhagavad Gita.

saśarīram ahō viśvam parityajya mayādhunā
kutaśchit kouśalādēva paramātmā vilōkyatē

'Transcending this world along with the body - by the skill of *jnana*, the supreme Self is experienced here itself!'. This is the voice of King Vaideha Janaka, when enlightenment dawns upon him after receiving Self-knowledge from sage Ashtavakra.

In the inward journey the entire cosmos comes to rest in the body, the body in the senses. The senses rest in the mind and when the mind rests and disappears in the heart, the whole story comes to an end. The absurd autobiography of the individual ego which sprouts with the thought of 'I' and 'mine' vanishes, and at that very instant, the supreme consciousness is revealed in all its glory. This method is clearly explained in Sri Ramana Gita. It is called *hṛdaya vidyā, dahara vidyā,* and so on. It is also known as *mahānyāsa*. The real *sanyāsi* is one who settles the mind in its source. This is the only way to renounce the world. Such a person, who has renounced the world, has no body or world that is separate from the Self, even though he may appear to others as living in a body.

sattāchitsukharūpamasti satatam
nāham nacha tvam mṛṣā
nēdam vāpi jagat pradṛṣṭamakhilam
nāstīti jānīhi bhō: – Proudanubhuti 16

'Beingness, pure awareness and Bliss alone is, ever resplendent. I do not exist, you do not exist, and the visible world also does not exist. Dear one, know this well.'

Who could ever gauge the inner depth of the liberated being who moves about singing this song of Self-experience?

VERSE SEVEN

...nērē—ninḍṛa

ulagaṛi-vu monḍṛā yudittoḍuṅgu mēnu

mulaga-ṛivu tannā loḷiru—mula-gaṛivu

tōnḍṛi-maṛai daṛkiḍa-nāi tōnḍṛi-maṛai yā-doḷirum

pūnḍṛa-mā makdē poru-ḷāmāl

ulagu aṛivum onḍṛāi	The visible world and the mind that is the seer, like twins
udittu oḍuṅgumēnum	though they rise and set
ulagu aṛivu tannāl	the world by the light of the mind
oḷirum	shines (the world will not shine by itself)
ulagu aṛivu tōnḍṛi maṛaidaṛku iḍanāi	the substratum whence the world and mind arise, and wherein they set,
tōnḍṛi maṛaiyādu	itself without rising and setting
oḷirum	and by itself shines
akḍē pūnḍṛamām poruḷ āmāl	that is the eternal perfect whole.

Paraphrase:

Though the world and the mind rise and set simultaneously, the world shines by the light of the mind alone, for it (the world), is not self-luminous. That substratum whence the world and the perceiving mind rise and set but which, by itself, without rising and setting, shines, is the eternal, perfect truth.

Commentary

In the previous *śloka*, it has been explained that the world arises only when the mind arises. In this verse, the attempt is to express the reality which is the source of the world and the mind. Where does the 'I' that sees the world, and the 'world' that is seen by me, disappear during sleep? Where do they arise from, on waking? On waking, the individual-'I' arises, and the world appears along with it as an object to be seen by me. Therefore, Bhagavan's reply to those who ask how the world was created has always been this counter question: "Who is the one who sees the world?" The world is seen only after the 'I', who is the seer of the world, has arisen. If one enquires: "Where does this 'I' come from?", then the 'I' - the individual ego - disappears entirely, without leaving even a trace. When the ego-'I' subsides, the real- 'I', the egoless substratum, the supreme Brahman shines forth. That alone exists. In this reality, *ahanta* and *idanta* - the ego-'I' and the visible 'world' - arise and appear like two branches *(idanta,* is *idam,* or the world that is seen). The illusory nature of this apparent duality is clearly experienced by everyone in the deep sleep state. Reflection on the nature of the deep sleep state *(suṣupti)* will clarify the meaning and intention of this *śloka*.

During the *brāhmamuhūrta (*early morning before dawn), immediately after waking up from deep sleep, when one is fresh and energetic one has to contemplate, enquire and plumb within: "Where was I a while ago? What was the nature of my personality during the state of deep sleep?" At first, the only response may be "I did not know anything...

The knowing 'I' was not there... It was blissful." By repeated reflection on this experience, sparks of insights will flash forth. Gradually that bliss, the experience of the deep fulfillment of the deep sleep state, will trickle down to the waking state through the crevices of the still-space in the intellect formed by contemplation. This revelation of the 'whole' through the windows of the quiet mind is *samādhi*. When the intellect hitherto tortured by thoughts, feelings and sleep becomes absolutely quiet, in the fullness of *ātmavichāra,* the celestial cool waters of the beyond will descend, healing all the hurts caused by the ego. Thus, reflection on the deep sleep state reveals the Self which is pure existence and that is intelligence and fullness. This centre where the 'I' merges and remains in its pristine purity is the serene realm of Brahman - *samprasāda* says the Brihadaranyaka Upanishad.

Bhagavan calls such a one who has grasped the truth, as *oru kuḍai nizharkōvē*, in Arunachala Ashtakam. That means he is the sole emperor who abides in the throne of his own heart. He is the ruler of an empire that will never be lost! Once, Swami Ramatirtha met the then President of United States. "I am Emperor Rama", said the Swami to the President, while conversing. Amused, the President asked him rather humorously: "Of which country are Your Highness the emperor?" The Swami replied: "Rama is the eternal emperor of the whole universe. The empire of Rama is one which will never be lost!"

Tōnḍṛi maṛaiyādoḷirum pūnḍṛamām akdē poruḷ - through yoga, one may experience certain kinds of states. All these states are within the realm of nature. Truth is not a state. It is the ever-attained reality. Realization is the recognition of the Existence-Consciousness, which never appears and disappears, but always 'is'. Bhagavan sings about this in Aksharamanamalai as *pōkkum varavumillā poduveḷi.*

The world by itself is not aware of its own existence. The self-luminous Atman or existence also is not aware of the world as world. That which is inert has no awareness while pure awareness does not know anything other than itself. The mind which arises in between this consciousness and inert matter, and which is termed as a *granthi* (knot), is the cause for the appearance and disappearance of the world.

BEYOND THE ROCKS

Beyond the hard, barren rocks of deep sleep,
Lies the solution, nay, dissolution of all our miseries!
It is the only authentic state, where
The inner being communes with you gently whispering,
"Dear! You are body-less, mind-less, ego-less, world-less!!"
Thus does Mother *śruti* reveal the ever-revealed Brahman.
When Lord Ramana spoke thus to me,
The words vanished, revealing the unknowable!
The dawn came to me in the deeps of awareness.
Gliding beyond all names and forms
'I' fell into the ocean of existence, peace and light.
Fruition, fulfillment was reached here and now.
This heart leaps in ecstasy; blessed is this life,
Blessed, blessed, blessed am I!

VERSE EIGHT

...yēnḍṛadām
yeppe-yariṭ ṭevvu-ruvi lēt-tinumār pēr-uruvi
lappo-ruḷaik kāṇ-vazhiya dāyinu-mam—meip-poruḷi
nuṇmaiyiṭṛa nuṇmai-yinai yōrndo-ḍuṅgi yonḍṛu-dalē
yuṇmaiyiṛ kāṇa luṇarn-diḍuga

yēnḍṛadām	it is possible
ār eppayariṭṭu	whosoever by whatever name
evvuruvil ēttinum	and in whatever form worships
pēr uruvil apporuḷai	nameless, formless that whole - the absolute
kāṇ vazhi adu āyinum am	the way to see verily is that though
tan uṇmaiyinai ōrndu	recollecting the truth of one's own real nature
am meip poruḷin	of that supreme truth
uṇmaiyil	in the real nature
oḍuṅgi onḍṛu-dalē	getting absorbed, non-dually as One
uṇmaiyil kāṇal uṇarndiḍuga	is true vision, know this

Paraphrase:

By whatever name or form, that nameless and formless supreme being is thought of and worshipped - it is verily a way to see that reality. Yet, establishing one's attention in one's own Self, losing one's individual 'I' in the reality, and becoming one with That, is realization; know this!

Commentary

In this *śloka*, while approving the worship of God with name and form, Bhagavan explains what realization *(tattva darśanam)* truly is. A seeker who has fully accomplished and transcended both the realm of action and the realm of worship (one who is a *kṛtakṛtya* and a *kṛtōpāsaka)* alone is competent to listen to Vedanta. Such a mature seeker will realize the Self by mere *śravaṇa* (listening) from a Master. Our bodies are fields filled with the seeds of *prārabdha karma*. It is impossible to terminate *karma* without going through it. However, if one performs actions with desire, he acquires more *vāsanās* and falls back into the whirlpool of more complex *karma*. 'One *karma* leaves only after sowing the seed of another and thus leads to unending *samsāra'* declares the Upadesa Saram. Hence *karmayōga* means performing one's obligatory actions with detachment, without any desire for their fruit and as an offering to the Lord. Thereby the seeds of *karma* will gradually come to an end. New *karmavāsanās* will not sprout and the mind will attain purity. In the pure mind will dawn the knowledge of the Self. This is the aim of *karmayoga*.

īśwarārpitam nēcchayā kṛtam
chitta śōdhakam muktisādhakam (Upadesa Saram)

Generally the seeker begins with devotion to a personal God with name and form according to his former spiritual tendencies. If the body is the field of action, the mind is the field of *upāsana* - meditation. Both action and meditation are based on the doer. They can be done, not done, or can be done wrongly. This applies to all worldly and Vedic *karmas*. The acts of worship are also like this. All these have to be performed by the seeker, strictly as instructed by his Guru. On the other hand *jnana* is to be known or experienced. It is *vastutantra*. A seeker whose 'body-debt' *(śarīra-ṛṇam)* has ended through *karma* and whose mind is purged of its impurities through devout worship or meditation will be able to focus his attention on the Self by listening to the meaning of the *mahāvākyās*. By *śravaṇa* itself, his attention *(śraddhā)* will turn towards the Self. The mind of a *mumukṣu* listening to the words of the Guru will go beyond their literal meaning and will become one with the implied meaning, the experiential-essence, and will get absorbed in it.

The name and form of the personal God is an anchorage for the soul, which has given up its hold on the world, in its inner voyage. The first part of the *śloka, eppeyariṭṭu... kānvazhiyadu āyinum,* sanctions this. However in the second part, the shift of attention is made from the seen to the seer - *ammeypporuḷin uṇmaiyil tan uṇmaiyinai ōrndu oḍuṅgi onḍṛudale uṇmaiyiṛ kāṇal.* Sri Bhagavan Himself was enchanted by the name 'Arunachala'. The divine sensation that Bhagavan had for this name is in ample evidence in Arunachala Ashtakam and in Aksharamanamalai. Even after the death-experience followed by the Self-realization that happened in Madurai, the name 'Arunachala' and the devotion towards it continued to remain with Ramana. It was by the powerful force of this divine fascination that Bhagavan, renouncing everything, arrived at Tiruvannamalai. On reaching here, he saw the form of Arunachala, reigning in resplendent silence! Thus Ramana experienced both name and form of the Lord. But immediately going beyond name and form, His mind merged itself in the seer, in his own Self.

'On beholding the unmoving hill with mind turned inward, I enquired within, 'Who is the seer?' The knower (seer, ego) disappeared; I beheld the non-existence of the seer. The 'I' (ego) did not arise to say 'I saw'. How then could the 'I' arise to say I did not see? Who has the power to convey it in words when in days of yore, Thou Thyself, as Dakshinamurthy, did this only by silence? Thou standeth motionless spanning heaven and earth as Arunachala Hill in all resplendence, only to reveal Thy transcendent state in silence!!' (Arunachala Ashtakam - 2)

This is the flight from worship to wisdom. A seeker once had a *darśan* (vision) of Siva as a result of intense worship. Carried away by the experience, he asked the Maharshi how to make it permanent. Bhagavan replied: "The visible Siva is not eternal. What appears and disappears is not the real Siva-*swarūpa*. The real Siva-*tattva* is the consciousness that ever remains unchanged during, before, and after the appearance of the vision of Siva. It is the consciousness that ever remains unchanged as a witness to the mind, which is the Eye of the eye that had the vision."

A devotee wished ardently for Krishna-*darśan.* So whenever he met a *sādhu*, he would prostrate before him, invite him to his house and pray for Krishna-*darśan.* A Vaishnavite saint initiated him with the 'Hare Rama' *mantra* and said that it would grant him Krishna-*darśan.* The devotee meditated upon the *mantra* with intense devotion and sincerity. But he did not obtain Krishna-*darśan.* While he was thus pining for a vision of Krishna, another *sādhu* visited him at his home far away at Punjab and advised him to go to Tiruvannamalai and meet Sri Ramana Maharshi. When, after some time he visited Ramanasramam, and saw Bhagavan, it was anger that this devotee felt; for, it was the same Ramana Maharshi who had come to his house and advised him to go to Tiruvannamalai! When he told others that this same *sanyāsi* had visited him earlier and played the game of self propagation, he was told that the Maharshi had never left Arunachala for almost fifty years! Although astonished at this miracle, this devotee felt no particular attraction towards Bhagavan or Ramanasramam or the other visitors in the Ashram. However, as he started chanting the name of Krishna sitting on the slopes of the Arunachala hill, he became absorbed in it and began to have visions of Krishna. He lost himself in these visions of the Lord, and began to develop a sense of pride in having them. He even felt like making fun of Bhagavan, and thought: "I must go and inform this to Ramana Swami. I must advise him to pray for Krishna-*darśan* rather than simply sitting there in silence!" With this, he approached Bhagavan who was sitting in great dignity and peace, absorbed in the bliss of the Self. There, while waiting for a chance to speak to Bhagavan, he found that devotion for Krishna would not rise in his heart however much he tried; instead, a pulsation, 'Who am I?'... 'Who am I?' began to arise continuously within him. He was trying to ignore this pulsation, when the following dialogue took place:

Bhagavan: Where have you been all these days?

D: I was on the mountain slopes doing *tapas.*

B: *Oho*! And what did you achieve?

D: Krishna-*darśan.*

B: Constantly?

D: No. He appears at times.

B: That which appears and disappears is not the truth. What is it that knows that which appears, and always shines as the Knower of all knowledge? Pay attention to that. That is *ātmaswarūpa*.

Saying this Bhagavan stared at the devotee. The divine glance made him merge in the heart. Gradually, the form that he was meditating upon disappeared, and in its place, the Self-enquiry, 'Who am I?' began to arise. This Self-enquiry led him to Self-realization. In later years, this devotee became a guiding light to many seekers. He declared later that the 'Hare Rama' *mantra* and meditation on the form of Krishna became the vehicle which took him to the presence of the satguru.

muktāśrayam yarhi nirviṣayam viraktam
nirvāṇamṛcchati mana: sahasā yathārchi:
ātmānamatra puruṣōvyavadhānamēkam
anvīkṣatē pratinivṛttaguṇapravāha:

– 'Kapilopadesa'; Srimad Bhagavatam 3–28–35

'The Lord's beatific form, which is the basis for meditation, disappears on its own at a particular stage. And when the Lord's form which was his sole anchorage disappears, the mind that has developed detachment and dispassion towards other objects as a result of meditation attains *nirvāṇa,* like the flame getting blown out devoid of fuel. In this state, without any hindrance, the flow of *satva* and the other *guṇās* subside, and uninterrupted Self-experience happens.'

Meditation on form *(rūpadhyānam)* and chanting the holy name *(nāmajapam)* will certainly be helpful in reaching Bhagavan's path of Self-realization. When Natesa Mudaliar sought Sri Bhagavan's grace, Bhagavan in a dream asked him to meditate on Siva in a particular form before approaching him. Later when he came to Bhagavan he prayed for grace. Bhagavan smiled and said to him "Who is asking for grace? Is it the Atman or the body? Of course the body cannot ask. If it is the Self, grace is its nature. If the self which misapprehends itself with body separates itself and realizes, then it will come to know that grace is indeed the Self." At that very instant the blessed devotee surrendered to the Master.

Vilacheri Mani known as rogue Mani - *pōkkiri* Mani - was a boyhood friend of Ramana. After many years of wayward life he went to Arunachala for the sake of his mother, on their way back from Tirupati. Even then he was unwilling to visit the Maharishi. But his mother, on her own, went up the hill to see Bhagavan. Vilacheri Mani then followed her just out of curiosity to see what had happened to his old friend. He went up, entered the Virupaksha cave and what did he behold! Lo! It was not his friend that he found there. He saw God sitting there in human form; a figure shining like burnished gold, eyes 'still' as a rippleless lake. Mani prostrated before that silent being and prayed holding on to the feet "Lord, redeem me". Bhagavan glanced at him with compassion and said in a familiar tone "*che, che* what is this? Mani, let go of the legs and remain quiet as

SIVA, SIVA." Mani let go the feet and danced in delight saying "Bhagavan has initiated me with the divine name!" From that moment he began chanting 'Siva, Siva' day and night. The name merged with his breath, blood-stream and heartbeat. It penetrated into the deep recesses of his mind and went beyond to shine as Self-awareness. He had a peaceful absorption in the end, repeating the name of Siva!

When the mind becomes pure, the attainment of a satguru who will give instructions to attain Self-knowledge will happen of its own accord. This is the gradual process. Very rarely some seekers directly come to the path of *jnana-vichāra*. Hence it is to be understood that worship of name and form purifies the mind to attain the right vision *(sat-darśanam)*. The mind made sharp and single-pointed by concentration and meditation, flows inward very easily. In other words, such a mind becomes qualified to grasp the pulsation of 'I'. For Bhagavan Ramana Maharshi, the mind became absorbed in the I-consciousness even without the instructions of an external Guru. Bhagavan has said several times that the presence of Siva in the form of Arunachala was the cause for it. Bhagavan has also glorified Arunachala as His Guru in his marvelous Five Hymns on Arunachala (Arunachala Stuti Panchakam).

Bhagavan Narada says in the Bhakti Sutra*: 'ātmarat-yavirōdhēna iti śāṇḍilya:'*. That is, worshipping the Lord with name and form, should not conflict with the delight in the Self. In other words, the Lord's form that we worship, instead of leading us to the Self, the seer within, should not entice our mind towards the seen. Very often devotion *(bhakti)* in the world is seen as a movement away from the Self, turning it into one more worldly activity. But those who worship the form of the Lord with the aim of Self-knowledge will never slip from the path. The indweller within, will grant them vision appearing in the form of their personal deity, and also lead them to Self-knowledge in the form of an external Guru.

THE DIVINE NAME

Lord! Thy Name is the key
With which I have opened the
Treasure-trove of bliss divine.
Ceaselessly did I chant Thy Name
And lo! The Name disappeared
Along with the repeater
You revealed there yourself!
Chanting the Name which is
Nothing but Thy form
Death died and birth no more,
The mind came in contact
With the 'Name' within;
Nāma which is not a spoken word;
Nāma which is not an uttered sound;
The sound which is verily
The essence of everything - the *śabdabrahma*!

(The *Secret Stream of the Sacred*)

VERSE NINE

...viṇmai

iraṭṭai-gaṇ muppu-ḍiga ḷenḍṛum-onḍṛu paṭṭṛi

yirup-pavā mavvon-ḍṛē denḍṛu—karut-tinuṭ

kaṇḍāṛ kazhalu-mavai kaṇḍa-va rēyuṇmai

kaṇḍār kalaṅ-gārē kāṇ

viṇmai	like the blueness of the sky
iraṭṭaigaḷ muppuḍigaḷ	dyads (all dualities like birth and death, good and bad) and the triads (like the knower, known and knowledge)
enḍṛum onḍṛu paṭṭṛi	always, by clinging on to the one, namely, ego
iruppavām	Subsist
avvonḍṛu ēdu enḍṛu	what is the truth of that ego, thus
karuttinuḷ kaṇḍāl	the mind turned inward within oneself and the truth enquired and known
kazhalum avai	dyads and triads will fall away
kaṇḍavarē uṇmai kaṇḍār	such who perceive the death of the ego are those who perceive the Self, the content of truth
kalaṅgārē kāṇ	such discerning people, know then, will not be agitated anymore by dyads and triads

Paraphrase:

The dyads (like birth and death, good and bad, pleasure and pain) and the triads (like knower, known and knowledge) merely exist, holding on to the ego as support. If one but turns the mind inward, within oneself and enquires into the truth of this ego, the dyads and triads will fall away. One who thus witnesses the death of the ego alone is the one who has seen the Self, or the truth. Such men of discernment will never again be agitated by such dyads and triads.

Commentary

The nature of the mind is to operate in the dualistic realm. Like the age old question 'Which came first, the hen or the egg?' the mind conjures up two mutually dependent objects and make us doubt and go round in circles, leading to a blind alley, unable to transcend the dualities. When both the egg and the hen get destroyed, earth alone remains. Earth alone is. We ourselves create the illusion of two and suffer. Similarly the mind itself imagines the duality of joy and sorrow, and creating attachment towards joy and aversion towards sorrow, it traps us in the mesh of duality. The same is the case with the triads - *muppuḍi*. 'I', 'the world' and 'the knowledge about the world' - all of these exist in the mind alone. In deep sleep, when the mind has subsided, none of these three entities is seen. When the mind arises, the seer and the seen appear too. The ego is the root of the mind. If one observes where the ego-'I' arises from, it will merge in the heart, and truth will be gloriously revealed.

na paśyatām sat chalanam kadāpi – Sat-darsanam

'One who has seen the truth, will slip no more from that state; will not be deceived by the apparent dualities'.

He will realize that all the dualities as well as the imaginary individual-'I', appear due to the inscrutable *māyā;* and that they are only an illusory appearance in the absolute reality like the mirage in a desert. Due to this very knowledge, he will not be deluded even if he sees them again. Even if a glimpse of Self-experience happens once, unless followed by relentless Self-abidance, the mind might bring back all the delusions with greater force! It is to annihilate the *tripuṭi,* to allow the lamp of Self-awareness to glow steadily, that sages choose solitary places and in silence spend time in Self-abidance. Once the *pratyabhijña* (recognition) of the Self has dawned, it may remain in memory, but to attain continual uninterrupted experience of the eternal Self through the destruction of *vāsanās*, it is essential to sit in solitude and absorb oneself wholly in Self-abidance - *ātmaniṣṭha*. When abiding in the Self becomes natural and spontaneous, one can move about as one wishes.

Even highly mature seekers used to complain to Bhagavan that desire and anger make the mind restless, that the feeling of emptiness is experienced at times and so on, which hamper their *sādhana*. Bhagavan's remedy usually for all this was to make them realize that such obstacles occur only in the mind, and that it is due to the deep-rooted identification with the mind that one is affected by these obstacles. If one loses hold of the 'I' all these hindrances crop up. If the 'I' is held in awareness, there will be no feeling of emptiness either.

When desire, anger and the like arise, one must ask: 'To whom do these arise?' The answer will be 'to me'. If you ask: 'Who is this 'I'?' the 'I' will dissolve and the ever-attained freedom and peace will radiate. The 'I' is the source of all dualistic thoughts. When the 'I' disappears, the dualities also disappear and the Self alone will remain. Those who have experienced THAT will abide in the eternal, uninterrupted, and pure consciousness. They will not have identifications such as 'I eat', 'I see', 'I sleep', 'I worship' etc. When the body eats and sleeps, the 'I' mingles with it and gives rise to *vikalpās* (identifications). If the 'I'-thought does not arise, even when the actions of the body occur, the awareness will shine cloudless. This 'state' is called *nirvikalpa*. In *nirvikalpa*, when the ego is born in the I-consciousness, the *samvit* gets divided. In the pure *samvit*, if the 'I'-thought ceases to arise, the absolute consciousness or *chit* alone remains. The dyads and triads *(iraṭṭaigaḷum muppuḍigaḷum)* arise in the divided *samvit*. The *śruti* (Veda) calls the limited *samvit*, '*alpam*'; and the unlimited *samvit*, '*bhūmā*'. *Bhūmēva sukham, na alpē sukhamasti,* is the famous teaching of Sanatkumara (Chandogya Upanishad 7-23-1).

FLICKERLESS FLAME IN WINDLESS SPACE

In the silence of the woods and solitary caves of the mountains
Did one sit to plunge within and behold the flickerless flame-'I am'
Wind from all sides raged with fury to blow out the flame
All the doors of perception were shut,
Flickerless was held the flame 'I am' in the windless inner space.
Years vanished in a twinkle, for timelessness was its light!
Perception plumbed its own bosom,
Mind swallowed its own self,
The self dived back to its womb
And the phantom was lost in the fathomless deeps
Where he gained eternal life by death!

VERSE TEN

iruḷpōn—maṇḍum

aṛi-yāmai viṭṭaṛi-vin ḍṛām-aṛivu viṭṭav

vaṛi-yāmai yinḍṛā-gu manda—vaṛivu

maṛiyā maiyum-ārkken ḍṛam-mudalām tannai

yaṛi-yu maṛivē yaṛi-vām

iruḷpōn maṇḍum	As a dense veil of darkness
aṛiyāmai viṭṭu	apart from the ignorance
aṛivu inḍṛām	there is no separate existence for knowledge
aṛivu viṭṭu av	likewise, apart from the objective knowledge
aṛiyāmai inḍṛu āgum	ignorance cannot remain
anda aṛivum	that knowledge
aṛiyāmaiyum	and the ignorance
ārkku enḍṛu	'to whom?', thus enquiring
am mudalām tannai	that primal 'I', the Self
aṛiyum aṛivē aṛivām	that which knows it, alone is true knowledge

Paraphrase:

There is no separate existence for knowledge apart from ignorance. To enquire, 'Whose is this knowledge? Whose is this ignorance?' and thus to know the primal Self, this alone is true knowledge.

Commentary

Jnana is the *swarūpa* of Brahman, the Self. The corresponding word for the Sanskrit term *jnana* in Tamil is *aṛivu*. This *aṛivu* generally comes into being along with the *tripuṭi* - the knower, the knowledge and the known. It is not possible to have any worldly or scriptural knowledge without these three entities. The expression 'knows' naturally implies the following: 'Who?' 'What?' and 'How?'. All such knowledge implying the knower, the act of knowing and the known, is in the realm of duality. All these happen within nature. Hence this knowledge is termed *aparāvidyā*. *Aparāvidyā* is actually *avidyā*; it is just ignorance. Therefore, this knowledge cannot be accepted as *brahma-swarūpa*. *Aparāvidyā* is ignorance, for, even when there is knowledge, ignorance exists as its companion. Worldly knowledge cannot exist without ignorance, and ignorance cannot exist without knowledge. This is how the *iraṭṭai* (duality) functions, always going hand-in-hand. Along with the *muppuḍi* - 'the knower, the known and the act of knowing', the *iraṭṭai*– knowledge and ignorance also arise.

Once, a simple-minded *sādhu* saw a number of scholars asking questions, and Bhagavan giving them suitable answers. After they left, this man asked with great humility and apprehension: "Bhagavan, all these people have studied various books and are learned. They are able to ask Sri Bhagavan questions of great depth and understand the answers whereas I know nothing. I am an ignorant person. What will be my fate? Is there any hope for me?" Bhagavan replied: "Yours is unlearned ignorance and theirs is learned ignorance; that's all!

You say, 'I am an *ajnani*'. If you enquire who this 'I' is, then real knowledge will dawn upon you! These scholars too, if they make their noisy minds quiet, and know their own Self, all their doubts will vanish and they will also become peaceful."

What is the knowledge of Brahman? *Tannai aṛiyum aṛivē aṛivāgum* - 'knowing one's Self alone is true knowledge'. All other knowledge exists in the form of *iraṭṭaigal* - as a mixture of knowledge of the objects of the senses, and ignorance. While a person may possess knowledge about a particular subject, he may be quite ignorant of many others. Omniscience is never ever possible in the realm of worldly knowledge. According to the *śāstrās,* a person should not be called a *paṇḍita* on account of his great scholarship in the knowledge about the world. *Paṇḍā* literally means *ātmaviṣayā-mati:* - that knowledge which makes the Self known. One who has that knowledge alone can be considered a *paṇḍita* says Sri Sankara in the Gita Bhashyam.

A Guru is not for teaching something new; on the other hand, it is to turn the attention of a *mumukṣu* towards the Self, towards the knower, the 'I'. The world is actually a mixture of *chit* - the 'I', the knower which is pure awareness and *idam* - the known, the objects. In short, this constitutes what we define as 'my world'. What we generally call as 'knowledge' is simply information that we gather through the senses with the help of the mind. All these ideas, images and informations are then framed in certain names and forms preserved in the form of thought-impressions in the brain. This process is defective at the very first step. For, the thought 'I', the first person, the centre of thinking, is itself illusory. All kinds of information that arise from this erroneous basic premise in the form of thoughts and linguistic expressions are mere waves in the mind (*vikṣēpa*). For a person who does not know English, the brilliant expositions of a great scholar or the primitive usages of an illiterate are both mere sounds! Hence 'knowledge' and 'ignorance' are only relative terms.

In Vedanta, 'knowledge' refers only to the pure awareness, the knowing-principle, the intelligence behind all knowledge. Terms like knowledge and experience, are synonyms for consciousness. This consciousness is what the Veda calls *jñapti*. The experience of 'I am' is the light which illumines both knowledge and ignorance. When we follow the quest 'Who am I?' with the eye of attention, the 'I' in the experience of 'I am' can be seen to disappear into the simple experience of 'am'. In this experience 'I am', 'I' is the personal element and 'am' is existence. It is existential-awareness that is expressed by Bhagavan as: *aṛivum aṛiyāmayum kaḍanda aṛivu* (the ultimate 'knowledge' that lies beyond knowledge and ignorance). It is consciousness that underlies and illumines both 'I know' and 'I do not know'. This awareness is existence, beingness - the *sat*. That indeed is the treasure that we are seeking. *Ammudalām tannai aṛiyum aṛivē aṛivām* - **knowing that Self, the primal beingness, is knowledge.** Remaining established in that original source, which is pure awareness is wisdom.

Bhagavan himself says in Upadesa Undiyar - *tānāy iruttalē tannai aṛidalām* - **abiding as the Self is, knowing the Self**. As all have the consciousness 'I', in and through all the experiences, it has to be asserted that every one of us, without exception, has the experience of the Self. The *śruti* also says that **this Self is hidden in the experience of all.** Yet the suffering continues as a result of mixing up the functions of the body-mind-senses with the consciousness-'I'. Eliminating the functions of the *upādhīs* from consciousness and holding the 'I am' ablaze in awareness is *Ātma-Yōgā*. When we perceive objects by the light of consciousness we claim that 'we know'. When we do not perceive objects we say that 'we do not know'. In fact it is consciousness that illumines both the presence and the absence of objects! The person who claims, 'I do not know' must be conscious to say so. That is, he himself is the consciousness! So Bhagavan generally remarks: "All are *jnanis*. There is no *ajnani* at all." Where is it possible for ignorance to stay? Just as darkness cannot remain in the sun, ignorance cannot remain in the Self.

THE STREAM

Get out of the stream of duality that breeds conflicts.
Waters of desire; ripples and waves of craving,
Flowing between the banks of knowledge and ignorance
Is this stream of suffering that brings in birth and death.
Jump out of this and watch the flow from the inner-space,
You will see the seer and the seen vanish!
The space, pure awareness alone will remain as the whole!

VERSE ELEVEN

...aṛiba

aṛi-vuṛun tannai yaṛiyā dayalai

yaṛiva daṛi-yāmai yanḍṛi—yaṛivō

vaṛi-vayaṛ kādhāra tannai yaṛiya

vaṛi-vaṛi yāmai yaṛumē

aṛiba aṛivu uṛum tannai aṛiyādu	Without knowing the true nature of oneself, the knower who knows the objects
ayalai aṛivadu	knowing the objects that are other than oneself
aṛiyāmai anḍṛi aṛivō	can this be true knowledge? Is it not mere ignorance?
aṛivu ayaṛku	the objective worldly knowledge and the absence of it which is ignorance
ādhāra tannai aṛiya	When the substratum, the Self, is known
aṛivu aṛiyāmai aṛumē	both knowledge and ignorance will come to an end

Paraphrase:

Without knowing the 'I' who knows all objects through the senses and the mind - by enquiring 'Who am I?' - knowing objects which are separate from oneself is indeed ignorance. This can never be true knowledge. When the Self, the substratum of 'knowing' and 'not knowing' is known, both knowledge and ignorance will come to an end.

Commentary

A knower knows objects separate from oneself. Is this real knowledge? The mind of the perceiver that perceives objects through the senses assumes the forms of those objects. The intellect gathers these received impressions, and even in the absence of the objects, continues to preserve them as memory under the guise of 'knowledge'. The subtle shadowy impressions gathered and preserved in this manner hide the inner light of the Self like a dark veil. This is not true knowledge. This layer of *vāsanās* or inherent tendencies of the mind that veils the light of the Self is actually ignorance. Only by the awareness of the Self, can this veiling be removed. The 'I'-consciousness alone is self-luminous - *swayamprakāśā*. All that we see - ranging from the ego-'I' to the entire visible world of creation - are all pictures seen with the light of the *chit*. It is only after the instruments *(karaṇās)* like the mind and the senses arise in the awareness-'I', that the knowledge about the world arises. When the senses, the mind and the 'I'-thought subside in the heart through enquiry, pure consciousness shines as 'I-I' *(aham-aham).* This consciousness is the substratum, *(aṛivu ayaṛkku ādhāra tān).* If one abides as this Self, knowing-*aṛivu* and not knowing-*aṛiyāmai* both will come to an end. **Consciousness that is neither knowledge nor ignorance** *(jñānavarjita ajñānahīna chit)* will glow in all its brilliance (Upadesa Saram).

From the Self which is pure intelligence, arises an inscrutable power as 'I', 'I'. This power, comes in contact with ignorance, and transforms itself as the mind. From the mind, with the power of sound, it manifests as space; with sound and touch it manifests as air; with sound, touch and form it manifests as fire; with sound, touch, form and taste it manifests as water; and with sound, touch, form, taste and smell it expands as earth. Thus, in this universe which is a mixture of the five elements, the source of all manifestations is pure intelligence experienced as the consciousness-'I'. When this indefinable power deviates from consciousness and assumes the forms of objects, it becomes the mind. The very nature of the mind is to create an illusion of objects other than the Self. This is called *vikalpa.* When the mind is directed towards the Self, it becomes *chit-śakti*. When the power of the Self, the *ātma-śakti,* that has become the mind, gets purified through non-motivated actions and *bhakti*, that mind becomes refined and subtle. At this stage if one happens to get an intimation about the immeasurable that shines in the heart as 'I', 'I', a strange fascination arises from the depths to sink within. The purified mind, when it hears the words of the Guru, gets transformed at once into *chit-śakti* and gets absorbed in its source. This meditative mind is called *pratyaṅgmukha manas* (introverted or facing the Self). When the mind transcends both knowledge and ignorance, it glides into the indivisible. This is the revelation of the immeasurable. The Upanishads call it the imperishable - *akṣara*. The Mundaka Upanishad defines *parāvidyā* as, *Yayā tadakṣaram adhigamyatē* - **the knowledge by which that imperishable is known**.

Once, a devotee approached Bhagavan Sri Ramana with a new notebook and requested Bhagavan to bless him by writing something in it. Bhagavan remained silent without any *saṅkalpa*. Praying again for Sri Bhagavan's blessing the devotee said: "Oh, Bhagavan! It is enough if Bhagavan writes just one *akṣaram* (letter)." On hearing this Bhagavan smiled, took the book, and wrote out a marvelous single-verse (*muktaka)*.

ēkam akṣaram hṛdi nirantaram
bhāsatē swayam likhyatē katham

'That imperishable, self-luminous One shines in the heart continually. How can one write it?'

From a young age we are taught that - *vidyādhanam sarvadhanāt pradhānam* - knowledge is the greatest treasure that can be gained. Bhagavan, however, maintains that all our learning about the outside world is actually 'ignorance'. '*Ajnana*' is defined thus: 'knowing the other without knowing the real nature of one's own Self'. Let us see the example of mistaking a rope for a snake. Often in dim light a rope is mistaken for a snake. In pitch darkness the rope itself is not seen. So the snake also is not seen. It is only in dim light that the rope is misapprehended as a snake. Likewise absolute ignorance will not do much harm; just as the rope is not seen in total darkness. What is harmful is the presence of the faint light of a little knowledge, in which one misapprehends the rope as the snake. In deep sleep one does not recognize the Self. In the waking state, not only is the Self not known but also the non-Self such as the ego, body, world and so on is projected on it. This is similar to the experience of 'non-seeing' of the rope and the 'seeing' of the snake. In pitch darkness when the rope is not seen, as well as in dim light when the snake comes into view, the rope remains absolutely unchanged. The rope is there as it is. In the same way the Self remains changeless, incorruptible in the waking, dream, and deep sleep states. But because of the two aspects of ignorance - *āvaraṇa* (veiling) and *vikṣēpa* (projection), one does not recognize the experience. The *āvaraṇa* brings about the darkness of 'not-knowing'; and *vikṣēpa* projects the knowing of the 'other'. Not seeing the rope is the result of *āvaraṇa*. Mistaking the rope for a snake is due to *vikṣēpa*. *Āvaraṇa* occurs in deep sleep; both *āvaraṇa* and *vikṣēpa* occur in the waking and dream states.

In deep sleep even though there is the operation of *āvaraṇa*, there is the blissful experience of the Self. Hence we say: 'I slept happily'. Who is the one that records this blissful experience and speaks about it? It cannot be the intellect, as the intellect is absent in deep sleep. In that case, who declares the presence of happiness in that state? Was it mere memory? No. It was pure experience of the Self that revealed itself in the transition moment between the sleep and the waking. The bliss of the Self, experienced during deep sleep in the absence of the body-mind limitation gives a glimpse of it in that moment where you are neither awake nor asleep. Once a seeker recognizes this treasure, the veil of ignorance will be removed from the intellect. Inability to observe this obvious truth is *āvaraṇa*.

sukhamātyantikaṁ yattad buddhigrāhyam atīndriyam

– Bhagavad Gita 6-21

An extremely subtle intelligence - the *śraddhāśakti* - lies dormant in everyone. If attention, distilled by austerity is focused on this *śakti,* it will clearly manifest as transcendental-intelligence, *samādhiprajña.* That intellect gains the power to penetrate into the realm beyond the senses. That *buddhi* emblazoned by grace glides beyond the waking state and dream-state and peeps into the happiness inherent in deep sleep. That intellect - *prajñā* - becomes pure and powerful enough to recognize the substratum - *adhiṣṭhāna.* The very nature of the substratum is *samādhi.*

samādhinā atyantasusūkṣmavṛtyā –Vivekachudamani

The experience of happiness in deep sleep comes from the heart, while the ignorance, 'I did not know anything' comes from the intellect. Although happiness is attained, due to inattention or *aśraddha,* the experience is lost hold of while coming to the waking state. It is somewhat akin to falling down from heaven when one's fruits of good deeds run out. Everyone constantly has the experience of the Self as 'I'. But this eternal experience has to be held in vision by the luminous eye of attention. Hence Self-enquiry is inevitable. *Vichāra* is indeed the magnificent eye for seeing the truth - *vichāra: chāru lōchanam* – Yoga Vasishtam.

When the Master points to this experience by means of intuitive reasoning - *śrutyanugṛhīta tarka* - granted by the grace of the revealed *śruti*, the seeker realizes that the Self is ever-attained. He comes to know that there is nothing new to be attained, and that hitherto, he missed seeing this treasure within, only because of his inattention *(aśraddha)*. Knowing the Atman that is of the nature of pure awareness, through awareness itself, one abides in it as awareness! When *vikṣēpa* and *āvaraṇa* are removed from the intellect, the experience of consciousness of the ever-attained 'I-I', will shine forth as liberation. This consciousness shines without any change in the three states of waking, dream and deep sleep.

THE WORSHIP

He indeed is the blessed one, who, in aloneness
Shuts all the five 'eyes' and with the lamp of attention
The inner chamber lit, incessantly worships
The adorable-being who shines within as 'I AM',
With the flowers of awareness and peace - *śraddha* and *śānti*.

VERSE TWELVE

...aṛavē
aṛi-vaṛi yāmai-yu maṭṭṛa-daṛi vāmē
yaṛi-yuma duṇmai-yaṛi vāgā—daṛi-dark
kaṛi-vittaṛ kanniya-min ḍṛāya-virva dāṭṛā
naṛi-vāgum pāzhan dṛaṛi-vāi

aṛavē	completely
aṛivu aṛiyāmaiyum	the knowledge that is
aṭṭṛadu aṛivāmē	devoid of knowledge and ignorance is true knowledge
aṛiyum adu	the knowledge that knows objects through the senses
uṇmai aṛivu āgādu	is not true knowledge
aṛidaṛku aṛivittaṛku	with nothing else for it to know, with nothing other than itself to make it known
anniyam inḍṛāy avirvadāl	it shines by itself without there being anything other than itself
tān aṛivu āgum	the Self which is of the nature of pure awareness is true knowledge,
pāzh anḍṛu aṛivāi	it is not void, know this

Paraphrase:

Self-knowledge is devoid of both knowledge and ignorance. The knowledge of the 'other' i.e., objects apart from oneself, is not knowledge. As it shines by itself, without there being anything else other than it to know or to make it known, the Self, the Atman is true knowledge. Know that, it is not void.

Commentary

This *śloka* emphasizes the truth already discussed in earlier *veṇbās,* that Self-knowledge alone is real knowledge. The Upanishads state that knowledge is of two types - *aparā-vidyā* and *parāvidyā*. As the names suggest, knowledge within *aparāprakṛti* is *aparā* and the knowledge related to *parā-prakṛti* or the *jīva* is *parā.* (See the Bhagavad Gita, ch.-7; for the discussion on *parāprakṛti* and *aparāprakṛti.)*

Any knowledge gained by the mind is limited. The mind can either think (*vikṣēpa*) or sleep (*laya*). What we mean by 'I know' is merely memories or imaginations or concepts; all are nothing but thoughts. 'My knowledge' is only a *vikṣēpa* - a projection of the mind. Projection is the waking state. In sleep, the mind temporarily subsides. Sleep and projection, otherwise known as *laya* and *vikṣēpa* are nothing but mind. These do not in the least tarnish our real nature. Real knowledge is the awareness of the Self.

True knowledge is beyond knowledge and ignorance. In pure consciousness there is nothing other than itself to know or to forget. The self-effulgent consciousness is *jñapti* -

the spontaneous knowing of itself. The experience of 'I' is self-luminous. The mind or the senses are not needed to know this. The 'I'-consciousness is knowledge in its fullness. It is this absolutely dense consciousness that shines as 'I-I'. The duality - knowledge and ignorance - is born when this perfect awareness is misapprehended as the limited ego. Knowledge and ignorance are mutually dependent and one cannot remain without the other. When the 'mind' which is their cause, is removed, the absolute substratum shines forth on its own.This is not nothingness. It is complete, whole, fullness itself. All that is other than the Self is mere illusion. 'I AM' alone is truth. When even divine visions are said to be unreal, what can we say about other appearances? All visions are only illusions that appear and disappear.

ādāvantē cha yannāsti vartamānēpi tattathā

– Gaudapadakarika

'Whatever was not in the beginning and ceases to be later is not real even if it appears to be seen in the present'. This is the definition that Gaudapadacharya gives for the unreal.

The Self is the eternal principle. Bhagavan addresses the Lord in Arunachala Ashtakam as *irundoḷir* which means 'self-luminous beingness'. True knowledge is realization, the *pratyabhijñā* - instantaneous recognition of the Self by a lightning-like flash of intelligence. It is the re-cognition of one's Self that occurs in the pure existence - the *sat*. This existence shines in us without any change as 'I-I' in the past, present and future, as well as in the three states of waking, dream and deep sleep. This is Brahman. This is also called *jñapti* - awareness. To those who ask whether there remains only void when both knowledge and ignorance are removed, Bhagavan Ramana says: *pāzh anḍṛu* - 'It is not void'. It is at this juncture of enquiry that Buddhism slipped into the theory of *śūnya-vādā*. The Maharshi has already rejected the theory of 'nothingness' by the very first word, *uḷḷadu*. In fact the existence behind the world is of the Lord. The very 'existence' is Brahman. The substratum of the reality of the world shines in us as the consciousness 'I-I'. Chandogya Upanishad expresses this as *satyasya satyam* - truth of the true or existence of the existent. Can an entity which is itself non-existent give reality to other objects? It is the light of the Self, which is reality itself, that gives light to the objects of the world. And therefore we declare that they exist! In Arunachala Ashtakam Bhagavan calls this: *iruṭṭinai viḷakkeḍuttu aḍuttiḍal* (approaching darkness with light).

At times, seekers may have a feeling of an emptiness and restlessness. Even then, they must attentively pursue the enquiry, 'Who am I?' The quest, 'Who sees this emptiness?' has to be pursued relentlessly. The boulders of emptiness can be demolished by the spear of Self-enquiry. Only when one loses hold of the pulsation 'I', is the sense of emptiness felt. Visions and the sense of void are not different from one another. All visions lie hidden in the void. What appears to us as nothingness is the latent mind that remains as darkness. The words in the *śruti* - *asad vā idamagra āsīt tatō vai sadajāyata* - at first there was nothingness, then existence was born - express this idea. The void *(śūnyata)* is the veiling *(āvaraṇa)* and visions *(darśanās)* are the projections *(vikṣēpa)*. Nothingness also is the mind. Visions too are the mind. Yoga is remaining in stillness as *jñapti.* Abiding in one's real nature without visions, thoughts or the sense of nothingness is *samādhi.* As the awareness-'I', the Self, remains clear and effulgent it is not nothingness; it is absolute Existence-Consciousness-Bliss.

SOLE LUMINOUS BEING

The mind sought its own seed in its bosom,
And dived within to the abysmal depth.
Neither being nor non-being was there.
Death whirled around in darkness; mere void!
Grace awakened the inner vision that saw through this,
And light was there, in the womb of darkness
Beyond all duals as the **One Sole Luminous Being**!

VERSE THIRTEEN

... seṛivāya

jñāna-mām tānē-mei nānāvā jñāna-mañ

jñāna-mām poiyām-añ jñāna-mumē—jñāna-mām

tannai-yanḍṛi yinḍṛaṇi-ga tām-palavum poimei-yām

ponnai-yanḍṛi uṇḍō pugal

seṛivāya	in abundance
jñānamām tānē mei	pure awareness, the 'I AM' alone is real
nānāvā jñānam	the knowledge of manifold appearances is actually
ajñānamām	ignorance
poyyām ajñānamumē	the unreal ajnana also
jñānamām tannai anḍṛi inḍṛu	is non-existent apart from oneself which is of the nature of - jnana - pure awareness
aṇigaḷ tām	ornaments are
palavum poi	though of many names and forms are unreal
meiyām ponnai anḍṛi uṇḍō?	do they exist apart from gold, which is real?
pugal	ponder over this and tell

Paraphrase:

The Self that is awareness, the 'I AM', alone is Real. The knowledge that knows 'many' is *ajnana* (ignorance). Even that ignorance, an unreal appearance, cannot exist apart from the Self. False are the ornaments. Can they exist apart from gold, which alone is true? Ponder over this and tell me!

Commentary

The awareness 'I AM' is a self-evident, immediate experience that even an atheist or a rationalist cannot deny. Indeed this is the experience of the Self.

asti ityēva upalabdhasya tattvabhāva: prasīdati – Kathopanishad

'One who focuses his attention relentlessly on one's beingness, will awaken into the truth of Brahman'. The meaning of the *mahāvākya* **That art Thou** *(Tat Tvam Asi)* itself is the realized state of the supreme principle (*tattvabhāvam)*. Sri Ramana Maharshi expresses the same idea in Aksharamanamalai.

tānē tānē tattuvam idanai
tānē kāṭṭuvāi aruṇāchala!

'That which shines as one's own existence, as 'I' 'I' *(tān)* is *tattuvam* (the supreme truth). To see this, there cannot be another 'I'. And so Arunachala Siva who is the supreme-being, who is one's own existence, blaze forth thyself as the primordial fire 'I AM'. Reveal thyself by thyself, O Lord!'

One's own existence *(astitvam)* which is experienced as 'I am' is Brahman. To know this, one has to look within and investigate the individual-'I' *(asmitvam)*. Then it will reveal itself as the infinite. Bhagavan has sung in Aksharamanamalai that Arunachala Himself has initiated him into this secret path of self-enquiry.

tirumbi aham tanai dinamahakkaṇ kāṇ
teriyumenḍṛanai en Aruṇāchala!

'Turning inwards, behold the 'I' 'I' continually, every day with the inner eye and you will surely come to know; O Arunachala! You did initiate me thus into thy *upadēśa - ātmavichāra.'*

The *mantra* 'Who am I?' is *the mahāvākya* that reveals the *tattuvam* - truth. Enquiry here begins with 'I' and ends with 'I'. 'I', the ego, is the door to the portal of the timeless. 'To erase the primal ignorance, the 'I', keep hold of the 'I-I' within, day and night. Then the 'I' will reveal itself as the *ātmadēva* and you will delightfully merge in Him.' Thus Bhagavan reveals the *upadēśa* given to him by Arunachala in Vivekachudamani - *maṅgala veṇba*. This is the exact *upadēśa* that Arunachala gave to Arunagirinatha also. In Kandaranubhuti, the saint sings that the Lord revealed the *tat-pada* as 'I-I' by erasing the 'I'.

Rather than simply abiding in 'what is', the Self, knowing this and that with the mind is sheer ignorance. Even this ignorance is illumined by that beingness only. When the cloud is seen to cover the sun, the fact remains that the very existence of the cloud is known only by the light of the sun! In the same way, even to say that 'I am ignorant', the light of consciousness is required to do so. Hence *jnana,* the Self alone, is. Bhagavan expresses this as, *jñānamām tannai anḍri inḍru*. Ornaments like bangles and chains are made of gold. A woman with likes and dislikes towards particular names, forms and patterns may say 'I want a chain not a bangle'; 'this chain is beautiful'; 'that one is not good'; and so on. But a goldsmith or a thief who sees only the gold will give no specialty for any particular item. Their concern is only with the basic stuff - gold. Theirs is what is called *kanakaika mahābuddhi:* (the knowledge of seeing only the gold). One whose intention is to steal gold has no desire for the patterns of the ornaments since the substance, the gold alone, is significant for him. In the same way a seeker who aims at seeing only the reality is not interested either in names and forms, or in the affairs of the world. He is looking for the divine behind them. Those for whom worldly affairs are of utmost importance will not have the courage to declare that the world is illusory, and that Brahman alone is real. Worldliness is the companion of ignorance. The seeker, who no more relies upon the dealings of the world, who depends only on reality, will find no difficulty in denying the names and forms and accepting only the truth behind them. Such anchorage in truth is **revealing intelligence** - *vyava-sāyātmikābuḍdhi*. This is indeed courage - *dhairya.* He can declare with conviction: *aṇikal tām palavum poi* - ornaments with various names and forms are illusory; gold alone is real.

In worldly affairs, seeking solutions for problems is inevitable. Chaotic and confusing situations demand or rather compel actions. With such a compulsion one will not have the courage to declare that problems are unreal and the knowledge needed to solve them, is ignorance - *nānāvām jñānam ajñānamām*. For, we attempt to find solutions to our personal problems with the help of a variety of knowledge, thoughts. But the seeker who aims at absolute release ascertains that all problems are merely of the mind, and so instead of attempting to solve them, renounces them internally by giving up the thoughts about them. Rather, instead of solving them, he dissolves them! There is no need to look for a remedy to cure the disease that troubles you in a dream. The moment one wakes up from the dream, the disease vanishes. When the *jīva* that has been sleeping since time immemorial wakes up from its slumber, the reality that is un-born, un-sleeping, un-dreaming, and non-dual *(ajam anidram asvapnam advaitam)* shines forth says Gowdapada. It is such an enlightenment that is the goal of a *mumukṣu*, not an external solution to problems. The irresistible fascination to get absorbed in the Self gives the power to ignore the relative for the real.

One day a villager came to Bhagavan Sri Ramana, explained all his worldly problems and wept. Bhagavan listened to everything patiently and then replied in his usual manner: "All these sorrows are of the mind. In deep sleep, none of these exist. Only when the mind arises do all these thoughts arise. Hence, consciously make the mind subside in its source. Then all your problems will disappear along with the ego." The visitor, after sitting for some time in Bhagavan's presence, left the place. Then another devotee said: "Bhagavan is teaching *brahmavidyā* even to laymen! They are coming here seeking a practical solution to their worldly problems. But Bhagavan advises them from the highest standpoint. Will it be of any help to them?" First Bhagavan said *"enakku idu tān teriyum ōye* - This is all I know!" Then he continued: "Two people are sleeping in a room. One of them dreams that all his property is being stolen by thieves and screams, 'Catch the thief!' Should the friend who hears this go and try to catch the thief? If you wake up the sleeping man there is neither the thief nor the theft. He will see that he alone exists in the room. Won't he? In the same way, when the ultimate truth dawns, one will clearly realize that all these worldly problems are mere dream and that he has never been trapped in the sorrowful world." This is the direct way. *jñānamām tānē mei* - the Self that is pure awareness alone is real. This is a definitive statement, a declaration. *nānāvām jñānam ajñānamām* - knowledge of many is definitely ignorance.

It is sheer ignorance to have attachment and aversion to names and forms without knowing the one behind them, as it brings misery. The one non-dual awareness appears as the world when seen through the ludicrous glass of the senses. This error in perception lies behind our attachments and aversions. According to Vedanta neither knowing nor non-knowing is *jnana*. *Jnana* is to transcend knowledge and ignorance and to abide as the Self which is pure awareness. Such abidance alone brings the peace that everyone cherishes.

When Paul Brunton, the Western seeker came to visit Bhagavan Sri Ramana, he entered Bhagavan's room with a number of questions. He expected verbal answers for his mental doubts but what he got was more than that. Bhagavan saved him not only from ignorance but also from knowledge. In Bhagavan's presence all the questions vanished like darkness in the presence of the sun. Moreover, in this tranquil and serene presence of absolute peace resembling the still, unruffled ocean, all of Brunton's thoughts were stilled. To quote his words: "Pin-drop silence prevails throughout the long hall. The sage remains perfectly still, motionless, quite undisturbed at our arrival... I look full into the eyes of the seated figure in the hope of catching his notice. They are dark brown, medium-sized and wide open. If he is aware of my presence, he betrays no hint, gives no sign. His body is supernaturally quiet as steady as a statue. Not once does he catch my gaze, for his eyes continue to look into remote space, and infinitely remote it seems.

It is an ancient theory of mine that one can take the inventory of a man's soul from his eyes. But before those of the Maharishee I hesitate, puzzled and baffled. The minutes creep by in unutterable slowness. I reach a point of visual concentration where I have forgotten the existence of all save this silent figure on the couch... There is something in this man which holds my attention as steel filings are held by a magnet. I cannot turn my gaze away from him... This strange fascination begins to grip me more firmly... I become aware of a silent resistless change which is taking place in my mind. One by one, the questions which I have prepared in the train with such meticulous accuracy drop away. For it does not now seem to matter whether they are asked or not, and it does not seem to matter whether I solved the problems which have hitherto troubled me. I know only that a steady river of quietness seems to be flowing near me, that a great peace is penetrating in the inner reaches of my being, and that my thought-tortured brain is beginning to arrive at some rest.

How small seem those questions which I have asked myself with such frequency! ... I perceive with sudden clarity that the intellect creates its own problems and then makes itself miserable trying to solve them. This is indeed a novel concept to enter the mind of one who has hitherto placed such high value upon intellect. I surrender myself to the steadily deepening sense of restfulness until two hours have passed. The passage of time now provokes no irritation, because I feel that the chains of mind-made problems are being broken and thrown away. And then, little by little, a new question takes the field of consciousness. “Does this man, Maharishee, emanate the perfume of spiritual peace as the flower emanates the fragrance from its petals?” I begin to wonder whether, by some radio-activity of the soul, some unknown telepathic process, the stillness which invades the troubled waters of my soul really come from him... I came here to question ... but now... I, who am at peace with all the world and with myself, why should I trouble my head with questions?” (A Search in Secret India)

Poyyām ajñānamumē - this can be interpreted as 'ignorance which is not real', *ajnanam,* or as 'that knowledge which is false'. 'That knowledge' implies the worldly knowledge mentioned earlier. Derivatively that also means 'ignorance'. *Ponnai anḍṛi uṇḍō* - do they exist apart from gold? Names and forms are false. If this becomes experiential knowledge, then meditation with eyes open can be accomplished. **All names and forms of the world are mere superimpositions on Brahman like ornaments superimposed on gold. Brahman alone is. Whatever is seen through the mind and the senses as well as the seer who sees them - All are One, the One and only truth - Parameswara Himself.**

In Aksharamanamalai Bhagavan sings thus: 'When I perceive various objects through the five senses, the thieves of attachment and aversion enter the temple of my heart and loot my peace. What is the solution?' Bhagavan himself gives the answer: *oruvanām unnai oḷittevar varuvār; un sūdē idu-Aruṇāchala!* 'Who else can enter stealthily as thou alone is? This is just your trickery O Arunachala!' (Aksharamanamalai - 12)

Un sūdē idu – 'This is just your trickery'. These five are simply sensory perceptions (or *pratīti).* They are the result of the divine illusion of the Lord. Such illusory perceptions are the result of the mind rising up in the pure consciousness. How is one to resolve this problem? The only way to see through this illusion is by holding on to the firm conviction that 'One' alone exists. The moment one experiences the 'One' behind many, the desire for sense objects disappears effortlessly. *rasōpyasya param dṛṣṭvā nivartatē* – The Bhagavad Gita. 'The taste for sense objects will completely leave one when the supreme is seen'.

When the desire for sense objects is merely controlled, it may subside, but the traces of desire will continue to linger in the mind. However, in the presence of the supreme truth, this *viṣayarasa* also will vanish completely. The fountainhead of all *rasās* is the *param,* the Atman that shines as 'I'. This is why *viṣayarasa* gets sublimated only when it comes into contact with the source of all *rasās*. And only when the *viṣayarasa* is sublimated, does one transcend the illusory nature of the world. Even if one gains an intellectual understanding that the world is an illusion, as long as there is any trace of *viṣayarasa* left, one cannot help being swayed by the experiences of the world. In order to be free from the habit of extroversion, one has to develop relentless withdrawing from the sensory plane and should make the mind habitually rest in the essence behind all names and forms. The essence behind all the names and forms shines within as the import of 'I'. It is *asti bhāti priyam* - **it exists, it shines, it is love**. And that is the essential material (gold) with which all the names and forms (the ornaments) are made. All objects possess *asti, bhāti, priyam, nāmā, and rūpā.* The first three are the nature of Brahman; the name and form alone belong to the world. So if you take away the name and form of any object, what remains is existence, effulgence and love.

Bhagavan loved a story connected to this that is found in Vasudevamananam. One person took to Vedanta *vichāra* under a Guru after a protracted span of family life. However much he heard the teaching, his mind refused to get established in the Self. When investigated, it was amusingly found that a she-buffalo to which he was attached in his former life was appearing in his thoughts again and again. This was the distraction. The Master told him to meditate on the buffalo as Brahman. That is to ignore the name and form of the animal and meditate on the essence the *asti, bhāti, priyam.* By doing so, that seeker soon realized that the essence behind the vision of the buffalo is his own awareness, the 'I AM'. He realized Brahman.

Thoughts and emotions arise in the mind because of attachment or aversion towards the objects of the world. It may also be said that the various objects of perception are the externalized manifestations of the thoughts in the mind. Just as gold gets transformed into various ornaments, in the presence or absence of the sense objects, (i.e. both in the waking and dream), mind manifests in various names and forms - as man or woman, name or fame, relatives or nations. As the mind is nothing but the power of the Atman, all these are nothing but the Atman. The stuff with which these various names and forms are made of is *tān* - the Self. This *chit,* the Atman is the truth. All emotions are like bubbles and waves that rise up in the ocean. Pure awareness is the water. *Salila ēkō draṣṭā advaitō bhavati,* says the *śruti* - **He who knows that water alone exists, sees water alone even when he sees the waves and bubbles; such a one gets established in advaita**. He will not stir from the essence by the storms of temptations or miseries. He is a *sahajātma sthita* - one who is established naturally in his own Self. His *samādhi* is not a result of a technique, but is his very awareness (*bōdha)*. This non-dual consciousness of the Self will never be lost; even if he has to act involved in the world all the time.

'Observing everything, the yogi moves about deeply involved in the world. Yet he is ever aware of Brahman. It is like the dancing village girl who, while dancing in abandon to the music, not for a moment loses her attention on the pitcher on her head' says sage Vidyaranya. *Meyyām ponnai anḍṛi unḍō pugal* - do the ornaments have any existence apart from the gold? If one thoroughly reflects upon this *mahāvākya* - **is there anything other than the Self**? - it is certain that one will get established in *sahaja samādhi.*

VERSE FOURTEEN

...uḍanā—nennumat
tanmai-yuṇḍēn munnilaipa ḍark-kaiga tām-uḷavān
tanmai-yi nuṇmai-yait tānāindu—tanmai-yaṛin
munnilaipa ḍark-kai muḍivuṭ-ṭṛon ḍṛāyoḷirun
tanmaiyē tannilai-mai tān

uḍal nān ennumat	(I am the body—this identification)
tanmai uṇḍēl	if the first person 'I' exists
munnilai paḍarkkaigaḷ	the notions of second
tām uḷavām	and third persons, namely, you and he also exist
tanmaiyin uṇmaiyait tān āyndu	if one investigates the real nature of the 'I', the first person
tanmai aṛin	and if the 'I' ceases
munnilai paḍarkkai	notions of you and he, the second person and the third person
muḍivuṭṭṛu	coming to an end
onḍṛāi oḷirum tanmaiyē tan nilaimai tān	the awareness 'I AM' that shines always as the One is indeed one's real natural state.

Paraphrase:

If the first person 'I' (the ego-sense or the 'I am the body' notion) persists, the notions of second and third persons, namely, 'you' and 'he' also prevail. If the truth of the first person, the ego-sense, is investigated within and is ended, the sense of both the second and third persons will similarly vanish. What remains is the 'I AM', one's own Self, always shining as the One non-dual awareness, and that is the true state of one's being.

Commentary

In the previous *śloka,* it was stated that the Self alone is real, and that the universe manifesting in all its variety is *mithya,* an illusion. It was clearly established that 'I am' or the Self alone is the truth; and that the world as different from the Self is seen due to ignorance. In this *śloka,* we enter the portals of the royal path, the direct path revealed by Bhagavan Ramana which is the enquiry into the Self- 'Who am I?'

Tanmai uṇḍēl munnilai paḍarkkaigaḷ tām uḷavām - The first person *(tanmai)* in the form of the 'I'-thought is that which sprouts up first, and pervades the other two - *munnilai* (second person) and *paḍarkkai* (third person). Only after the 'I' arises do the thoughts about 'you' and 'he' come up. In deep sleep, when the 'I' subsides, the illusions of 'you', 'he' and 'the world' do not remain. So it is obvious that **the second and third persons that appear after the ego-'I' arises, are objects born along with the subject-'I'**. 'You', 'he', etc., appear as 'outside objects' (*dṛśya*) or the known, separate from the subject-'I' that arises as a particular individual, the knower (*dṛk*). This is the essence of Bhagavan's words.

Later in *śloka* twenty-six, the same idea is expressed as: *ahantai uṇḍāyin anaittum uṇḍāgum, ahantai inḍṛēl inḍṛu anaittum*. In Arunachala Ashtakam, Bhagavan makes a definitive statement - *aham enum ninaivu inḍṛu enil piṛa onḍṛum inḍṛu* - **if there arises no 'I'-thought, there will be no other thought.** In the same way if we examine the *tripuṭi* of *jīva, īśwara* and *jagat, īśwara* and *jagat* appear only after the *tanmai,* the *jīva* appears. Individuality alone is the source of all illusions. The individual ego is the first sprout in the absolute existence. If, with subtle intellect, one enquires into the source of this primary offshoot, one will be able to feel its current. Bhagavan calls this, the **I-current**, the *dhāra.* In the waking and dream states, the individual-'I' arises only by identifying itself with a body. The individual-'I' that is available in waking and dream states is the 'I' identified as 'I am a man', 'I am a Brahmin', 'I am a family man', 'I am a *sanyāsi'*, and the like. But in deep sleep there is absolutely no identification for the individual-'I' as 'I am this' or 'I am that'; nor is there the sprout of the ego-'I'. In the deep sleep state, the 'I' which is absolute bliss in its essence remains as simple 'existence'. It is the 'I' limited by the body that sprouts forth as the ego. **The experience of happiness or wholeness, that everyone experiences devoid of any limitations (adjuncts or *upādhīs*) during deep sleep is *prajñānam*, the Self or Atman which is pure consciousness.**

In deep sleep, as the 'I' does not sprout forth as the ego, there are no thought modes like 'you', 'he', *jīva, jagat* or *īśwara*. Since the ego or *tanmai* arises in the waking and dream states, and subsides during deep sleep, it is not real. Therefore, it is clear that this individual-'I' is not the true, unchanging I-consciousness, the Self. Thus the individual-'I' is just the ego or the *aham vṛtti*; only a wave that arises and sets. That which shines forth as the bliss of existence even during deep sleep (in the absence of the body, mind or any identification that 'I am this' or 'I am that'), is the real Self, *aham-padārttha* - the import of the 'I'. It is this *aham-padārttha* that Bhagavan speaks of as *tanmayin uṇmai*.

What is this secret path of enquiry, the quest, the *mahāyōgā*? It lies in directing one's attention inwards and keenly observing the pulsation of 'I' - tracing the 'I'-thought to the source. If our inner gaze is directed towards the sense of individuality that arises within as 'I', it will be observed that the ego or personality turns elusive and loses its foothold. If our power of attention *(śraddhā śakti),* that normally gets scattered outwards, is directed towards this *tanmai* or the pulsation of 'I', this false ego will merge and vanish into its source or the heart.

As far as we know, nowhere else have we seen this path of enquiry revealed with such simplicity and clarity as has been done by Sri Ramana. The scriptures of all religions talk about erasing the ego. However, for a seeker to actually accomplish the egoless state, nowhere else can one find such a clear process of inward quest. Bhagavan has said that this Direct Path alone can dissolve the limited ego into the *bhūma* or infinity. That the ego ought to be erased and that one should uncover one's true nature has been taught in spiritual traditions from time immemorial. Just as science conducts research with material objects, there have been several such experiments in the spiritual field too with the mind and various theories have been postulated to provide answers to the riddle. This supreme knowledge of merging the ego in its source, into absolute consciousness or the *bhūma* also has been talked about in such scriptures as the Yoga Vasishta. Being a secret science, however, the knowledge has only been transmitted through the *guru-śiṣya parampara.* The tradition also proclaims that the power of grace which is *rahastarpaṇa tarpita* - secretly transmitted - will function only if the knowledge is received directly from the Guru. It is this same secret that has been revealed by Bhagavan Sri Ramana Maharshi. It may have been the need of the hour, a need felt by sincere seekers that prompted the supreme to reveal this traditional secret to all. Though Bhagavan has brought the method out into the open, it is obvious that it will not function without proper devotion and sincerity in the seeker to invoke the grace of the Guru. Ramana Vidyā is a secret although revealed; and an open revelation, though a secret!

When the power of attention is focused on the ego-'I' through the enquiry 'Who am I?' - all identifications such as 'I am this', 'I am that' dissolve in its source, the heart, wherein pure existence shines forth as the infinite. Here the eternal, conscious reality, the real Self alone shines resplendent as 'I-I'. That which shines forth as 'I-I' is the real Self. That is the real-'I'. After the recognition of the Self as 'I AM', if one abides steadfast in this ego-less state, without any trace of limitation born of identification with body or mind, one gets established in *sahajātmaniṣṭhā* - **natural abidance in the Self**.

Bhagavan used to narrate the puranic story of Nidagha and Sage Ribhu to illustrate how a Master guides a seeker to realization. Nidagha was a very studious disciple of the Sage Ribhu. After completing the learning of Vedas Ribhu wanted to impart the knowledge of the Self, *brahmavidyā* also, to the disciple. But as he was found not ripe enough for that, he was sent back to the world where he became the Guru of the king and led a comfortable life. After many years Ribhu went to his disciple disguised as an old village rustic. At that time the king, sitting on an elephant, was in a grand procession along with all his retinue. Nidagha was standing on the side of the road watching this. Ribhu approached him and pretending ignorance asked him:

R- Sir, what is happening here?

N- Can't you see? The king is in a procession along with his retinue.

R- Sir, I am a villager. So I do not know such things. Please show me the king.

N- The person sitting majestically on the elephant's back is of course the king.

R- Sir, which is the elephant and which is the king?

N- You fool! (Pointing) That is the elephant. It is below; the giant creature. The king is sitting above, on its back.

R- Wait, wait. See, I am a fool. Show me what is below and above. (Nidagha became frustrated and livid with anger to hear this. He made the old man bend down and sat on his back.)

N- See, now I am above and you are below.

The great Master asked him with telling effect. **"Dear one! Tell me now, what is this 'I' and what is this 'you'?"**

Nidagha, hearing that, was transfixed for a moment. His mind was riveted on the 'I' within. He was immersed in *samādhi* for some moments. After that he jumped from his Master's back and fell flat at the Master's feet shedding tears of remorse, gratitude and devotion and said. "O Lord! Out of ignorance I failed to recognize you. You embodiment of compassion! All these years I learnt so much but ignored my own Self. By thy grace alone, now I have stumbled upon this precious treasure. Bless me so that I will be established in 'That'." Pleased by this, the Sage taught him the Ribhu Gita.

tadyuṣmadasmad mativarjjitaikā
sthitirjvalantī sahajātmanasyāt – Sat-darsanam

A young swami once came to Sri Ramanasramam. He wished to ask the Maharshi some questions. But he felt uncomfortable to ask them in the presence of others. As he was thinking thus, some of Bhagavan's devotees who were present there got up and went out. Bhagavan was seated alone. Considering himself very fortunate, he approached Bhagavan and said, "Swami, I want to ask some questions." Bhagavan turned his divine, steady gaze towards him and replied: "Let everyone go."

V: All have left. I alone am here.

B: Let that 'I' also go.

These words struck the visitor like a bolt of lightning, like *saṭōri*.

THE PRIMORDIAL FIRE

To be aware of One Self is to be aware of the Eternal.
Bury your mind in the deeps of 'I AM'ness.
Hitherto unknown feeling of strength and peace you'll gain.
Move not from that centre.
Stay there rooted as a pillar of power.
You'll cease to be a petty self.
A column of fire will be thy form.
The fire which arose in the beginning of time
The inscrutable fire that baffled even gods
Will blaze forth, in the centre of your being.

VERSE FIFTEEN

...nidamu — mannum

nigazh-vinaip paṭṭṛi yiṛap-pedirvu niṛpa

nigazhkā lavaiyu nigazhvē—nigazh-vonḍṛē

yinḍṛuṇ-mai tērā diṛap-pedirvu tēra-vuna

lonḍṛinḍṛi yeṇṇa vunal

nidamum mannum nigazhvinaip paṭṭṛi	Always, holding on to the current of the present, that is now
iṛappu edirvu niṛpa	the past and the future happen to exist
nigazhkāl avaiyum nigazhvē	at the time of happening, the past and the future are only the present
nigazhvu onḍṛē inḍṛu uṇmai tērādu	therefore without recognizing the fact that the present, which is 'here and now', alone is real
iṛappu edirvu tēra unal	Investigating the past and the future
onḍṛu inḍṛi eṇṇa unal	is like attempting to count without the digit 'one'

Paraphrase:

Only by holding on to the current of the present that is now, do the past and future exist. At the time of their occurrence, the past and the future are also known as 'present'. The 'present' alone is real. To investigate the past and future without knowing the truth of the present, the 'here and now', is like attempting to count forgetting the digit one.

Commentary

The Vedanta *vichāra* enters into a fascinating realm of insight in this *śloka*. In the previous verse Bhagavan has revealed the importance of the first person, the 'I'-thought in the process of Self-enquiry. Though the first person also is a thought like the second and third persons, only by probing into the 'I', can one touch the source. That is shown with certitude by Bhagavan. In this *śloka* Sri Bhagavan comes to the same truth by enquiring into the triad of time - the past, present and future.

What is time? The rishis define time as 'a gap in the awareness of infinity' *(khaṇḍasamvit)*. In stillness there is no time. Time arises when thoughts begin to arise in that stillness. Thoughts create the illusion of time in waking and dream states. In the deep sleep state there is neither thought nor time or space. When the mind arises the world manifests itself with time, space and causation. A devotee once attempted to discuss with Bhagavan the *yugās* such as *satyayuga, kaliyuga* and their respective durations. Bhagavan responded: "I do not consider time as real. Time appears only when the mind arises. Time does not exist for one who constantly abides in the bliss of the Self. Therefore such discussions do not have any value." *Śāstrās* regard all these – time, space, causation, karma, mind - as synonyms for the Lord's power which has manifested itself as the visible universe.

A very simple division of time is the triad - the past, present and future. In language and in the mental plane these three divisions of time have great significance. But, do these three divisions of time exist in our actual experience? What is the 'past' that we speak of? It is just thoughts that I have now about events that are said to have occurred earlier, based purely on my memory. At the time of experience, they happened in the present. The future is mere imagination, just an expectation. That also is not there now in experience. It becomes true only in the present. What is experienced as 'now' is the present. That alone is experience. **The awareness 'I AM' is the present which is 'now'**.

Thoughts and emotions of the mind cannot touch the 'present'. The moment thought touches the now, it is already the past. It is nothing but memory. The present - the NOW - is consciousness itself. The past and the future are of the mind. The present is the 'I AM'. 'When can one know this?' The answer can only be 'now'. Now or never is the law to know because, all time is now.

iha chēdavēdīdatha satyamasti
nachēdihāvēdīd mahatīvinaṣṭi: – Kenopanishad

'If you know it here and now, it is certain that you have got it. If you ignore the now, the here, alas, great is thy loss!' With the mind introverted one must stay in the consciousness 'I AM', here and now (i.e., at the very moment when one listens to the instruction of the Guru) It is not possible to experience it at some imagined future. Nor is it possible to know it experientially in the past. If we fail to recognize it in the present, it is a great loss.

pratibōdha viditam matam; amṛtatvam hi vindatē –Kenopanishad

The stillness of pure awareness that reveals itself as 'I-I' between successive thoughts must be recognized and identified as *ahamasmi* (I am 'That'). That is the nectar of the timeless. In the eternal present which is the stillness of awareness, thoughts arise and float like clouds in the sky. They happen in the intellect without touching the experience of 'now'. If the attention falls on thoughts, the past and the future will be felt. If the attention falls on the pure awareness, the timeless 'now' alone will shine forth as the truth.

vartamānam anāyāsam bhajadbāhyadhiyākṣaṇam
bhūtam bhaviṣyadabhajadyāti chittamachittatām

–Yoga Vasishtam

'By fixing the attention lightly or effortlessly in the present without allowing it to wander into the past or future, the mind becomes 'no-mind'.'

The 'now' is the heart. The present is the fullness of stillness where even a trace of thought does not arise. *Īśwara* is the eternal present. The unbroken present is *samādhi.* If the thoughts are in the form of memories, they belong to the past; if they are in the form of imagination, they are the future. The mind constantly moves between the past and the future like a pendulum. When the pendulum stops moving, time also stops. If the mind remains in the present there is no time.

'Days pass, nights pass, months and years flash by,
Immersed in the infinite expanse of beingness
Awakened to the land of eternal light, the blessed one
Knows not, the events of the sense-world.
Immersed in the sacred trance he drinks deep the elixir of *parā*'

Bhagavan refers to this in Aksharamanamalai as: *rāppagal illā veṛuveḷi.* 'Arunachala! Come and be one with me in the ever-illumined resplendence of the heart, where the time as night and day dissolves in the supreme delight of *nirvāṇa.*'

To the question, 'How many numbers are there in arithmetic?' even learned persons often reply, 'countless'. In fact, there is only one number - 'one'. One added to one becomes two. In this manner, it goes on increasing infinitely as three, four, and so on. Actually it is one that appears as the infinite. In the same way it is the present, experienced now, that appears to be infinity. What is always experienced is the present - 'now'. This progresses till infinity, as 'now', 'now', 'now'. When the mind begins to move, it prevents one from experiencing the 'now', and brings in the past and the future. '**Only that which exists now, exists always**' is a *mahāvākya* of Sri Bhagavan. Bhagavan, firmly established in this truth, never gave any importance to previous births, future births, aeons, creation, destruction, and so on. Once a devotee asked, "How can I know what I was in my last birth?" Bhagavan said, "Leave aside the thoughts of the last birth. Are you born now? If yes, who are you now? What are you now? Enquire in this manner."

A seeker must see the truth clearly here and now. Take note of Bhagavan's words, *inḍṛu uṇmai tērādu iṛappu edirvu tēra unal.* The body is the past. The mind is the future. Consciousness, the Self is the present. The mind is the future body. It is the past mind which has now taken the form of the body. When prominence is given to the body and the mind, it is impossible to remain in the present. When you remain in the present, you will not be aware of the body or the mind. It was explained in the previous *śloka* that although the triad 'I', 'you' and 'he' are illusions, if one fixes one's attention on the 'I' and enquires into its source, the illusory-'I' will disappear; and the real-'I', the Self, will reveal itself. In the same manner, the triad - the past, present and the future - is also an illusion. In deep sleep no one is aware of space, time and causation. When the first cause, the 'I' appears, the mind arises. When the mind arises, time and space also arise along with it. Nevertheless, the time-less is available in the now. By holding on to the present, the 'now', the timeless reality can be reached. It can also be experienced that in the present, time does not exist, and that pure consciousness alone is the 'now'. The 'I', when investigated vanishes and when one stays in the 'now', the mind ceases to operate.

Once someone asked Bhagavan a doubt related to that day's lunar date (*tithi*). To this Bhagavan replied: "I am not even sure whether it is day or night now. How can I say whether it is *chaturthi* or *ēkādaśī* (the fourth day or the eleventh day of the lunar month)? Sometimes when the eyes were open, it would be day and sometimes it would be night. At times, even an entire day would have passed; I never noticed these things." Bhagavan said this referring to the time he was sitting in self-absorption in Gurumurtam. Here is another exchange with Ramana Maharshi regarding the illusory nature of time.

Devotee: Bhagavan! Is it possible that one may be born again elsewhere within two years after death?
B: Not only that he may be born again, he may even be seventy two years old! (Talks)

TIME

The mind is a pendulum which swings between past and future.
It is a cloud which covers the brilliance of the divine orb.
To be free of time is to be free of the mind.
Know that the 'now' alone is;
Past and future are the cobweb the mind weaves
Do not believe your mind, listen to the divine whisper.
In between the thoughts, listen to the voice 'I am'.
'I-I' is the ever ringing Mystic syllable, the mantra.
Go deep and find this ever rolling inner rosary within.
'I am' is another name for liberation.
It is neither in the past nor in the future.
It is the eternal Self which is here and now.
Be aware of the truth-eternal, the present moment.
It is Self, it is God, it is the timeless immeasurable.

VERSE SIXTEEN

...uṇara—nindṛaporuḷ
nāmandṛi nāḷēdu nāḍēdu nāḍuṅ-kā
nām-uḍambē nāṇāṭṭu ṇām-paḍuva—nām-uḍambō
nām-inḍṛan ḍṛenḍṛu-monḍṛu nāḍiṅ-gaṅ geṅgu-monḍṛā
nām-uṇḍu nāṇāḍi nām

nāḍuṅkāl uṇara ninḍṛa	When clearly
poruḷ nām anḍṛi	investigated, apart from the self-evident awareness 'I AM'
nāḷ ēdu nāḍu ēdu	where is time and where is space?
nām uḍambēl	if we ('I') are the body,
nāḷ nāṭṭuḷ nām paḍuvam	we will be bound by time and space
nām uḍambō?	are we this body? (no)
nām inḍṛu anḍṛu enḍṛum onḍṛu	today or then, at all times, we are the same and always the changeless One
nāḍu iṅgu aṅgu eṅgum onḍṛāl	in every place (here there or everywhere) we are one
nām uṇḍu	we, the Self, exist
nāl ṇāḍu il nām	neither time nor space is, we alone are, timeless and spaceless 'I AM'

Paraphrase:

When investigated deeply, where is time and where is space apart from the awareness which is self-evident as 'I AM'? If we are the body, we will be bound by time and space. But are we the body? No. We are the same form of awareness here, there and everywhere. Always we alone are, timeless and spaceless 'I AM'.

[In this *śloka*, the Sanskrit words *dēśā* and *kālā* are translated as *nāḍu* - place and *nāḷ* - day in Tamil. Bhagavan has effectively used these fresh terms for arresting our attention.]

Commentary

It has been already established that existence is experienced as 'I am' (*aham*) and that existence lies beyond time and space. Time and space are born when the awareness 'I' identifies with the illusory body-mind. When we sleep, the mind dissolves and along with the mind, the body and world also disappear. When the mind dissolves, place and time both disappear. Without the body-adjunct, time and space will not be perceived. Now, are we the body?

The awareness 'I AM' shines in us at all times without any change. This awareness is untouched by the body. This 'I AM' has been the awareness that illumined the stages of the body - childhood, youth and old age. It lies behind all the states of waking, dream and deep sleep. However that awareness is not a state. It is the eternal constant reality. The 'states' belong to the field of the known - *prakṛti*. They change constantly. Here, there, now, then - all these expressions indicate different stages and states. When I identify only with the body, I will be affected by differences of place such as Arunachala or Hardwar and the differences of time such as night or day. Yet, the awareness- 'I' shines radiantly as the eternal, constant experience of truth without submitting to any change even when the body changes.

What does a person mean when he sees his childhood photograph and refers to it as 'I' or 'that is my picture'? To the question, 'hasn't the body changed?' the answer would be, 'yes, certainly'. Each and every cell of the body has changed. But the experiential knowledge behind the affirmation, 'this is my photograph' is because of the cognizance that the same I-consciousness which was there in childhood continues to remain unchanged even in old age. As this 'I'-experience has been ignored, the experience of the Self has not resulted till now. The moment that instantaneous intuitive recognition happens, the inner power of knowing glides beyond time and space.

Nām uḍambēl nāḷ nāṭṭuḷ nām paḍuvam - If we are the body, we get trapped in time and space. The awareness has its existence in awareness, not in the body. *Nām inḍṛu, anḍṛu, enḍṛum onḍṛu* - although the body changes in childhood, youth and old age, the awareness - 'I AM' - continues to remain changeless. One who abides in the 'I AM' will never get affected by these states. This fact about the awareness that persists in all states, must be pondered over deeply.

All our misunderstanding is due to the topsy-turvy knowledge that the world is there, that the body has happened in it and that the 'I' inhabits the body, whereas the ego, mind, body, the world and the like are mere appearances on the Self. This will become very clear if the attention is relentlessly fixed on this 'I'. If attention leaves the 'I AM' and gets scattered externally, the first falsehood that arises is the individuality-'I'. With this individual-'I' as the root, the mind, the body and the world expand as branches of this huge world-tree *(samsāra vṛkṣa)*. The ego-bird consumes the joys and sorrows which are the fruits of this self-created illusory tree. Behind this ego-bird, the resplendent bird with golden plumage perches aloof as a witness consuming nothing. Until one experiences this resplendent Atman, the illusion will continue. Time and space are a continuation of the illusion that the ego is real. For the same reason, in deep sleep when the ego subsides, time and space disappear. The reality that exists in the deep sleep state prevails unchanged in the waking and dream states and also in childhood, youth and old age. This is what Bhagavan means by saying *nām uṇḍu* - 'I exist'. A verse composed independently by Sri Bhagavan is quoted below:

nāmanḍṛi nāḷēdu nām nammai nāḍādu
nāmuḍalenḍṛeṇṇil namai nāḷuṇṇum—nāmuḍambō?
nām inḍṛu senḍṛa varu nāḷenḍṛum onḍṛadanāl
nāmuṇḍu nāḷuṇḍa nām

'Time as a limitation has no existence without the awareness 'I AM'. Does time exist apart from our beingness? If we fail to investigate our Self and misapprehend the body as the Self, time will certainly devour us. Are we the body? If we enquire thus and know the immeasurable, we will swallow time like delicious food. Time as present, past and future will be no more. 'I AM' alone will remain as one eternal existence. When extroverted, time devours the mind and when mind rests in the Self it devours time.'

While simply sitting, one gets bored. But is there any boredom in sleep, even if it is for ten hours? In that state we are doing nothing; there is no entertainment, nothing to talk, nothing to think or see. So even this boredom is a mysterious phenomenon! It too hints at our inherent nature. Somewhere in the depths of our being lies the experience that we are beyond time. So when we are limited by time we get frustrated and we want to overcome the limitation of time. That is why we get bored. But we don't know the technique to eat up the time-space stuff and be finished with it. We do it regularly in sleep. Are we conscious of time or space in sleep? No. Thus by abiding in the Self consciously, we can swallow time and it will be the most sumptuous food. Never will we feel hungry again. We have no anxiety, no boredom or other disturbances in deep sleep. Why? There we strip off the mind and stay naked as the timeless being. So too, consciously still the mind and know here and now the infinite, the whole.

VERSE SEVENTEEN

...ūna—māmiv
uḍanānē tannai yuṇarārk kuṇarn-dāṛkk
kuḍa-laḷavē nānṭṛa nuṇa-rārk—kuḍa-luḷḷē
tannuṇarn-dārk kellai-yaṛat tānoḷiru nān-iduvē
yinna-vartam bhēda-mena veṇṇu-vāi

tannai uṇarārkku	For those who have not realized the Self
uṇarn-dārkku	as well as for the Self-realized jnani
ūnamām ivvuḍal nānē	the limitation, i.e. this body, is 'I'
tan uṇarārkku	to the unrealized ajnani
nān uḍal aḷavē	the awareness of 'I' is limited to the size of the body
uḍal uḷḷē tan uṇarndārkku	to those who have recognised the nature of 'I AM' within the body
nān tān ellai aṛa oḷirum	the 'I' will shine forth as boundless awareness
iduvē innavar tam bhēdam ena eṇṇu-vāi	This indeed is the difference between the two; know this for certain.

Paraphrase:

For those who have not realized, as well as for the Self-realized *jnani*, the limitation, i.e. this body, is 'I'. For the unrealized *ajnani*, the awareness of 'I' is limited to the extent of the body. But to those who have recognised the nature of 'I AM' within the body, the 'I' will shine forth as boundless awareness. This indeed is the difference between the two; know this for certain.

Commentary

The significance of this *veṇba* has to be realized through deep enquiry. *Uḍal nānē tannai uṇarārkku uṇarṇdārkku* - the statement that to both - the *ajnani* who has not become aware of the Self and the *jnani* who has realized the Self - the body alone is the 'I', might sound contradictory to the teaching of Vedanta. Its true significance is made clear in the following lines. *Tan uṇarārkku nān uḍalaḷavē* - for one who has not known the Self, the 'I' is restricted only to the body. What about the *jnani* who has clearly recognised the real nature of the Self? *Nān tān ellai aṛa oḷirum* - the 'I', 'I' will reveal itself as boundless, eternal, infinite, pure consciousness.

The space within the pot - the *ghaṭākāśa* or pot-space - appears to be limited by the pot. But on enquiry, it will be revealed that space can never be limited inside the pot and that the pot itself is a mere appearance in infinite space. Even when the pot space is seen, the knower knows that it is nothing but infinite space. In the same way, when the I-consciousness, *jīva bhāva,* that pulsates as though it is within the body, is subjected to enquiry, it will reveal itself as not within the body but as the eternal, infinite consciousness and the body being only an appearance in it. Both the *jnani* and the *ajnani* say 'I'. The experience of *aham* (I) is common to both. While to the question what this 'I' is, the *ajnani* responds in terms of a series of imagined identities such as name, caste, creed and status, the *jnani* who has rejected all misapprehensions and has become consciousness itself, is constantly aware: 'I am the all-pervading Self'.

nāham manuṣyō na cha dēvayakṣō
na brāhmaṇa kṣatriya vaiśya śūdrā:
na brahmachārī na gṛhī vanasthō
bhikṣur na chāham nijabōdharūpa: –Hasthamalakeeyam - 2

'I am not a man or a *dēvā* or a *yakṣā*. I am not a *brāhmaṇa* or of any other caste. I am not a *brahmachārī* or of any other order. I am the pure consciousness that remains when all these super-impositions are removed.'

samastēṣu vastuṣvanusyūtamēkam
samastāni vastūniyam na spṛśanti
viyadvad sadā śuddhamaccha svarūpa:
sa nityōpalabdhisvarūpōhamātmā – Hasthamalakeeyam - 13

'I am that Self that ever remains as the unbroken awareness in all things and that which is untouched by any object; that which is ever-pure and untainted like space, and ever-attained by all."

These two *ślokas* proclaim the experience of a *jnani*. If this *śloka* is carefully studied, the difference between the state of a *jnani* and an *ajnani* will become very clear. How such a tiny misapprehension leads to so much misery! In deep sleep, there are no distinctions felt such as being a *brāhmaṇa*, a *brahmachārī* or a man or woman and so on. It is when the mind arises as the individual-'I' that all these distinctions appear. It is not possible for anyone to say that he did not exist in deep sleep. The real-'I' is that which remained as bliss itself in the ego-less state of deep sleep. It is the eternal, ever-attained Self. This world that arises in the Self is in fact not apart from the Self, like the waves and bubbles that arise in the ocean. Viewed from this plane of consciousness, that which appears as this mind and body is the same as the Self. What appears as ornaments - chains and bangles - is nothing but gold. Yet the forms of the chain and the bangle by themselves are not gold. Just as an ignorant one considers the bangle as the gold, the worldly person considers the body as the Self. But the *ātma-jñāni* (knower of the Self) knows that this body is only a bubble in the ocean of absolute consciousness. Is there any gain or loss for the ocean whether a bubble appears or disappears?

kumbhō vinaśyatu tiṣṭhatu vā yathēṣṭam

'Whether a pot exists or is broken, the space within the pot remains unaffected'.

After receiving the *upadēśa* from Ashtavakra, the enlightened King Janaka exclaims: "When the wind of the mind blows on the Self, the infinite ocean of consciousness, countless worlds appear and disappear as waves. But that causes no increase or decrease in 'Me'." One day, a lady devotee served certain special foods only to Bhagavan. Bhagavan asked: "Why have you served this only for me? Oh! You are showing your devotion to the swami? You must see that the swami is present in everyone. Do you think this body alone is 'swami'?

You must practice seeing the 'One' in everyone." This sense of oneness is the eternal constant experience of a realized soul!

tannuḷ tanu irukka tān ajjaḍa uḍalam
tannuḷ iruppadāl tān unnum—annavan
chittirattin uḷ uḷada chittirattukkādhāra
vastiram enḍreṇṇuvān pōlvān – Ekatma Panchakam

'Contrary to the reality that this body remains within the Self, the *ajnani* regards the Self as residing within this inert body. This is like saying that the screen on which the pictures move lies within the picture!'

When one views the Himalayas from a distance, the mountain range seem to be contained within our eyes. But if one goes near and starts ascending the Himalayas, one turns into a speck in its great vastness. Likewise, when one observes from a distance of *aśraddha* (inattention), the 'I' appears to be only a spark within the body. When the same 'I' is approached and attended to intimately with *śraddha*, the ego-'I' along with the body vanishes into the seamless consciousness - *ellai aṛa oḷirum tānil.* The 'me' when scrutinised, will extend and extend beyond the body, the mind, the intellect, the emptiness, the bliss, into the infinite.

To enlighten one who thinks that he is only the body, the *śāstrās* have this methodology to lead the attention from the known to the knower: "You are not the body, nor the *prāṇa* nor the mind, nor the intellect nor *avidyā*. You are the 'seer' who illumines all these seen objects. When you reject all these one by one as 'not this - not this' *(vyatirēka yukti),* the residue of pure experience that ultimately remains can neither be accepted nor rejected. The Self alone will shine forth, divisionless, whole. Until then, continue this *vichāra*." In this *vyatirēka mārga* (path of negation), as the rejecter and the rejected, the seer and the seen, continue to remain separate, it cannot be considered a complete path. It is only a preliminary aid to realization. For the *jnani* who has seen that his real nature is eternal, pure, self-effulgent and ever-free, all that was rejected earlier now shines forth as his own Self. Just as sun rays are not different from the sun, he beholds clearly that the body and the world are but the rays of his own Self (this is *anvayā*). Here, the import of the *mahāvākya - sarvam khalvidam Brahma* (all this is verily Brahman) is experienced. He directly realizes that the world arises, remains and dissolves in Brahman, the Self, and that this does not cause any change in the eternal, pure, self-effulgent, ever-free awareness. First the rope is seen as a snake, and later the misconception is removed and the rope is seen for what it is - however, all along, the rope itself has remained unchanged. This may be defined as *vastutantra jñānam*. It cannot even be postulated that the rope was the substratum for the illusion of the snake. The illusion of the snake is only in the mind of the seer, not in the rope. Similarly the illusion of the world is in our mind and has not veiled the Self in the least.

The knowledge which is highlighted in this *veṇba* is the yardstick to identify a *jnani*. Normally, people get carried away by those exhibiting *siddhīs* and external signs and consider such a person as an awakened-one. They gather around such *siddhās*. These *siddhās* hold on to the 'I am the body' idea and consider the world as real. These *siddhīs* of the *siddhās* mesmerize the spectators and strengthen the egos of the *siddhās* and make them miserable. Both suffer as in the case of 'a water snake that has swallowed a huge frog' says Sri Ramakrishna. Even without any *siddhi*, the *jnani* who revels in himself, rejoices. A *jnani* who abides firmly in the advaitic experience will be least affected by fame or insult. Although one has become a great *siddhā* and has attained name, fame and wealth, yet, if he has not realized the truth, intense inner emptiness will haunt him all his life and he has to die in that pain.

Some pointers

While the *ajnani* regards the limited body as the Self, the *jnani* considers the infinite substratum as the Self. As long as worldly affairs remain important, the mind will not be prepared to give up 'I am the body' idea. This habit of regarding oneself as a limited individual is *ahaṅkārā* (ego) which is made of *dehābhimānā* ('I am the body' idea). The body and the world always remain together. 'I am the body' idea inevitably follows worldly affairs. Involvement in worldly life always demands body-identification. This limitation always dogs ignorance. Society, doctrines, fame, power of influence, differentiation between gods or idols of worship, pride in one's status and class are all ignorance associated with the body and the world. If these are accepted, the ego will force itself in and impose restrictions, attachments, aversions and so on. If the ego does not cease to operate, the indivisible awareness, the 'One without a second' will not be revealed. Societal rules and customs have been made based on the assumption that the body is the Self and *avidyā* is truth. Even rituals prescribed in the *karmakāṇḍā* of the Vedas are based on this false premise, superimposing divisions of caste and status (such as *brāhmaṇa* and *gṛhastha*) on the Self. Although body identification is inevitable for worldly affairs, it has no reality for the awakened one. Hence, Sankaracharya considered worldly interactions as opposed to Self-knowledge.

na sūrayō hi vyavahāramēnam

tattvāvamarśēna sahāmananti - Srimad Bhagavatham 5-11-1

'The sages do not consider this worldly interaction as in any way significant from the standpoint of real knowledge' says the sage Jada Bharatha to the King Rahugana when the latter confused worldly *dharma* with *jnana.*

Here a question may arise in the minds of seekers whether worldly affairs should be renounced for the pursuit of Self- enquiry? It is not possible for anyone to completely renounce worldly affairs as long as the body exists. In the state of ignorance, neither is it necessary to give up the Vedic disciplines retained as a spiritual practice. It is enough to mentally renounce the priority for worldly affairs. Self-enquiry must be given priority. It is enough if one has the conviction to suffer any loss for this purpose. This readiness to suffer is real sacrifice or maturity. Whatever be the difficulty that might befall one's family, society, class or status, fame or power, due to one's devotion to truth, one has to endure that happily and consider these as favourable to the destruction of the ego. If one develops this quality, it implies that he has internally renounced worldliness. This is the *sanyāsa* upheld by Bhagavan. Keeping these points in mind one must meditate upon the meanings of both, this verse and the next one.

VERSE EIGHTEEN

...munnām
ulaguṇ-mai yāgu muṇar-villārk kuḷ-ḷārk
kulagaḷavā muṇmai yuṇa-rārk—kulagi-nuk
kādhāra māyuru-vaṭ ṛārum-uṇarn dār-uṇmai
yīdā-gum bhēdamivaṛk keṇṇuga

uṇarvu illārkku	Both for the ignorant who do not have the awareness of the Self
uḷḷārkku	and for the sages who have the awareness of the Self
munnām ulagu uṇmai āgum	the world that is seen by the senses is real
uṇarārkku uṇmai ulagaḷavām	for the ignorant, the reality is limited by the world
uṇarndār uṇmai ulaginukku ādhāramāi	for the awakened-one, reality is the substratum on which the world appears and disappears
uru aṭṭṛu ārum	and it shines forth as formless effulgence
ivarkku bhēdam īdu āgum eṇṇuga	know that this is the difference between the two i.e., jnani and ajnani

Paraphrase:

Both for the ignorant who do not have the awareness of the Self and for the sages who have the awareness, the world that is seen by the senses is real. For the ignorant, the reality is limited by the world whereas for the awakened, it shines forth as the formless effulgence - the substratum - on which the world appears and disappears. Know that this is the difference between the *jnani* and *ajnani.*

Commentary

In the previous *śloka*, the unique difference between a *jnani* and an *ajnani* with respect to their body idea (*dēhātma buddhi)* was explained. This *śloka* refers to the difference in their perception of the world. Here too, Bhagavan first makes an apparently contradictory statement that the world is real for both the *jnani* and the *ajnani*; and then resolves it. For the *ajnani*, the visible world alone is the truth. For the *jnani*, the 'I am' shines forth as perfect, nameless and formless awareness, the substratum and witness of all that is visible. In the sixth *śloka*, it was clearly explained that the visible world is mind-projected. It was also clearly proved that this appears only through the body which is made up of the five *kōśās*. Then, how do we explain this contradictory statement that the world is real for the *jnani*?

The *jnani* realizes that the awareness which illumines the world is the Self. To him the world is also a reflection of that reality. There is no body, mind or world apart from the Self. One who, by the words of the Guru, is convinced that there is only one non-dual reality, *(ēkamēva advitīyam)* experiences eternal solitude, says Sri Sankara. He perceives not the body, the mind or the world. He beholds only the Atman. In the Tamil translation of Devikalottara - Jnana Vichara Patalam, Sri Bhagavan states:

bhēda - ulagamum illai ulagappaṭṭṛuḷḷa loukikan tānum ilaiyē
'There exists neither the pluralistic world nor the worldly person who is attached to the world; the Self alone is'.

tānē disaiyōḍu dēvarumāi niṛkkum
tānē uḍal uyir tattuvamāi niṛkkum
tānē kaḍal malai ādiyumāi niṛkkum
tānē ulagil talaivanumāmē

'I alone shine forth as all space, and directions and divine beings; I alone shine forth as body, life and the innumerable principles; I alone shine forth as oceans, mountains and so on; I alone shine forth as the Lord of the world!' Thus states Tirumoolar in the Tirumandiram expressing the enlightened vision that the entire world is a manifestation of the truth, 'I am' *(tān).*

For the *jnani*, the world with its names and forms is not real. For him, consciousness, its substratum, is the truth. Therefore, his attention does not come into contact with the dream-like objective world. His vision is always rooted in the eternal reality. The names and forms of all objects that the *jnani* sees become irrelevant, and Atman shines forth in his heart. For an *ajnani*, the sight of names and forms create mental modes. Wherever the *jnani's* mind goes, his inner beingness remains unaffected by those perceptions or thoughts. Sri Sankara says '*yatra yatra manō yāti tatra tatra samādhaya:*'. The knower abides in *samādhi* even with his eyes open. He experiences the Self alone through all his senses. The world is a picture or movie or series of movies seen on the screen of the Self. In this state, it is true that *viśwam*, the world, is Vishnu.

Pārttaviḍamellām paraveḷi declares Tayumanavar: 'Wherever one looks there is only *chidākāśā* or consciousness'.

When the world is seen, *paramātma* is not seen. When the Self is seen, the world is not seen. A small child seeing an elephant made of wood excitedly says, "Here is an elephant!" His mother, who sees the same toy and who knows the truth says that it is wood. For each of them, the object seen is the same. Yet, the child sees it as an elephant; whereas the mother says that there is no elephant there but only wood. For the child, the truth is simply the name and form which is seen with the eyes. For the mother, the truth is the knowledge that it is wood. The seer of truth is like the mother who perceives only the wood. He sees that the Self alone appears as the world. Those who, like the child in the analogy quoted above, stubbornly believe that this world of appearances alone is the truth, though they may claim to be rationalists, are only irrational and childish.

The unintelligent say, 'see, the world exists.' But the 'isness' that is expressed as 'exist' is not of the world; it belongs to the Self of the seer. The Self is expressed as *satyasya satyam* - the reality behind the existence. Existence, which renders reality to the visible world, shines within as 'I' (*aham)*. This experience is the basis of all that is seen. This is what Bhagavan calls *uru aṭṭṛu ārum* - the formless effulgence behind all forms. In the light of this truth, names and forms vanish. Until a seeker attains Self-realization, he must accept the world as an illusion, so that he does not get trapped by the world by superficially accepting the proclamation that the world is Brahman. It must be held with certitude that this phenomenal world of names and forms is not real, but an illusion. In order to see the light within, which illumines the world, the extroverted mind must be trained to look within and the enquiry, 'Who am I?' must be pursued. This is not possible as long as the sensory world is regarded as true. Therefore, the conviction that the world is an illusion must come first. Later on, it will be experienced that truth alone is. The entire phenomenon is Atman.

The main purpose for maintaining complete certitude of the illusory nature of the world is to help one to wriggle out of its spell. However, if such a conviction instead of bringing about detachment, becomes a license to live as one pleases, then though at the mental level, one might consider the world and the objects as illusory, yet in practice one will continue to treat them as real. We have seen innumerable seekers fall into this trap. Their intellect becomes their greatest enemy. Therefore, while maintaining this certitude regarding the illusory nature of the world, the mind should be made introverted through Self-enquiry. Every statement in Vedanta must be used as food to nourish *jnana*, devotion and dispassion and not for selfish ends - *bhakti jñāna virāgāṇām sthāpanāya* (Srimad Bhagavata Mahatmyam 2-71). Bhagavan Sri Krishna instructs his dear devotee Uddhava as follows:

yadidam manasā vāchā chakṣurbhyām śravaṇādibhi:
naśvaram gṛhyamāṇam cha viddhi māyāmanōmayam

Know that whatever is grasped by the mind, eyes or ears - they are all evanescent, illusory and are only mere conceptions of the mind'. (Srimad Bhagavatam 11-7-7)

The same Lord instructs the Sanatkumaras, the *siddhās*, that all that is grasped through the senses is the Self alone.

manasā vachasā dṛṣṭyā gṛhyatē anyairapīndriyai:
ahamēva na mattō anyaditi buddhyaddhvamanjasā

'Whatever is grasped through the mind, through words, through any of the senses, O awakened ones! Know them to be nothing other than Me. 'I alone am all these', thus do recognise here and now. This indeed is the direct simple truth.'

(Srimad Bhagavatam 11–13–24)

Note the reply given by Bhagavan Ramana to a question regarding the creation of the world: "Does the world say that I exist? Or, do you say so?" What is seen is the world. The attitude of the viewer is reflected in the world. If you consider yourself as a mortal body with name and form, the world will also appear likewise with name and form. If you direct your mind away from the objects and make it abide in the seer by the quest 'Who am I?', the ego that sees will subside and the eye of wisdom will emerge. Then the *dṛśyā* reveals Brahman - *dṛṣṭim jñānamayīm kṛtvā paśyēt brahmamayam jagat.* Body consciousness and worldly affairs are all based on the ego. If the ego is given up, everything is given up. This is called '*nirōdha*'. What is *nirōdha*?

nirōdhastu lōka vēda vyāpāra nyāsa: – Narada Bhakti Sutra -1

'*Nirōdha* is renunciation of worldly and Vedic transactions.' The vision of one who has given up the individual ego and has achieved *nirōdha*, will be of immortal awareness.

VERSE NINETEEN

...bhēda
vidhi-mati mūla vivēka milārkkē
vidhi-mati vellum vivā-dam—vidhi-matikaṭ
kōrmuda-lān tannai yuṇarn-dā ravai-taṇandār
sār-varō pinnu-mavai sāṭṭṛuvāi—sār-bhavai

(bhēda)	(Mutually contradictory)
vidhi mati mūla vivēkam ilārkkē	only those who are devoid of the knowledge of the root of destiny and free-will
vidhi mati vellum vivādam	will alone entertain the debate whether free-will prevail or fate
vidhi matikaṭku ōr mudalām tannai uṇarndār	those who have awakened to the Self which is the common source of fate and free-will
avai taṇandār	are those who have completely transcended both fate and free-will
pinnum avai	will they again,
sārvarō sāṭṭṛuvāi	get caught in the misery of those two and be affected by them? Do think and tell

Paraphrase:

This debate whether fate prevails over free-will or free-will over fate is only meant for those ignorant ones who know not the source of both. Those who have known the source of the ego - the Atman, transcend both. Will they ever slip back to the misery born of the ridiculous puzzle thereafter? Do think clearly and tell.

Commentary

Sri Bhagavan, in a very simple manner, solves an age-old problem which has baffled intellectuals. Puzzles that defy easy answers such as, 'Does the hen come first or the egg? Does the tree come first or the seed?' are commonly posed by children to trick others. Yet, the answer is actually very simple. If the seed is broken and put into the soil, or if the tree is felled and put into the soil - both will turn into the same earth. The earth is thus the only reality, *(mṛttikētyēva satyam – Ch. Up.)*. The earth itself manifests both in the form of the seed and the tree, yet creates the illusion that one has emerged from the other. This is also the case with the analogy of the hen and the egg. When destroyed, both turn into earth. Then there is no seed, tree, hen or egg. That the earth alone is - this is the truth. Note the Upanishadic statement: *ēkamēva advitīyam nēha nānāsti kiṅchana* - 'There is only one reality; Nothing else exists.' Never does a seed remain simultaneously as a seed and a tree; there is either the tree or the seed. Later, a seed comes out of the tree, which will in turn, grow into another tree. The question as to which arose first is posed keeping in mind one seed and another tree. This is the defective logic resulting from mutual dependence.

Our efforts become our destiny. Destiny creates impressions of experience. This in turn becomes the innate dispositions and lurks behind our effort which appears as free-will. Thus the vicious cycle of effort-result-destiny is kept going round and round. This problem can never be resolved in the realm of the mind. The question as to whether we are mere puppets in the hands of destiny or whether we can conquer destiny by our self-effort, has been tormenting mankind since time immemorial. Self-effort and destiny are factual when considered from the point of view of the individual ego. When the illusory nature of the ego is realized, the question regarding self-effort vs. destiny will vanish and the pure, ever-free existence will reveal itself. *Prārabdha* is destiny. *Āgāmi* and *sañchita* are self-effort. The body is in the realm of destiny; the mind is in the plane of self-effort. Self-effort will change into destiny, and destiny will also affect self-effort. This is perplexing, isn't it? This is the problem if questions are asked within the realm of *māyā,* which is itself illogical. When the intellect out of sheer exhaustion from thinking about this unsolvable riddle, surrenders to the inner being and becomes absolutely quiet and still, then there will arise that state of supreme release which is beyond effort and destiny.

Let us revert to the topic at hand. *Vidhi mati mūlam* - what is the source of destiny and self-effort? In the dream, a person climbs up a mountain. On the way, he slips and falls down. He gets up and continues to walk. The fall and the walk in this experience are for his imaginary dream personality. And this has happened due to an illusion caused by sleep. Once he wakes up, there is neither the mountain nor the climb nor the fall. That person too does not exist. The problem was not solved; it simply vanished on waking up or rather, never existed to begin with! In a similar manner, enlightenment happens by the quest, 'Who is the 'I' that is at the source of both destiny and free-will?' *Vidhimatikatkku ōr mudal* - The source of both destiny and free-will is the ego. That too is mere thought. Once its non-existence is understood, pure consciousness alone remains as the one and only substratum.

One day, a *sādhu* belonging to a certain order came to see Bhagavan Sri Ramana. He went round the ashram. Noticing that there was no particular ritual followed in the ashram, he asked Bhagavan out of curiosity: "Swami, what is the tradition that you follow?" Sri Bhagavan did not reply, but continued to remain in His natural quietude. When this visitor kept repeating the same question several times, a devotee who was present there replied, "Not following any tradition is our tradition. Tell us about your tradition." The *sādhu* said, "We wake up before sunrise, we practise *japa,* service to the Guru and other rituals till sunset. In the evening, we offer the fruit of all our actions to our Guru. Thus, renunciation of the fruit of all our spiritual practises is our main custom." Hearing this, Bhagavan said laughingly, "*ōhō*! You perform *sādhana* and offer the fruit to your Guru? This is like keeping the principal intact and offering the interest. So this is what you offer to your Guru! Well done!" Listening to this, Sri Muruganar remarked, "Their Guru has at least left the *mudal* (principal) intact! Here, our Guru (Bhagavan) swallows the capital itself. Where is the question of there being any interest left?"

Without eradicating the ego, and continuing to perform actions with the sense of doership and later on surrendering the fruit of such actions is what is indicated by the statement, 'offering interest while keeping the capital intact'. If the ego or the sense of doership is itself erased, who is there then to perform action? The grace of the satguru wipes out the ego. Along with it, destiny, free-will, *āgāmi, sañchita* and *prārabdha,* good and bad actions, all subside. Pure absolute awareness alone remains. This is why Sri Muruganar refers to it as 'swallowing the principal'. The ego of doership is like a balloon which is inflated with the fuel of *pūrva-karma samskārās* (tendencies born of past actions) and the consequent experiences. If the ego vanishes as a result of Self-knowledge, the sense of doership will also disappear. Then who is there left to make any effort? Who is there to experience destiny, which results from past action? This problem dissolves instantly like the bursting of a balloon.

One day, a devotee wept at the feet of Bhagavan for a long time talking about his misfortunes caused by destiny. With a silent gaze Maharshi listened attentively to his litany of woes. After everything was said, a few moments passed by in silence. Then, turning His gaze towards this devotee Bhagavan said: "You are weeping saying, 'this happened to me', 'my sorrow' and so on. In this manner, your lament was full of words like 'to me', 'my' and 'I'. Who is this 'I'? What is this 'I'? From where did it arise? Did these sorrows exist in deep sleep where the 'I' did not arise? No. Then, from where did these miseries come now? You may say 'from my mind'. As the mind does not exist in deep sleep and as you remained as pure bliss without the mind in deep sleep, it can be concluded that the sorrows of the mind do not affect your real Self. Even in the waking state, if you enquire 'Who am I?' the ego 'I' will dissolve and truth alone will remain. No sorrow remains there. Destiny can never affect the Self. *Yasmin sthitō na du:khēna guruṇāpi vichālyatē* – 'That which remains unaffected even by the gravest of sorrows is our real Self. When a person is established in that, he is in 'Yoga'!' (Bhagavat Gita) Listening to this, another devotee asked: "Swami, how can *jnana upadēśā* (spiritual instruction) provide the solution for personal and domestic sorrows?"

M: What to do? All problems are due to *prārabdha*. As long as there remains an ego to experience this, there is no ultimate solution for them. Knowledge alone is the solution. Knowing the Self, leave the body-mind adjunct to *prārabdha*. However grave and serious the individual and family may seem to you, in the eyes of a *jnani* they are your delusions only. Hence, the aim of a *jnani* is to awaken you from this delusion. A person who is dreaming that he is being robbed, shouts 'thief, thief'. What will his friend lying awake nearby do? Will he run to catch the thief?

D: No. He will wake up the sleeping man.

M: Yes. Such is the case with the sorrows of the ignorant. The only solution is to wake them up.

"Depending on each one's *prārabdha,* the ordainer Lord makes each one perform certain actions. Whatever is not ordained will not happen - try as you might. What is supposed to happen will not stop - whatever you do to prevent it. Hence the best course is to remain silent." This was the *mahā upadēśa* (great message) which Sri Ramana gave his mother Azhagammal.

If the body is a puppet in the hands of fate, where is freedom? Freedom is the Self. Be still and know. Remaining still is the same as the absence of doership. That itself is variously termed as *śaraṇāgati,* Self-realization and so on. Due to ignorance, we wrongly believe that the individual-'I' is real, the body and other objects are mine, and that these objects, actions and thoughts are either beneficial to me or bring me sorrow. When through Self-enquiry, this 'I' itself is erased, all sorrows fall away. This is the only way out. This method is also very practical. Even in the midst of deep sorrow, we must have the *śraddha* (faith) to enquire who is the 'I' that experiences the grief - that is all. If this is done, at that very moment our individuality will vanish into the quietude of *chidākāśā* (inner space). If one never forgets to do this, this alone is enough. If one practises merging the mind in consciousness, then peace will become natural. Other than Self-enquiry, there is really no other permanent way to solve any of our problems. This is Bhagavan Sri Ramana's teaching.

All the adjuncts, ranging from the ego to the body and the external world seen around us serve as the field for the play of destiny and self-effort. This field is called in the Srimad Bhagavad Gita variously as *prakṛti, kṣētra,* and so on. There is no abiding peace within this field; whereas the still absolute consciousness is the abode of peace. It is eternally free. That is our real Self. If that *puruṣa,* the *kṣētrajñā* is known, the field (or nature) will dissolve like the water in a mirage when we go near. This experience is referred to as *nirvāṇā*. For a knower of truth, asking questions and discussing the experiences of the false ego is as absurd as 'casting the horoscope of the son of a barren woman'.

ETERNAL FREEDOM OF ONENESS

The One Self alone prevails in all states, devoid of the other
In it appears the ridiculous 'two' as the seer and the seen,
'Me' and God, destiny and will, bondage and liberation;
O, the ignominy of that misapprehension that creates a puny 'I'
And weaves the cob-web of a bizarre world of duality around it!
In that cocoon, threads of dream, is bound this 'me', a non-entity
To regain the glory of that primordial Oneness,
'Awaken to the truth',
Seek 'Who am I?', the 'I' will vanish in the radiance of knowledge;
The puzzle of fate and free-will vanishes like a dream at dawn;
No more dream, no more misery; eternal freedom of
Oneness - OM!

VERSE TWENTY

...sār-bhavai

kāṇun tanai-viṭṭut tān-kaḍavu ḷaik-kāṇal

kāṇu manōmaya-māṅ kāṭchi-tanaik—kāṇu-mavan

ṭrānkaḍa-vuḷ kaṇḍā-nān tan-mudalait tān-mudalpōit

tānkaḍavu ḷanḍṛi-yila dāl

sār-bhavai	(The objects that are seen before us)
kāṇum tanai viṭṭu	ignoring the 'I', the seer
tān kaḍavuḷaik kāṇal	oneself seeing God (like any other object)
kāṇum manōmayamām kāṭchi	is only a vision projected by the mind
tān-mudal-pōi	once the 'I' , the primal thought is erased
tān kaḍavuḷ anḍṛi iladāl	what remains as the Self is nothing other than God
tan mudalait tanaik kāṇum	one who sees the pure awareness that is the essence of one's 'I'
avan tān kaḍavuḷ kaṇḍānām	he alone has really seen God

Paraphrase:

To see God, ignoring 'the seer' who sees, is but to see the form of one's imagined mental projection. Once the 'I', the primal thought is erased that which remains as the Self is none other than God. Therefore, the one who has seen the essence of one's 'I', the pure awareness, the source of the rise and subsidence of the ego, alone has seen 'That', the supreme.

Commentary

Yacchakṣuṣā na paśyati
yēna chakṣūmṣi paśyati
tadēva brahma tvam viddhi
nēdam yadidam upāsatē – Kenopanishad 1-6

'That which is not beheld by the eyes but by which the eyes see, is alone Brahman; know that what you meditate on is not Brahman but by which you meditate is Brahman'. Thus the *śruti* reveals to the meditator whose mind has become one-pointed by intense devotion or *upāsanā* - *nēdam yadidam upāsatē*. That is, the visible object you worship with name and form is not Brahman. That which is seen with the eye is not Brahman. Brahman is that reality which is behind the eye, behind the mind, behind the intellect, the presence that enlivens these. It is the eye of the eye; the 'I'.

During Bhagavan Ramana's time, a devotee called Natesa Iyer was working in the ashram kitchen. He was an ardent devotee who performed *Śivapañchāyatana pūjā* every day without fail. Bhagavan himself guided him to perform it in the cow shed. During *dīpārādhana,* Bhagavan would pass that way, and watch; and at times even touch the idols. This practice continued for two years without a break. After two years Bhagavan stopped this visit abruptly. Natesa Iyer felt upset and one day approached Bhagavan and said: "Oh Bhagavan! You did not come today!" Bhagavan replied, "Are you still continuing the *pūjā*? You have done enough." On hearing this, the devotee said, "But Bhagavan I do not know anything else!" To this Bhagavan said "You know the knower who says 'I do not know'. Know that 'I', that is enough." From that day, he stopped the external worship. This devotee, who had received the necessary grace of the Guru, transcended the stage of external worship and turned his attention towards his inner Self. External worship is helpful for a seeker till his mind turns inwards.

Jīvanmuktās who are fully aware of the inscrutable course of *karma* and *upāsanā,* guide each individual from the point where he stands. Ungerminated seeds of *karma* lurk in the innermost realm of the person and cause obstructions. The body is the field- *kṣētra* - of such innumerable seeds. Those who perform their actions *(swadharma)* with detachment and without expecting their fruit, in due course, transcend the identification with the body. The *aham vṛtti* ('I'-thought) flows through the nervous-system in the form of self image ('the body is me' idea). This psychic realm becomes pure through desireless action. *Upāsanā* or *bhakti* is necessary to transcend the projections of the mind. The mind becomes pure and one-pointed through *bhakti*. The method of worship and the form of one's *iṣṭadēva* differs from person to person. Hence Lord has revealed innumerable forms of worship. If the purified mind is directed deftly from that which is seen to the seer, realization dawns in the heart. If one does not understand that freedom is the goal, all actions and worship will serve only to bind him and lead him to new bonds. The purpose of this *śloka* is to make us aware of this.

Kāṇum tanai viṭṭu - Don't let go of the seer. Attention must never turn away from the seer, the consciousness 'I'. In such abidance the experience of the Self dawns. *Ātma samsthiti: swātma darśanam* - Being oneself is indeed seeing oneself, says Bhagavan in Upadesa Saram.

tannai upādhi viṭṭu ōrvadu tān īśan
tannai uṇarvadām undī paṛa
tān āy oḷirvadāl undī paṛa – Upadesa Undiyar 25

'Abiding in one's consciousness separated from the body-mind adjunct is itself God-consciousness. God shines as the I-consciousness.'

If attention turns away from this I-consciousness, the ego-'I' and the *tripuṭi* - the seer, the seen and the act of seeing - will emerge. The experience of the Self will occur only when this *tripuṭi* disappear. *Manōmayamām kāṭchi* - without knowing the witnessing-'I', and believing the names and forms as truth, is an illusion of the mind.

One day the following conversation took place between a devotee and Bhagavan.

D: Swami, once I had the vision of Lord Siva as a result of my *sādhana.* It gave me great happiness. How can I get this *darśan* again?

B: Who is the one that saw the form of Siva? Where did Siva arise from, remain in and subside? The Siva who was seen, the 'I' that saw Siva, and the act of seeing Siva - all took place in the consciousness 'I am'. This is a *tripuṭi*. By enquiring, "Who is the 'I' that sees all this", and turning your attention towards the pulsation 'I', the ego and along with it, all visions will disappear. The seer alone will remain, self-effulgent as pure Experience-Consciousness-Bliss *(kēvala anubhavānanda swarūpā)*. This is the real Siva-experience. That which comes and goes is not permanent.

Once another devotee asked Bhagavan: "Bhagavan, what will you ask for, if Lord Arunachaleswara Himself appears in front of you?"

B: I will say to him: "Do not play this trick of appearing and disappearing before me." Do not ask me such questions and try to deceive me. Siva is the Self. All forms belong to the 'seen', the world. Siva is the real Self of the seer. He is pure consciousness.

Devotees see God in form in accordance with their *upāsanā*. Actually it is the Self of the *sādhaka* that gives this vision in the form of the beloved deity. The consciousness that is behind the vision is that of the worshipper himself. For some seekers the disappearance of the worshipped form and the experience of the Atman happen spontaneously. The moment the form of the worshipped Lord disappears from the mind which has become mature through *upāsanā*, the Self shines forth.

muktāśrayam yarhi nirviṣayam viraktam
nirvāṇamṛcchati mana: sahasā yathārchi:
ātmānamatra puruṣō avyavadhānamēkam
anvīkṣatē prati nivṛttaguṇapravāha:

–Srimad Bhagavatam; Kapilopadesam 3-28-35

'When freed of the refuge of name and form, the mind is extinguished like a lamp that is dried up of oil and the seeker continuously experiences the Self without any hindrance'.

Dṛgēva na tu dṛśyatē - 'It is not possible to see the seer' declares Adi Sankara. The nature of the seer is itself experience; it is not 'experiencing' something. The pure experience of 'I' is the nature of the seer, which is the Self. When the entire seen is ignored as non-self, the seer abides in the Self as Self. This is Self-realization. This is the state of the Self, and thus it need not even have the appendage 'realization'. This alone is real. Therefore, even the term 'realization' *(sākṣātkāram)* is redundant. When our sense of doership *(kāram)* gets removed, this becomes clear once and for all.

Tān mudal pōy - the nature of the individual ego is the sprouting of the 'I' and its identification with such mental pictures as, 'I am a *sādhaka'*, 'I am a family man', or 'a rich man'. This 'I' is rooted out only through Self-enquiry. What is it that remains when this is removed? The Self, which remained even in deep sleep is revealed. The *śruti* refers to this truth as: *ēṣa sarvēśvara: ēṣa sarvajña: ēṣa antaryāmi:* - 'This is the lord of all, the omnipotent one, this is the omniscient one, this is the inner being'. When the fascination for keeping oneself separate from the whole is removed through right knowledge the inner being reveals himself as the supreme being - Brahman which the Mandukya Upanishad refers to as *ēkātmapratyayasāram, prapañchōpaśamam, śāntam, advaitam* i.e., 'the essence of the experience of one changeless Self, the source where the universe is subsumed, the peace that is whole, non-dual'! This indeed is the Self, this indeed is God.

One can never see the Lord who abides in the depth of consciousness of the seer if attention deviates from the 'I', and focuses itself on 'you', 'he', 'this' and 'that'. So the in-dwelling Self itself appears in the form of the Guru in order to turn our attention on the 'I-I'. The 'I'-thought is the door to infinity. 'I' is the thread that leads one to the heart. (See *śloka* 14)

adanai nōkkādē idanai nōkkādē
edanaiyu nī nōkkādiruppin—madan sēr
iruppu nōkkālē ellaiyil chidākāśa
parappu nōkkām poruḷ āvāy

Look not at that, look not at this.
If you cease looking at anything,
But stay still, in your own beingness;
Boundless space of awareness will be thy being.

(Sri Muruganar, Guruvachaka Kovai 647)

Bhagavan expresses the same idea as, *tān kaḍavuḷ anḍṛi iladāl* - 'one's beingness has no existence apart from God'. Worshipping God with name and form is *sādhanā-bhakti*. Self-knowledge dawns by enquiring: 'Who am I, the seer?' and focussing the attention on the seer-'I' which reveals the reality. Abiding firmly in this non-dual I-consciousness and drinking the nectar of the Self is called *parābhakti*. This experience which follows Self-knowledge is indicated by terms like *parānurakti, ātmarati,* and *jīvanmukti*. Whatever be the term used, this is the bliss that transcends the division of the seer and the seen. Here the experiencer, the experienced, and the act of experience are all pure I-consciousness alone, and nothing else. Only the one who has attained such a state of bliss in the Self is the seer of God - *avan tān kaḍavuḷ kaṇḍānām* - Bhagavan states categorically.

Lord Krishna conveys the truth of the Self to the *gopis* in a message through Uddhava, in order to relieve them of their suffering due to separation from Him. The Bhagavatam says that the *gopis*, full of devotion to Krishna, realized the Self and transcended the sorrow of separation.

tatastā: kṛṣna sandēśair vyapēta virahajvarā:
uddhavam pūjayāñchakrur jñātvātmānam adhōkṣajam

– Srimad Bhagavatam 10-47-53

'Having been relieved of the fever of separation by this message of Krishna, they realized that Krishna is the Atman. Feeling blessed and fulfilled, they worshipped Uddhava with great devotion.'

In the Bhagavatam, Sage Vyasa has spoken in detail that however attractive the vision of God with form might be, the experience will never be complete unless one has attained Self-realization. Listen to what Sri Suka says about the *gopis* searching for the missing Krishna enquiring of the plants and trees about him, during the occasion of *rāsakrīḍā*.

papracchurākāśavadantaram bahir
bhūtēṣu santam puruṣam vanaspatīn

–Srimad Bhagavatam 10-30-4

That is, they asked the trees and plants about that *puruṣa* - the supreme being, who, like the infinite expanse - *ākāśa* - pervades all creation, within and without. That the *gopikas* had this knowledge due to their association with Krishna, is proved clearly from their own words before the *rāsakrīḍa*.

kurvanti hi tvayi ratim kuśalā: sva ātman
nityapriyē patisutādibhirārtidai: kim

–Srimad Bhagavatam 10-29-33

'The wise ones place their delight only in the Atman, the real Self. The Self alone is the eternal beloved. Husband, child and such relations serve only to lead one's attention away from the Self and cause misery.'

In spite of having such clear wisdom, the *gopikas* forgot it temporarily because of seeing Krishna's delightful form. Lord Krishna's purpose in sending the message through Uddhava was to get them established in Self-knowledge. Some of the close devotees of Sri Ramana also suffered the pangs of separation when Bhagavan left the body. Yet their Self-knowledge born of their association with Bhagavan helped them and redirected their attention to the Self. Some of them have directly spoken of this to the author. The name and form of the Guru or God will help us to detach ourselves from the names and forms of the world, and will grant us *bhāvabhakti*. But to abide firmly in the Self, this too must be transcended.

āsai aṛumin āsai aṛumin
īśanōḍāyinum āsai aṛumin –Tirumoolar

'Give up desire, give up desire; even for the Lord, give up desire.'
External visions, however divine they may be, will leave us one

day causing intense grief. That which never leaves us is the Atman alone, who is the Eye of the eye, the seer.

kaṇṇukku kaṇṇāi kaṇṇinḍri kāṇ unai

kāṇuvadevar pār aruṇāchalā! - Aksharamanamalai

'You shine forth, O Arunachala, as the Eye of the eye and see without the eye. Who is there to see You O self-luminous One? By your grace, glance at me O Arunachala!'

When Maharshi left Madurai for Tiruvannamalai, He left a note saying: "I am going to see my father". Later, coming to Arunachala He saw the holy hill. At once, the mind withdrew deep into *jñāna vichārā* (Self-enquiry) asking internally: "Who is the one who has seen? No 'I' arose to say 'I saw', or to say 'I did not see'. Only the non-dual Self shone forth in that silence. Ignoring the Self and seeking God outside is like seeking darkness with a lamp in one's hand." says Bhagavan, in Arunachala Ashtakam. Bhagavan once said to a seeker who used to get all sorts of visions as a result of *yōga-sādhanā*: "Everything should subside; be peaceful. Mere existence, 'I am' *(tān)* alone is realization."

The above *śloka* has been explained elaborately with several examples in view of its subtlety of meaning and importance. Note the conversation in the Anubandham - sixth and seventh verse.

6. Disciple: Who is God?

Master: He who knows the mind.

D: My Self, the spirit, knows my mind.

M: Therefore you are God; and also the *śruti* declares that there is only One God, the knower.

7. M: By what light do you see?

D: The sun by day, the lamp by night.

M: By what light do you see these lights?

D: The eye.

M: By what light do you see the eye?

D: The mind.

M: By what light do you see the mind?

D: My Self.

M: You then are the light of the lights.

D: Yes, That I am, O Lord! (Ekasloki by Adi Sankara)

THE PATH OF LIGHT

Dear! See not the scene, learn to see the seeing;
Through 'innering' enter the stream of 'seeing';
The path of light behind the eyes, the *devayāna*
The light with which the senses are made
And swim in the waters of effulgence back to the inner Sun,
Glide back to the source, the Seer and abide there.
That is the blessed terminus of the inner-path.
There alone is auspiciousness, peace and immortality!

VERSE TWENTY-ONE

...uyirāt-tān karudum
tannait-tān kāṇa tṛalai-van tṛanaik-kāṇa
lennum-pan nūl-uṇmai yennai-yenin—tṛannait-tān
kāṇalevan tṛānonḍ-ṛāṛ kāṇa-voṇā dēṭṭṛa-laivaṛ
kāṇaleva nūṇādal kāṇ

uyirāttān-karudum	one who considers himself as a jīva
tannait tān kāṇal	seeing one's Self
talaivan tanaik kāṇal	is actually to see the Self, the primal-being, God
ennum pal nūl	declare many books on jnana
uṇmai ennai enin	if asked what their import is
tān onḍṛāl	as the experience of 'I am', is One without a second
tannait tān kāṇal evan	how can one see oneself like an object? Who is the one to see?
kāṇa oṇādēl	as it is not possible to see the Self
talaivan kāṇal evan	who is the one to see the Lord, the primal being?
ūṇ ādal kāṇ	to become food for Him is indeed to see Him

Paraphrase:

All books on *jnana* declare that to see one's own Self is to see God, the primal being. The import of this saying is that the awareness 'I am' is but singular, how can one see the Atman shining as one's own Self? Who is the seer then? Since seeing oneself by oneself is not possible, how can one see God, the primal being? Becoming 'food' for God is to see Him.

Commentary

All scriptural texts speak of divine visions - *ātmānamīkṣēta param prapaśyēt*. Seeing the Self is to see the Lord. But how is it possible to see the Self? This is the problem here. *Ātma samsthiti: swātma darśanam* - In Upadesa Saram Bhagavan Himself says that just being the Self is seeing the Self. Remain in the existence, 'I am', or rather mere 'am-ness'. There is none other than consciousness to see or know consciousness. Consciousness is the self-luminous awareness that knows its own existence. If the illusion of objects existing apart from it is removed, consciousness will shine forth. Since that consciousness is absolute experience, there is no 'other' to see it. So it means that it is not possible to see the Self. Then how is one to see God?

nivṛttabuddhyavasthāna: dūrībhūtānya darśana:
upalabhyātmanātmānam chakṣuṣēvārkamātmadṛk

– Srimad Bhagavatam 3–27–10

'With an inward facing intellect and doing away with the habit of seeing the 'other', abide in the Self. Such abidance itself is seeing. As the eyes behold the splendorous sun, the eye of awareness recognises the Self.'

Ūṇādal kāṇ - The individual 'I' must become the food for the inner Self which is the substratum. *Vayam dēvasya bhōjanam*, says the Veda. Nammazhvar, the great Vaishnava saint sang of his experience thus: "When I saw the Lord, overwhelmed by love, I felt like swallowing Him but instead He consumed me."

sāppāḍunnai sārnduṇavāyān

śāntamāyp pōvan aruṇāchalā – Aksharamanamalai 28

Bhagavan Sri Ramana exclaims: 'O Arunachala! I thought I would eat (consume) You. (I wanted to experience You). But, my individual ego became Your food. Now, there is perfect peace.'

Sri Narayana Guru too expresses this vision in these lines:

'The divine boar of yore searched down below and the swan flew up to the head

And lo! They failed to see Thy beginning or end!

O hill of fire! You swallowed me along with my senses

And thou dancest in my heart, the import of *NAMA*: *ŚIVĀYA*!'

(Sadasiva dasakam - Malayalam verses)

And in the words of Arunagirinatha:

yān āgiya ennai vizhuṅgi veṛum tān āy nilai ninḍṛadu tatparamē

–Kandaranubhuti

'Swallowing the 'I,' which is the me, the supreme being shone forth boundless as 'I am'.'

Balimapi balimatvā - In Srimad Bhagavatam, the *gopikas* say that King Mahabali was swallowed by the Lord just as the sacrificial offerings are consumed by the *dēvata*. In this manner, the seers of truth, even when they belong to different schools, speak about this *annībhavanam* i.e. becoming food for the Lord.

Jīva is the individual-'I'. *Ūṇādal* means the dissolution of this *jīva* in the heart which is its source. Every day in deep sleep this limited *jīva* merges with the reality. If this individuality is dissolved consciously in the waking state, the experience of the reality will occur. This itself is the vision of God, the pinnacle of all attainments *(paramapuruṣārtha)*. Here the term 'vision' stands for the light of the Self that shines forth when the *tripuṭi* of 'the seer-the seen-the act of seeing' disappears. This is the experience that the *bhaktas* regard as *śaraṇāgati*. The individual ego of the devotee vanishes into the Lord that is the Self. The Self alone remains in the form of deep, profound peace. This has already been spoken about in the second *maṅgaḷācharaṇa śloka.*

The *purāṇās* express the same idea when they describe how those who are 'killed' by the Lord attain *mukti*. The vanquishing of the ego by the in-dwelling Self either from within or by assuming an external form is the act of supreme grace. The same is called the *gurutattva - tad vadhāt prāṇinām vadha:* (Srimad Bhagavatam - 7). Real killing means the killing of the ego. If the physical body alone is killed, the ego will create another body and enter into it. The Guru is one who feasts on the ego of the disciple even when the body is alive. Bhagavan Ramana addresses Arunachala as *uyiruṇṇi* (one who eats the ego). Sri Muruganar used to refer to many devotees of Bhagavan who had received His grace as *'yānai vizhuṅgiya vḷāmpazham.'* When an elephant *(yānai)* consumes this fruit *(vḷāmpazham)* and defecates, the whole fruit appears to have come out unchanged, exactly in its former shape, but actually it is only the hollow covering that is thrown out after the inner essence has been consumed by the elephant. Similarly, when one becomes the recipient of grace, one might appear to be the same externally, but the individual ego would have been totally eliminated.

Irukkum iyaṛkaiyāl īśajīvargaḷ oru poruḷē āvar, declares the Upadesa Undiyar. The awareness of pure existence is the same in *īśwara* and the *jīva*. That is, the *jīva* is experienced in the consciousness 'I'. *Īśwara* also is to be realized in this very same consciousness. The 'I am' devoid of the body-mind adjuncts, is the experience of God. Bhagavan calls Arunachala, *irundoḷir* (Self-luminous existence) in the Arunachala Ashtakam. When the association with the body and mind is removed, the 'I' shines as infinite consciousness.

Sri Bhagavan used to narrate an entertaining story of a person who went to the forest wishing to see a tiger. After much adventurous searching he found a tiger's den and went in. That was all; the fascinating story ends abruptly. He never came back! Bhagavan used to say that such is the case of the individual ego that enters the heart-cave seeking God. In the same way, when the *jīva* wishing to see God, follows the path of *bhakti,* the ego and pride in the form of 'I' and 'mine' slowly get reduced. The fire of *bhakti* burns up the inner *vāsanās*. This is expressed in the 'Kapilopadesa' (Srimad Bhagavatam) as *nigīrṇamanalō yathā*. Just as the *vaiśvānara* fire burns whatever goes into the stomach, the fire of *bhakti* burns all desires within and in the end, burns up the ego that remains as the '*bhakta*'. As all differences *(vibhakti)* are wiped out here, this experience is called *bhakti*. This indeed is the *nān aṭṭṛa annilai* mentioned in the third verse.

VERSE TWENTY-TWO

...evaiyum-kāṇum

matik-koḷi tan-dam matik-ku ḷoḷi-ru

mati-yinai yuḷḷē maḍakkip—pati-yiṛ

padittiḍu-da lanḍṛip pati-yai mati-yān

madit-tiḍuda leṅgan mati-yāi

evaiyum kāṇum	that which sees everything
matikku oḷi tandu	that which illumines the intellect and mind
am matikkuḷ oḷirum patiyil	in the Lord who shines within that intellect
matiyinai uḷḷē maḍakki	instead of turning the mind inwards
padittiḍudal anḍṛi	and making it abide firmly (in the Lord)
patiyai matiyāl	by merely knowing about God with the intellect
madittiḍudal eṅgan mati-yāi	how can the immeasurable be measured by thought!

Paraphrase:

The Lord shines in the cave of the heart illumining and enlivening the intellect and the mind and through them everything else. To know Him one has to withdraw the mind from the world and should make it abide firmly in the Self, the Lord. Without merging thus, how can one measure the immeasurable being with the mind?

Commentary

Matikku oḷi tandu - the entire *anta:karaṇa* (the inner knowing-sense) is included within the term 'mati'. And the Self is the consciousness which is the witness of this intellect. Srimad Bhagavad Gita says: *yō buddhē: paratastu sa:* - That which shines beyond the intellect is 'He'.

vācham yaccha manō yaccha prāṇān yacchēndriyāṇi cha
ātmānamātmanā yaccha na bhūya: kalpasēdhvanē

– Srimad Bhagavatam 11-16-42

'Subsume the senses in the mind; control the thoughts with the intellect. Finally, silencing the activities of the intellect, repose in the stillness of Self-experience - this is the inner spiritual journey. Never again will you fall into this whirlpool of *samsārā*.'

Bhagavan expresses the same idea as, *matiyinai uḷḷē maḍakki*. The pure intellect is transformed as the power of the Self *(vibhūti*). It has the ability to act or to withdraw. When the intellect is directed outwards, it results in *pravṛtti*; when it is turned inward it results in *nivṛtti*. An intellect focussed externally turns into power - *siddhi*. When the same intellect is introverted, it reveals the experience of the Self-peace. The uninterrupted inward flow of the intellect happens truly due to Guru's grace. This is what is to be attained through *satsaṅga*.

Patiyil padittiḍudal - Here the word *pati* is used as a synonym for both Atman and *Īśwara*. In the earlier verse, the word *talaivan* was used. Although such words are used in Śaiva Siddhanta, Bhagavan Ramana uses them in a different sense. This description itself - *matikku oḷi tandu am matikkuḷ oḷirum* - indicates that the reference is to the Self that resides in the heart-cave. The term *mati* in *matikkuḷ* stands for the heart-cave. The mind is the inscrutable power that arises from the Self. Merging this power again at its source is what is meant by *patiyil padittiḍudal*. Bhagavan Ramana says in Upadesa Undiyar: *udikkum iḍatthil oḍuṅgi iruttal* - merging in the source from where it arises. In the stillness that results when the mind is subsumed in the heart, the true nature shines forth. That which shines as 'I am' is hidden by the concepts of the mind. To experience the pure awareness 'I' 'I' purged of all objects is Yoga.

The mind gets restless due to *laya, vikṣēpa* and *kaṣāya*. The mind agitated by thought-waves is in the state of *vikṣēpa*. *Laya* is the sleep-like *tāmasic* state which happens when one tries to control one's thoughts. A state of insipid inactivity induced by stupor is *kaṣāya*. If one wishes to be free of these three defects, one must hold on firmly to the 'I' and without losing hold of it, it should be subsumed in its source. It is only in a *sātvik* state of mind that one can grasp the movements of 'I'. Moderate and *sātvik* food, *satsaṅga* and devotion are the *sādhanās* that help to make the mind *sātvik.* The process of merging such a pure mind into the heart, without allowing it to sleep, move or become dull is referred to as, *matiyai maḍakki patiyil padittiḍudal.* This yoga of remaining firmly and unmovingly in the Self as 'I-I' will be discussed in detail in the forthcoming verses. Bhagavan Sri Ramana Himself has named this process as Maha Yoga.

Pati, paśu and *pāśam* are considered eternal by the Saiva Siddhantins. But in Vedanta, if the *jīva,* that is, *paśu* (creature) removes the individual ego or *pāśam* (rope) that binds it, then the *pati* (Lord) alone shines there. This is the truth. In this way, only if the intellect dissolves and becomes still by merging into its source, can one realize the Self. Without doing so, how can one know the Self by the thoughts born of the intellect? Thoughts can never touch the Self. When thoughts subside by themselves, the Self shines on its own as 'I' *(tānāi).* Kathopanishad talks about yoga in the following words:

buddhiścha na vichēṣṭati

tām āhu: paramām gatim – Kathopanishad 6-10

'That is the state of yoga where, after the senses and the mind are controlled the intellect also becomes absolutely still'.

On certain days the moon is sighted even during the day. But who cares to notice the moon when the sun shines brilliantly? Likewise, even in the *jnani,* his mind, lit up by the glow of the Self, is still visible. But just like the moon seen in broad daylight, the mind of the *jnani* is insignificant. If one wishes to know God who is resplendent as the Self within oneself, as 'I am' or as consciousness, the mind should become 'food' for the in-dwelling *īśwara* as mentioned in the previous verse. For this to happen, the mind must turn inwards seeking 'Who am I?' Then, the *chit śakti* (grace) gathers momentum and relentlessly draws that mind towards the heart-centre, totally engulfing it within itself. When the tiger in the cave gets the scent of the visitor, it will pounce on him and swallow him up. Likewise, the divine power of the Self will simply swallow (engulf) the introverted mind *(āṭkoṇḍu-viḍum).* Sri Ramana has said that when His mind became introverted due to the fear of death, the fire of wisdom which was glowing within the heart swallowed the mind. This is becoming 'food' for the Self. Just as a cotton doll cannot exist after embracing the fire, the mind cannot remain after contact with the Self. This is the essential meaning of *patiyil padittiḍal.* There is no other suitable method to destroy the ego than *ātmavichāra*. To conclude, Self-realization means the destruction of the ego, and not mere intellectual understanding.

THE BUBBLE AND THE OCEAN

Stop thinking, enough of knowing; Be still.
Do not measure the immeasurable with thought.
The bubble knows the ocean by death!
Mind will know the unfathomable by sinking into the source.
Enquire, plumb within, holding the thread of 'I'.
Relentlessly pursue the quest 'Who am I?'.
With the laser beam of attention, look at the 'I';
Trace the 'I'-thought to its source till it sinks
In the waters of Self-experience and ceases to rise again.

VERSE TWENTY-THREE

...mati-yiladāl

nānenḍṛid dēha navilā duṛak-kattu
nā-ninḍṛen ḍṛāru navil-vadilai—nānon
ḍṛezhun-dapi nellā mezhu-minda nān-eṅ
gezhu-menḍṛu nuṇ-matiyā leṇṇa—nazhu-vum

mati-yiladāl	As it does not have the awareness if its own existence
id dēham nān enḍṛu navilādu	this body will not express itself as 'I'
uṛakkattum nān inḍṛu enḍṛu ārum navilvadu ilai	no one denies the existence of the 'I' in deep sleep where the body is not
nān onḍṛu ezhunda pin	only after the emergence of the individuality as 'I'
ellām ezhum	all other thoughts appear
inda nān eṅgu ezhum	from where does this movement 'I' emerge?
enḍṛu	Thus
nuṇ-mati-yāl eṇṇa—nazhu-vum	when with a keen intellect enquired into, the ego sense vanishes

Paraphrase:

This body, being inert, will not say 'I' on its own. No one denies one's existence by saying 'I do not exist' in deep sleep. Only when the 'I'-thought arises (in the form of I am so and so) on waking, all other thoughts (God, *jīva,* world) follow. Investigate with a keen intellect whence the 'I' (the ego sense) emerges. When thus sought, the ego sense merges in its source and vanishes.

Commentary

All religions talk about world, God and the individual. Sri Bhagavan has so far spoken about the world and God. Now the focus is on the 'individual'- the 'I'. In the following four *veṇbās*, Bhagavan talks about how the individual-'I' arises, persists and how ultimately it merges in its source. After that in three *veṇbās*, Bhagavan gives instructions on Self enquiry - the direct path of enquiring into the source of the 'I'- thought.

Dēham nān enḍru navilādu - In the process of Self-enquiry, the first outward step is the assertion - *dēhōnāham* - 'I am not the body'. The awareness 'I' is not of the body. Even in people who have lost their arms or limbs or any other part of their body, the experience of the 'I' remains undiminished. The presence or absence of the limbs does not affect this awareness of 'I' in any manner. This is a clue for us to know that the 'I' has nothing to do with the body. The very fact that we refer to it as 'my' body implies that there is a vague awareness within, that 'I am not the body'. Nevertheless, by mixing up this awareness with the actions of the body, there arises an affinity with the body, which assumes 'I walk', 'I talk', 'I eat', 'I do', and so on. This assumed 'I' is only an illusion. But since the attention is entirely swallowed up by this 'I'-thought, the reality, the substratum, that which 'is', is not recognised. When the attention is given to this 'is-ness', it will become crystal clear that, it has absolutely no relation with the body at all.

It is the mind that has arisen in the body due to ignorance, which claims 'I am the body'. Bhagavan's question is whether the body says so on its own. If that be the case, even a dead body should have such a sense. As the corpse does not say so, the body does not possess the consciousness-'I'. Bhagavan says in the Anubandha *śloka - dēham mṛṇmayavat jaḍātmakam aham buddhi: na tasyāsti ata: nāham tat*. That which says 'I' in us now, but does not glow as 'I' in the corpse, exists apart from the body even now. To the question, 'Will this feeling continue to remain even if one leaves the body at the time of death?' the answer can only be that after death there will be no one there to describe the experience. But a state similar to death, in which the body is not, is available in sleep. In sleep, there is no body or mind or individual ego. Yet, no one feels their non-existence in deep sleep. What is more, 'I was happy' is the genuine experience of deep sleep for everyone. In deep sleep, in the absence of the ego, mind, body and the world, there was unalloyed happiness. Happiness was the Self then. This experience is undeniably the absolute experience of Brahman. In deep sleep I exist without the experience of the body. *Tadabhāva sūpti samayē siddhātma sadbhāvata:* - 'In deep sleep where there was no body, the existence of the Self is undeniable' - thus continues the *śloka* in the Anubandham. How astonishing! In spite of having been endowed with this experience, man, ignoring this ever-attained experience, leads a beggarly existence; he behaves like a beggar who sits on a chest full of gold, and begs, quite unaware of his own invaluable treasure. This indeed is *māyā*!

From all this, it becomes very clear that the body does not say 'I am'; that the body is not me; and that in deep sleep when there is no body, the experience of existence is undeniable. Yet, there is a vast difference between the 'I' in deep sleep, and the individual 'I' in the waking state. Contemplate on this deeply. Stop not till you crack the shell of non-understanding. The 'I' that is present in the deep sleep state is the 'I' devoid of the body, mind, the individual ego as well as the world perceived by the senses. There is not even a trace of duality. When the ego-'I' sprouts from this state, the mind, body and the world arise. This 'I' is one that rises and sets. The 'I' existing in the deep sleep state is eternally un-changing and non-dual. The individual-'I' in the waking state is pluralistic and subject to change. In deep sleep, differences such as caste, creed, status or gender, do not exist; even the feeling of being a human does not exist. There is only existence. Existence, experience and Self were one there. The 'I' in the waking state exists as myriad images and modifications. The existential essence that was in deep sleep is present behind the dream and waking states also as their substratum. Here reality is veiled by the body, mind and the individuality. That is why it is not clearly experienced. After a movie, the screen alone becomes visible. Nonetheless, even while the movie was being watched, the screen was always present as the substratum giving each frame that appeared on it a seeming reality. But as the attention was fixed on the movie, the screen went unnoticed. However, while watching the movie you were watching just the screen.

Only when the individual-'I' sprouts, do the body, mind, time, space etc. become perceptible. The subtle intellect has the ability to observe the rising of the individual-'I'. Bhagavan calls this *nuṇmati*. *Sādhanās* such as *japa*, meditation and other austerities, and actions performed with detachment *(niṣkāmya karmānuṣṭhānās)* are all prescribed only to purify the mind (to obtain this *nuṇmati*). When the 'I'-thought arises from the state of bliss in deep sleep, the first throb in stillness can be perceived. This stir creates dreams. Gradually, the ego takes the form of the personality; and then the physical body and the world become perceptible. This is a phenomenon we notice every day as we wake up from sleep. What becomes clear from this is that, it is with the rising of the ego that we lose the bliss of the Self. It has already been stated earlier that only if *tanmai* is there, do *munnilai* and *paḍarkkai* arise. Sri Bhagavan says that if we consciously observe the 'I' *(tanmai)* in the wakeful state, it will dissolve in its source, and we will be able to recognize the state of pure existence-consciousness which was there in deep sleep, here and now. This indeed is the sacred teaching of the Upanishads.

Inda nān eṅgu ezhumenḍṛu nuṇmatiyāl eṇ - In these words Bhagavan Ramana expounds his direct path of Self-enquiry. As we wake up from deep sleep, the feeling of 'I am so and so' arises. If we carefully observe wherefrom this 'I' arises, it disappears just like the mirage that vanishes when one goes near. This is *ātmavichāra*. Tracing the source of this 'I' is the technique of *hṛdaya vidyā* or *Ramaṇa vidyā.* This is explained in detail in the forthcoming *veṇbās*. Sri Bhagavan turned all these forty-two *veṇbās* into one *kaliveṇba*. This is a literary device in Tamil in which one verse is linked with the subsequent verse, thereby connecting all the verses stylistically into one *veṇba,* when it is then transformed into a *kaliveṇba*. This *śloka* that ends with '*nuṇmatiyāl eṇ*', when changed into *kaliveṇba,* was expanded as *nuṇmatiyāl eṇṇa nazhuvum*. With purified intellect, when the source of emergence of the 'I' is investigated, the 'I'-thought disappears and the pure, eternal, Existence-Consciousness-Bliss alone remains as the residuum. The same idea is expressed in the words, *tēḍināl ōṭṭam piḍikkum* - seek it and the ego flees (v. 25).

The Atman, the existence of which is experienced in deep sleep in the absence of the body, how is one to know it now? Bhagavan mentions the three levels: '*dēham nāham, kōham*, and *sōham*' in Anubandham. The story of a little girl may be cited in this context. G.V. Subbaramayya, a devotee of Bhagavan used to come frequently from Andhra Pradesh to visit Bhagavan Sri Ramana. He was a simple devotee who worshipped Bhagavan as his own father. He had two daughters, Lalita and Indira. Both these girls were blessed with Bhagavan's loving grace. Lalita would get into the hall and play with Bhagavan's walking stick, books, and other things there. Now and then, Bhagavan would ask this mischievous little five-year-old, "Hey, what are you doing?" She would reply, "I'm not doing anything!" Hearing this, Bhagavan would smile and remark, "Aha! Always remaining like this is *jnana*. Even after doing all this mischief, she says, 'I am not doing anything'. This is the truth."

Now, let us see the story of the three-year old Indira. This little girl had received Bhagavan's boundless grace. Once a devotee happened to listen to what Bhagavan was saying with great emphasis to this little girl. This learned devotee was amazed when he heard the words that Bhagavan was teaching her. Bhagavan was advising the little girl to memorise the lines: "*Dēham nāham* (the body is not me); *kōham*–then, who am I?; *sōham* - I am the Self." Hearing this, the devotee asked, "Bhagavan, will this little girl understand the meaning of these lines, which even learned scholars find hard to grasp?" Bhagavan, fixing his gaze on the devotee said, "What? Is that alone knowledge which can be grasped by the intellect?" The gravity of the question filled the devotee with fear and guilt. These words reminded him that it is grace alone that bestows knowledge.

A few days after this, Subbaramayya got ready to return to Andhra with his children. He saw Sri Bhagavan going for His usual walk to Arunachala, and took leave prostrating before Him. As Indira prostrated to take Bhagavan's blessings,

He made her repeat the teaching: '*dēham nāham...*' once again. He told her, "Don't forget this. You go to your home. I am going to mine." So saying, Bhagavan affectionately patted her with His stick and proceeded up the Hill. Very soon, the reason for this special behaviour of Bhagavan was revealed. Within a few months after this, little Indira left her body, with this teaching on her lips!

OCEAN OF EXISTENCE

Learn to turn within and look at the 'I' by the 'I'
Pour the water of attention into the Heart
Heart is the ocean of existence, awareness and peace
Let the mind like a bubble drop into the expanse of Being
Let the iceberg of the ego move or melt in the waters of existence
Let the froth of thoughts move or vanish in the sea of the Self
Water alone is; Oneness, non-dual awareness alone reigns.

VERSE TWENTY-FOUR

jaḍa-vuḍanā nennādu sacchit tudi-yā
duḍal-aḷavā nānon ḍṛudikku—miḍaiyi-litu
chit-jaḍakki ranthi-bandhaṅ jīva-nuṭpa mei-yahantai
yicchamu-sāramana meṇ

jaḍa uḍal nān ennādu	The inert body by itself will not say 'I'
sat chittu udiyātu	being-awareness too will not arise as 'I'
iḍaiyil uḍal aḷavāi	between the two with the body as its measure
nān onḍṛu udikkum	as 'I', a feeling arises
itu chit jaḍa giranthi	this knot that binds awareness with matter, is the chit-jaḍa-granthi
bandham jīvan nuṭpamei ahantai icchamusāram manam eṇ	this is called variously as bondage, jīva, subtle body, ego, samsāra, mind and so on. Know this.

Paraphrase:

The inert body will not say 'I' on its own. *Sat-chit* (being-awareness) too will not arise as 'I'. Between these two, something appears as 'I' with the body as its limit. This 'I', connecting the *chit* (awareness) and the *jaḍa* (the matter), binds them in a knot. Know that it is called variously as *chit-jaḍa-granthi,* bondage*, jīva, sūkṣma śarīra* (subtle body), *samsāra* (the cycle of birth and death) and the mind.

Commentary

Now we are entering the core of Bhagavan's teaching. Though it was already stated in the previous verse that the body does not have the pulsation 'I', it is in a different context that Bhagavan repeats the same in this verse. In the previous verse, it was pointed out that in deep sleep nobody says, 'I do not exist'. The 'existence' mentioned there is the consciousness devoid of the ego-'I'. That reality will not arise as 'I' 'I'. The body which is inert disappears in sleep and does not say 'I exist'. In between the inert body and pure consciousness, that which emerges as the ego-'I', is only an illusion connecting consciousness and the body. The visible world and the seer, which are contrary to each other in nature like darkness and light, appear to be one and the same because of this illusion *(ābhāsam)*. The nature of the Self is thus superimposed upon inert matter, and matter is super-imposed on the Self; thus leading to *parāspara-adhyāsa* (a mutual superimposition). Consciousness and inert matter are thus bound together, and this knot is called *hṛdaya granthi* or *chit-jaḍa granthi*. This is the centre of ignorance which is variously referred to as bondage, *jīva,* ego, world, mind and the subtle body. Liberation is the complete annihilation of this centre. It is this same centre that makes the *jīva* suffer in the state of ignorance by causing all kinds of misery. Actually the individual ego itself is its form. The method of dissolving this centre at its source is the path - *hṛdaya vidyā* - which is going to be explained hereafter. In the previous *śloka* itself Bhagavan has stated this in the lines - *idu eṅgu ezhumenḍṛu nuṇmatiyāl eṇṇa nazhuvum*. This verse is an explanation of the ego which is said to 'slip away' *(nazhuvum)*. As it slips away from the grasp of enquiry, the word *nazhuvum* is used.

In the *śāstrās* they say that 'the ego is a mere reflection of consciousness on the mirror of the mind' – *'chittagata chit-pratibimba-lakṣaṇō jīva:'*. Even though it is only a reflection, the misery that comes out of it is verily unbearable! Hence, well-wishers (the kind-hearted rishis) try to find out how this misery can be removed.

ahaṅkāravaśād āpad ahaṅkārād durādaya:
ahaṅkāravaśādīhā nāhaṅkārād parōripu: –Yoga Vasishtam

'All misery, evil and desire are created by the ego. There is no foe other than the ego' says Sri Rama to Vasishta. "Please heal me of this" prays Rama.

In the booklet 'Who am I?', the first book of Bhagavan Sri Ramana, it is stated that there is no method other than Self-enquiry which can eliminate the ego. In that book Bhagavan has also prescribed the method for Self-enquiry. The power of grace that is required for practising Self-enquiry lies hidden in the very words of the book. Seekers must read this little book repeatedly with great attention and utmost devotion, like taking a course of medicine. This book has in it the power to awaken *vichāra jñānā*.

Na alpē sukhamasti (Chandogya Upanishad) - the illusion of the limited personality is *alpam*. The Upanishad declares that 'there is no happiness in *alpam'*. Where this differentiated illusion of 'I' and 'the other' exists, there exists the ego as *alpam*. Where this differentiated illusion of 'I' and 'the other' is absent, and the absolute, non-dual consciousness alone is recognized as pure existence, there the infinite *bhūmā* shines forth. *Bhūmā* alone is bliss. In deep sleep, without the feeling of 'I' and 'the other' there is happiness. Yet, as *vichārā* is not possible in deep sleep, realization also is not possible in this state.

In deep sleep, there is not even a speck of duality. From that state the 'I'-thought arises, passes through the mind, creates the senses and the body, and takes pride in becoming the individual. This is something like a beggar who dreams he is wearing the royal robes of a king and believes that he really is a king, and takes pride in it. The dream king gets angry if someone tells him that the kingdom and power are only illusions. On waking up, all this vanishes. This illusory individuality is a super-imposition on the pure consciousness (Self), similar to the dream king or the superimposition of the snake on a rope. If in the waking state itself, one examines this 'I'-thought, it will vanish and the substratum, the Self, shines forth. In this way *jāgrat-suṣupti* (waking-deep sleep) happens through Self-enquiry. That is, the ego which is the cause for ignorance falls away. At that instant, the superimposition gets removed and the substratum shines forth. This must happen in the waking state itself. The ego described as *'nān onḍru uḍalaḷavāy udikkum'* will get destroyed and *sat-chit* alone will remain.

sattāchit sukharūpamasti satatam
nāham nachatvam mṛṣā
nēdam vāpi jagatpradṛṣṭamakhilam
nāstīti jānīhibhō: (Sri Sankara's Proudanubhuti - 16)

'Dear one, know this - existence, happiness and awareness - alone is, at all times; neither you, nor me, nor this world exists.'

na nirōdhō na cha utpatti: na baddhō na cha sādhaka:
na mumukṣur na vā mukta: ityēṣā paramārtthatā

– Gaudapadakarika

Bondage is a synonym for *chit-jaḍa granthi* (the knot that binds consciousness and matter). There is no bondage in the Self. In reality, there is neither bondage, nor a *sādhaka*, nor a *mukta*.

Q: Yet, we still feel bound, do we not?

A: Who is the one who feels bound?

Q: I do.

A: If one enquires who this 'I' is, the 'I' will disappear and the eternally free reality will blaze forth.

PEACE UNSURPASSABLE

Keep quiet, stay in the centre; peace unsurpassable is there.
Centre is perfection, circumference is cacophony
Centre is life, circumference is death
Freedom reigns in the centre, fate prowls on the surface
If you splash, a stir arises in the centre
You are irresistibly pushed to the circumference!
There cannot be harmony on the surface
Trace your way back to source and abide - BE STILL!

VERSE TWENTY-FIVE

...ennē—vicchai

urup-paṭṭṛi yuṇḍā murup-paṭṭṛi niṛku

murup-paṭṭṛi yuṇḍu-miga vōṅgu—muruviṭ

ṭurup-paṭṭṛun tēḍinā lōṭṭam piḍikku

muru-vaṭṭṛa pēyahantai yōr-vāi

ennē-vicchai	what a wonder!
uru aṭṭṛa pēi-ahantai	having no form of its own, like a ghost, the formless ego
uru paṭṭṛi uṇḍām	clinging onto a form (body), as 'I', comes into existence
uru paṭṭṛi niṛkum	holding on to the form, it stays
uru paṭṭṛi uṇḍu	continuing the hold, feeding on the food of the senses, experiencing pleasure and pain, and by the strength of the vāsanās of these experiences
miga ōṅgum	waxes strong
uru viṭṭu uru paṭṭṛum	when one form (body) perishes, grasps another
tēḍināl	when enquired into its truth
ōṭṭam piḍikkum ōrvāi	it takes to its heels, leaving no trace, know this

Paraphrase:

What a wonder! Holding a form the ego arises; holding a form it stays; continuing the hold, feeding on the food of the senses, experiencing pleasure and pain, and by the strength of the *vāsanās* of these experiences, it thrives. Leaving one form, it takes hold of another; when sought, it flees. Such is the ego-ghost with no form of its own.

Commentary

The nature of the ego is described in this verse. The ego does not have a form or existence of its own. Its birth, persistence, growth and nourishment are all dependent on a body. As it does not have a form and body of its own, it is also very difficult to grasp it. What we call as personality is none other than this ego. Patanjali calls it *asmitā*. While he considers it as one of the afflictions of a *jīva*, Bhagavan states that this alone is the root for all miseries.

The ego has a body that is made up of concepts, will, desire, moods and imaginations *(bhāvanā)*. Doership and enjoyership are its prominent characteristics. 'I am doing' is doership *(kartṛtvam)* and 'I am enjoying or experiencing' is enjoyership *(bhōktṛtvam)*. The ego arises out of the *samskārās* or past impressions resulting from ignorance, desire and indulgence in the past. Its foundation is the 'I' that conceives the subtle forms of the sense objects. This ghost cannot survive without constantly feeding on pleasure and pain. Therefore it will instigate the person to indulge in many motivated actions. It is this ego which makes the *jīva* into a *samsāri,* who is attracted to joy, and averse to sorrow. It loves play-acting. It is not contented with peace or rather gets bored with peace. Therefore, Sri Sankaracharya calls him *śailuṣa* (actor). It has no existence without a thought or feeling *(bhāvanā)*. It is the ego itself that imagines - 'I am a father', 'I am a mother', 'I am a son', 'I am a daughter', 'I am a *sanyāsi*', 'I am a *samsāri*', and so on and so forth. It is afraid of pure stillness - *mouna* - the thoughtless state. In order to thrive, it possesses some persons and makes them declare: 'One can attain Self-realization or God-realization only by retaining a separate identity.' All religious doctrines are its creation. It gets strengthened by conflict. So it is the ego that propagates religious conflicts as well as jealousy and arrogance even in the ashrams of great *mahātmās*. It cannot survive without conflict. Hence it creates holy wars. It will take on roles such as that of 'social welfare activist', or 'political worker', and sanctimoniously fatten itself. It even assumes the role of being a special incarnation or that of a great yogi. Even after attaining high spiritual experience, the ego will revive itself and gloat over such achievements. At all such junctures one must hold on firmly to the enquiry, 'Who is this I?' When pride wells up as 'I am so and so', if one observes the 'I'-thought closely and enquires 'Who is this I?', the real transcendental state of pure consciousness *(bhāvanātīta sadbhāva susthiti:)* alone will remain. When we see little children playing games, where they act out roles such as, 'I am the mother, you are the father' and so on, we can see the first sprout of this ego sense.

Even though the ego is only an appearance in the mind, it appropriates to itself the *astitva* (existence-principle) of consciousness and brings in a sense of *asmitva* (I am-ness). Instantly, remaining in the individual body, it creates innumerable problems. *Amānitvam* (absence of pride) is natural and spontaneous in a *jnani* whose ego is completely erased. He has no imaginations about himself. His centre of experience is the pure consciousness, the real-'I'. He can only say 'I am that I am' and the sage is effortlessly still. The *muni* abides in himself, tranquil and detached, even as he sees the common folk possessed by the ego-ghost offering justifications and explanations for their thoughts and imaginations, and engaging themselves in vain arguments and conflicts. The calm and peaceful sage does not run after name or fame and remains free of lust or anger. Absolute peace of *Brahmanirvāṇā* like the coolness of the comely full moon wafts around him.

Tēḍināl ōṭṭam piḍikkum - Although it has no form of its own, the ego assumes a multitude of forms, and is averse to enquiry. On enquiring, the ego vanishes like darkness in the presence of light. The ego is only an illusory superimposition on the Self, imagined in ignorance, like the seeing of the snake on the rope or the ghost on the post. It disappears when exposed to the light of Self-enquiry. The ghost is the progeny of darkness. All ghost stories are associated with midnight. There is no one who has seen a ghost in broad daylight. Similarly the ego-ghost dances in the darkness of inattention. Sri Bhagavan used to narrate a story entitled 'Bridegroom's Friend' to illustrate the nature of this ego, which is neither matter nor consciousness, but something that arises between the two and creates suffering.

Once upon a time a clever wayfarer entered a wedding hall. He joined the wedding group and pretended to be the friend of the bridegroom. The groom's people put up with his arrogant behaviour, thinking that he belonged to the bride's party; and the bride's people thought that he belonged to the groom's party. With assumed authority he ordered everyone around and caused a lot of trouble to both the parties. Finally when this became unbearable, both the parties began to enquire about him. The moment this investigation started, he left the place. No amount of searching could locate him. Likewise, Bhagavan says, "The ego will disappear on investigation."

Bhagavan has used the word 'form' in this verse. It has been stated that the ego depends on form. 'Form' is not confined to the body alone. The subtler layers of thought-forms are the more important factors on which it depends. Patanjali calls this *vṛttisārūpyam* i.e., the ego becoming one with the modes of the mind. Thought-waves flow constantly from the causal body to the subtle body. These thought-waves are extremely subtle forms of energy (pure undifferentiated *panchabhūtās*). It is these energy diffusions that get projected externally as gross forms. When attention falls on these forms (thoughts), and when it identifies itself with them, the ego thrives. This energy field unfolds itself as likes, dislikes, and *layā* or torpor. The 'I' thought mingles with this energy field and projects the personality image. This ego hides the pure existence just as dark clouds hide the blue sky. This slip of attention from the Self to the ego is the primal ignorance.

In the *sūtrabhāṣyā* Sri Sankara says that all secular and religious activities are based on this primal ignorance. So the egoless *tattvavid* transcends all activities in a natural manner. The ego stays linked with activities in the form of doership; with the fruit of actions in the form of enjoyership; with objects and personalities as attachment; and with thoughts in the form of images *(abhimāna)*. At times, when possessions are lost, or when loved ones die, the intensely suffering individual lets go of the identification with the ego, and experiences the peaceful rest in the Self. Such spasmodic experiences occur in the lives of most people at least for a short period of time. Rarely the castle of ego itself might collapse and get erased when some catastrophe happens to the object of its identification. In some, it may become the cause for absolute surrender, which will surely erase the individual-sense.

sāhankārasya dravyasya yōvasthānam anugraha:

–Srimad Bhagavatam

'The destruction of an object of pride is an act of grace.'

When there is nothing to be identified with, one experiences the ever-auspicious Self. Sorrows that visit us in life are often the hidden forces of grace that erase our ego. Attachment to any ideal, object, person, or position - good or bad - binds us to the body-mind adjunct and distances us from the Self. If the destruction of any such object causes pain to us, it implies that we are still caught in the grip of the ego. The annihilation of this attachment is the highest attainment. The inner feeling that is associated with any object is *ahankāra* (ego). Therefore the destruction of an object is a blessing, if it brings about the destruction of the ego.

In the story of Mahabali in Srimad Bhagavatam, Bhagavan says: *yasyānugrahamicchāmi tadviśōvidhunōmyaham* 'Whomsoever I wish to bless, I destroy his sense of attachment'.

If the attachments to objects or persons do not get erased when these are destroyed, the *abhimānā* would continue to stay within, in a subtle form. When the body dies, or sleeps, the ego that has not given up the inner attachment, and remains in the subtle body, will create another form (as in dreams) which could be a world similar to or different from the present world. All this is decided by the subtle body of this *jīva.* Bhagavan describes this as *uru viṭṭu uru paṭṭṛum*. Liberation is the destruction of the imaginary ego while one is alive. Other than Self-enquiry, there is no method to eradicate this ego.

rāma: svātma vichārōyam kōham syāmiti rūpaka:
chitta durdrumabījasya dahanē dahana: smṛta: – Yoga Vasishtam

'The Self-enquiry 'Who am I?' is the fire which scorches the seed of the poisonous tree that is the mind.'

Uru paṭṭṛi uṇḍu miga ōṅgum - The enjoyment of the objects of the senses is the tonic *(rasāyana)* for this ego. Even if it is attenuated by Self-enquiry, the memory of the objects will strengthen it again like the seed of the banyan tree sprouting in the rain. *Uruppaṭṭṛal* refers to the identification of the ego with a particular individuality. *Uruppaṭṭṛi uṇṇal* means identifying with the assumed personality, and consuming the sensory objects. *Uruppaṭṭral* means superimposition *(adhyāsa).* Just as the rope is misapprehended as a snake, the Self is misapprehended as being associated with the body.

ahambhāvasya dēhēsmin niśśeṣa vilayāvadhi
sāvadhānēna yuktātma svādhyāsāpanayam kuru

– Vivekachudamani 286

'Negate the superimposition with great care and alertness, until the ego that considers this body as 'I', is totally rooted out.'

The feeling that 'I am an individual with specific characteristics is firmly ingrained in us. We see others through the mirror of this feeling and develop corresponding likes and dislikes. When the ego disappears, and one observes from the standpoint of Self, the 'other' will not be seen. This is *ananyatā*. Whenever (with the feeling of 'I am so and so') the mind jumps out towards the objects of the world to feed on them, enquire attentively 'Who is this 'I'?' and go inward. This is the way. At that very moment the no-ego state or being will reveal itself. In this manner, if this egoless-state becomes clear moment by moment, experience after experience, then the immortal being will be revealed. This is the awareness of the Self, which is the seat of immense vitality. In this manner, if one develops the habit of making the ego subside at its source relentlessly, the habit of image forming will get over-powered by the force of Self-enquiry. With this, the ego born of *avidyā* will vanish. This is undeniably the *avabhṛtam* the most auspicious culmination of *jñāna yajñā*. (The ritual bath that is taken at the conclusion of a *yāgā* or *yajñā* is called *avabhṛtam.*)

VERSE TWENTY-SIX

...karu-vām
ahan-taiyuṇ ḍāyi nanait-tumuṇ ḍāgu
mahantaiyin ḍṛēlin ḍṛanaittu—mahan-taiyē
yāvumā māda-lāl yādi-denḍṛu nāḍalē
yōvu-dal yāvumena vōr

karuvām ahantai uṇḍāyin	When the primal seed of ignorance, that is the 'I' arises
anaittum uṇḍāgum	all appearances rise with it
ahantai iṇḍṛēl	where the 'I' is not
anaittum inḍṛu	all perceptions cease to appear
ahantaiyē yāvum ām	this ego-'I' alone is everything
ādalāl yādu idu	therefore, investigate 'What is this 'I'?'
enḍṛu nāḍalē	thus to enquire, to seek
ōvudal yāvum ena ōr	is itself renunciation of all, know this

Paraphrase:

When the ego, the cause of everything, rises as 'I', all the world appearances and perceptions rise along with it. If the ego rises not, all perceptions disappear. The ego verily is all, appearing as all. To seek, to enquire and to know its nature and whence it rises is to renounce everything.

Commentary

'Karu' actually means embryo, the first sprout of life. The ego is indeed the germ of *samsārā*. The primal seed of life is the throbbing of 'I', 'I'. It is around this throbbing, the body is formed. In this verse, Bhagavan Sri Ramana reveals to us the characteristics of *sanyāsa* at a very subtle plane. Sri Sankaracharya at the very beginning of the Gita Bhashya says that Self-knowledge is the characteristic feature of *sanyāsa*. Maharshi also defines *sanyāsa* in similar terms in Sri Ramana Gita:

sanyāsō nirmalam jñānam
na kāṣāyō na cha muṇḍanam

'*Sanyāsa* is clear knowledge of the Self and is not the mere wearing of the ochre robe or tonsuring of the head.' The state of realization or knowledge is that in which the ego does not arise at all. This is the state that is to be attained by Self-enquiry. A spiritual life is one where there is supreme peace without the least trace of ego.

Ahantai uṇḍāyin - The first thought that surfaces when one wakes up from sleep is the 'I'-thought. It is only after this thought arises that the body, the place and the names and forms arise. The last thought that subsides on falling asleep is also the same 'I'-thought. This 'I'-thought is the door that leads to the dream and waking states. In other words, it is the same 'I' that expands and manifests itself as the dream and waking world *(ahantaiyē yāvumām)*. In the deep sleep state, where there is no 'I'-thought, there is only pure existence without any differentiation between 'I' and the 'other', or between the 'knower' and the 'known'. From this state, when the ego arises, everything else manifests. Though this is the common experience of all, due to the veiling power of *avidyā,* it is not noticed until pointed out by the Guru.

Although Brahman is experienced in deep sleep, the realization, 'I am He' *(sōhamasmi)* does not occur since the veiling of *avidyā* still remains. The identification with the 'I' brings about unending miseries. One pays attention to the illusory individuality, without seeing the Self, like seeing the super-imposed snake without seeing the rope. However, when light is focussed on it, the rope becomes clearly visible. In the same way when closely observed with a clear intellect, the ego vanishes, and in its place, the eternal, pure, ever-free conscious reality reveals itself. Bhagavan refers to this as *yādu idenḍṛu nāḍal*. It is the individual-sense which bears the entire universe says the Bhagavad Gita - *'jīvabhūtām mahābāho yayēdam dhāryatē jagat'* (Ch.7- 5). The *jīva* itself is an illusion. If analysed, it will merge into the infinite Self just as the waves merge into the ocean. There the triad consisting of the *jīva-jagat-īśwara* will vanish like a dream. This is the only way to renounce everything. Bhagavan says that even the word 'everything' *(sarvam - yāvum)* is a synonym for the ego. If the ego is renounced, everything is renounced. Paul Brunton once asked Bhagavan Ramana: "Should we not renounce all our possessions?" Bhagavan responded, "the possessor too."

If the ego disappears when possessions are renounced, that is fine. But it is often seen that the ego continues to remain even after material possessions are given up. For the ego to disappear, one must enquire: "What is this 'I'-thought; Where does it come from?" - *yādideṇḍṛu nāḍal*. Such a one, who consciously enquires and makes the ego subside in the heart, will naturally be a *sanyāsi*. Bhagavan calls this 'renouncing everything' - *yāvum ōvudal*.

Sanyāsā

Let us digress a little here and analyse *sanyāsa* for the benefit of the seekers. It is a fact authenticated by the *śruti* that only those who have become inwardly pure *(śuddhasatva)* through renunciation - *sanyāsa* - will attain Self-realization. But, what exactly do we mean by *sanyāsa*? As we have already seen, Sri Bhagavan Ramana declares in the Ramana Gita that mere saffron robes and shaven head, without Self-knowledge, are not the signs of *sanyāsa*. In olden days enlightened souls had taken up ochre robe and begging bowl in order to be free of all social, filial or scriptural obligations. This *āśrama* gave ample time for spiritual pursuit as neither the world nor the Vedas imposed any duty on a *sanyāsi*. But in due course, this higher ideal and teaching got diluted in the hands of mediocre men. Those who lacked this inner awakening also took to this path either to be free of the disciplines imposed by Vedas or for mere respect that this attire and position brought for them. Instead of living up to the ideal they possessed more wealth and relationships than *gṛhasthās* and thus brought a pitiable fall to that sacred way of life. As rituals like 'accepting *sanyāsa*' and 'conferring *sanyāsa*' became more established, the true import of the term *sanyāsa* itself was forgotten. *Sanyāsā* is not something to be given or accepted. It is the inner purity to be attained by following the way of life prescribed as *'sanyāsa yōgā'* in the Bhagavad Gita. *Sanyāsa* is essentially the renunciation of the ego. The ego consists of the sum total of *āgāmi, sañchita* and *prārabdha karmās*. The ego is the driver that controls the course of life according to the forces of *karma*. The desire for enjoying the fruit of action, sense of doership in action, and attachment towards objects seen, are all natural movements in the centre *(granthi)* that identifies itself as 'I am so and so'.

If the ego is destroyed through *jnana*, all these will be annihilated; and the Self will be realized - this is *samnyāsam (ōvudal)*. Bhagavan Sri Ramana never encouraged his close disciples to adopt the *sanyāsi* robes. Bhagavan himself did not wear ochre clothes. Yet, he was himself the king amongst *sanyāsīs*. Many of the disciples of Bhagavan like Muruganar, Viswanatha Swami and Annamalai Swami were *sanyāsīs* of the highest order. Although they lived only on their daily alms *(bhikṣā),* Bhagavan did not ask them to wear *kāṣāyā* or change their names. Their attention was focussed only on the inner *sanyāsa* or the destruction of the ego. This does not mean that Bhagavan disparaged external *sanyāsa*. If *prārabdha* makes one who is internally a *sanyāsi,* accept the external signs too, that is fine. In the case of Kunjuswami he had to take external *sanyāsa* from Hrishikesh due to some reason. In his case Bhagavan accepted that completely. However, the mere adoption of the external signs of a *sanyāsi* while indulging in actions that are against *sanyāsa dharma* is not acceptable to the *śāstrās.* In a society, working for the upliftment of people is essential. But, why does one need to wear *sanyāsi* robes for that purpose? The *turīyā* or the fourth *āśrama* cannot be helpful in the area of social service. *Turīya āśrama* is meant for a life of withdrawal where *vairāgya* and *jñāna-vichāra* (dispassion and Self-enquiry) alone are important. The fact that renunciation of the ego and a multitude of worldly activities do not go to-gether has been clearly understood by seekers from experiments and experiences based on their own lives. With the renunciation of the ego, all activities other than one's *svadharma* (that is, actions that are not one's *prārabdha*) will fall off by themselves. Even *svadharma* will be performed without any doership or enjoyership. Sri Sankaracharya explains in the Gita Bhashyam that action performed by a *jnani* is not *karma, but akarma - viduṣā kriyamāṇam karma akarmaiva.*

Here Sri Bhagavan talks about inner *sanyāsa* that takes the nature of *naiṣkarmya*. The only way for this to happen is *vichāra*. Through enquiry alone the ego will vanish. The ego will remain like the ghost in a post or water in a mirage until one enquires into its source. And on enquiry, it will vanish leaving behind not even a trace. Therefore the enquiry into its source itself is actually *sanyāsa yōgā*. Let us proceed now to discuss *ahamgraha upāsana* which is variously termed as *hṛdaya vidyā, ātma-vichāra or* Self-enquiry.

***Ahamgraha Upāsana* - Points to ponder**

Traditionally *śravaṇa, manana* and *nididhyāsana* are the three steps generally prescribed for Vedanta *vichāra*.

'*Sanyasya śravaṇam kuryāt*' is the instruction for *śravaṇa*. In other words, renouncing all attachments, one must do *śravaṇa*. The external signs of *sanyāsa* will help one from being pulled back again to activities by one's relatives and society of the previous *āśrama*. One who renounces with this purpose is known as a *sādhaka* or *vividiṣa sanyāsi*. In this manner if a seeker with the right sense of direction renounces his ties with children, wife, society, wealth, and all else, and enters the path of Self-enquiry, it is indeed commendable. But even when one leads such a solitary life doing Self-enquiry or *śravaṇa* and *manana*, it cannot be said that he has attained absolute *sanyāsa*. For in solitude, one finds that all the things that one renounced, continue to linger subtly in oneself in the form of thoughts and emotions. Only when these subtle *vāsanās* are scorched in the fire of knowledge, does one truly become a *sanyāsi*. The ego-'I' is the source of all thoughts and feelings. One needs to search for it diligently, and find its source. Sri Bhagavan calls this the inner reflection - *antarmananam*.

Listening internally to the 'I-I' or grasping the pulsation of 'I-I' is what is called inner *śravaṇa*. The inner *manana* is the focussing of attention on this 'I'-thought without deviation. By constant attention the 'I' will leave its association with the body- mind limitation and shine forth as pure *chit* - consciousness. Abiding for long durations in this state is *nididhyāsanam*. This is also termed as - *ahamgraha upāsana* - meditation by holding to the 'I am'. This enquiry alone will open the door to the inner path of light and pave the way for the dawn of realization. Once *jnana* arises in a *sādhaka,* he is a *sanyāsi* wherever he may choose to stay.

'Sanyāsi' is not a name for the body. It is the name of the Self. The Self is a *nityasanyāsi* (eternal *sanyāsi).* As one who knows the Self becomes the Self, he is also a *nityasanyāsi*. The Self is never ever attached to anything at any time. *'Asaṅgō hi ayam puruṣa:'* says the Upanishad. In other words this *puruṣa*, the Atman, the Self, has absolutely no attachment to anything. It is never possible for it to be attached in any manner whatsoever. One who knows the ever-free Atman, will become everfree himself. This is the nature of *vidvat sanyāsa* attained through *jnana*. In this manner, he who has known himself transcends all *āśrama dharmas* and becomes an *atyāśrami* (one beyond all *āśramās*). This is what is implied by *yāvum ōvudal.*

RENUNCIATION

'Renunciation', the very sound is music to the soul!
It alone is the herb that heals all the hurts caused by desire
It alone is the *mantra* that drives out the vampire, ego
The robe and bowl of the awakened one is the insignia of freedom
The heart purged of all desire emits the perfume of great peace
The fragrance of renunciation attracts divine beings to that centre
All the *dēvās* pass through that person to touch the inner-presence!
Such was the sage par excellence, Sri Ramana
Who walked the earth emitting the fragrance of *ātmānubhuti*
The Master who gave up all for the good of all
And took the begging bowl of compassion
An emperor amongst monks, the great knower of Brahman!

VERSE TWENTY-SEVEN

...mudalpōn—mēvu-minda
nānudiyā duḷḷa-nilai nāmadu-vā yuḷḷa-nilai
nānudikkun tānamadai nāḍā-ma—nānudiyāt
tannizhapp-pai sārva-devan sārāmaṛ tṛānadu-vān
tannilai-yi niṛpa-devan sāṭ-ṭṛudi

(mudal-pōl mēvum inda)	(As if appearing as the one primal resource)
'nān' udiyādu uḷḷa nilai	that state where this 'I' rises not
nām 'adu'-vāi uḷḷa nilai	is the state where we are 'That'
nān udikkum sthānam adai nāḍā-mal	without seeking the place whence the 'I' arises
nān udiyā tannizhappai sārvadu evan	how can the state where the ego does not arise - the annihilation of the jīvabhāva - be attained?
sārāmal tān adu-ām tan nilaiyil niṛpadu evan	without eliminating the ego who could verily abide in the state in which one is 'That'?
sāṭ-ṭṛudi	tell me

Paraphrase:

The pure state where the 'I' does not arise is the state where we are 'That' - the Atman. Without plunging deep in enquiry to find from where the 'I'- thought arises, how can the extinction of the ego be achieved? Without the ego thus getting eliminated, how can one abide firmly in the state in which one is 'That'? Tell me.

Commentary

This is one of the most important verses in the text.

- *Prajñānam Brahma* - Brahman is pure consciousness
- *Aham Brahmāsmi* - I am Brahman
- *Tat Tvam Asi* - You are That
- *Ayam Ātma Brahma* - What appears as this *jīva* is Brahman

These four dicta are the *mahāvākyās* (Great Upanishadic Sayings). Bhagavan explains the meaning and significance of all these four *mahāvākyās* in this twenty-seventh verse. The two words *nām adu* (we are that) means that *nām* or the *jīva* is the same as 'That' or Brahman. If we enquire what it is that appears as the *jīva, prajñāna* - pure awareness alone will remain and that is indeed Brahman. *Nān udiyādu uḷḷa nilai* - When not even a trace of the 'I'-thought arises, then there will be the uninterrupted radiance of 'That'. Without using the names Brahman or God, Bhagavan uses the pronoun 'That' to imply the Self. Though the experience of the Self exists in deep sleep, we can conduct Self-enquiry only in the waking state. So if 'That' has to be experienced in the waking state, the finite-'I' has to merge in the infinite. 'That' must swallow 'this'. Then that is called the *sahaja nirvikalpa* state or realization. It is the individual ego-'I' that constantly creates *vikalpās* and makes the unbroken consciousness appear to be broken and limited. If this 'I' does not arise, the infinite consciousness will radiate here and now. *Nān udikkum tānamadai nāḍu* - The heart is the place of origin of the ego. *Prāṇa* also arises from the same place.

ahamayam kutō bhavati chinvata:
ayipatatyaham nijavichāraṇam – Upadesa Saram 19

'If one vigilantly enquires where this 'I' arises from, then the 'I'-thought dissolves at its source. This is *nijavichāraṇam* (Self-enquiry).'

Without allowing the 'I'-thought to emerge, subsuming it at its source, is variously known as *antarmukham, pratyaksthiti:* and *ātmaniṣṭhā.* If one seeks the source of the 'I'-thought and arrives at the heart even once, he will have a glimpse of the 'whole'. Even then, in order to overcome this beginningless habit of acting as an individual, one must consciously and continually observe and investigate the 'I' - thought.

anātmavāsanājālaisthirōbhūtātmavāsanā
nityātmaniṣṭhayātēṣām nāśē bhāti svayam sphuṭa
– Vivekachudamani 275

'The fragrance of the Self is veiled by the preoccupations with the desires to enjoy the non-Self. When these have been erased by constantly abiding in the Self, the Atman is revealed by itself.'

If the *samskāra* of *ātma vichāra* overpowers the *samskāra* of the ego, *nān udiyādu uḷḷa nilai* - the state where the 'I' does not arise - will become natural.

jnātēvastunyapi balavatī vāsanā anādirēṣā
kartābhoktāpyahamiti dṛḍhā yāsya samsārahetu:
– Vivekachudamani 267

'Even after having the glimpse of the Self, the powerful tendencies of the ego will forcefully surface again and again as 'I am the doer' and 'I am the enjoyer' and thus misery - *samsāra*–continues'. What is the solution for this?

pratyak dṛṣṭyātmani nivasatā sāpanēyāprayatnāt
muktim prāhustadiha munayō vāsanātānavam yat

–Vivekachudamani 267

'This *samskāra* of the ego-'I' must be overcome by making the individual-'I' subside at its source, and by abidance in the Self. Liberation is the total eradication of *vāsanās* born of this individual ego.'

Liberation is our real nature. The experience of 'I' itself is liberation. This is implied by the *mahāvākya, Aham Brahmāsmi*. I do not have to become Brahman, nor meditate, 'I am Brahman'. The true essence of the word 'I' is not an individual or a *jīva*; it is the absolute Brahman itself. How do we know this? It is when the individual-'I' subsides and does not arise, that we realize that 'We are That'.

ahamināśabhājyahamahamtayā
sphurati hṛt svayam parama pūrṇa sat – Upadesa Saram 20

'When the ego is destroyed, the absolute truth shines forth as 'I-I' - *ahamahamtayā*. Then that which shines is not the ego. It is the whole, existence. That itself is heart - *hṛt*.'

When we enquire into the nature of this 'I', it will disappear, and the absolute Self alone will remain as 'I-I'. This is Brahman. This is the meaning of the *mahāvākya*. One need not think or meditate, 'I am Brahman'. If we go deep within and grasp the true meaning of the 'I', then what is revealed is Brahman. In Kashmiri Saivism the Guru gives the disciple only one *mahāvākya* - '*Aham*' ('I'). This *mahāvākya* is known as *anubhūti mahāvākya* or the *mahāvākya* of experience. That is, the experience of 'I' (the Self) is ever-attained by us. As the 'I' makes us aware of the Self, it is called *anubhūti mahāvākya*. When the 'I' as a mere feeling or thought gets dissolved, the 'I-I' or the Self will shine forth in its place as pure consciousness. This is the meaning of the statement: We remain as 'That' when the 'I' does not arise.

If we want to abide naturally in the Self, the egoless-state must become steady and natural. Bhagavan calls this '*tannizhappu*' (loss of individual sense). This is the most potent word in spiritual experience. One will have the experience of the Self if *tannizhappu* is attained, whatever be his religious doctrine. Acharyas like Ramanuja, Madhva, Vallabha and Chaitanya were not advaitins. Yet, there is no conflict between them and the true advaitins regarding *sādhana*. A true advaitin knows the truth that if one's doctrine or *sādhana* helps a seeker to attain extinction of the ego, he too will have the experience of advaita. Following a doctrine is entirely different from having the actual experience. In practical life, even the profound all-encompassing teaching of advaita turns out to be the cause of pride in some people. Therefore those who have not attained the egoless state get into debates with the followers of other doctrines, little realising that the very idea of 'other' flies in the face of advaita.

For the ego to subside, a mighty presence is required. It happens often very easily when the grace of a *jīvanmukta* falls upon a seeker or rarely by the direct interference of the divine as in Bhagavan's case. It seldom happens with such effortless ease with the spiritual disciplines of one's own choice. Virtues like humility, an attitude of surrender, devotion, and absence of pride or conceit are more important than mere intellectual understanding of the scriptures. Viewed from this angle, Vedanta depends more on bhakti yoga than on the cleverness of the intellect. So those, sincerely and single-mindedly following visishtadvaita, dvaita or other such systems also may attain Self-realization through surrender which will lead to total annihilation of the ego.

Kannudaya Vallalar in his Ozhuvil Odukkam says: 'How and by what skill can one attain the loss of the ego? The wild ego elephant will surrender only in the presence of the lion that is the satguru. This is the only way to attain *tannizhappu*; it can never be attained by intellectual knowledge.' Whatever be the doctrine, the seeker's attention must continually and intensely flow towards the source from where the 'I' arises.

One day a young seeker came to Sri Bhagavan. He seemed rather eccentric and agitated. Standing before Sri Bhagavan he said: “Swami, you must show God to me here and now. Or else, I will strangle myself to death right now in your presence.' So saying, he actually attempted to strangle himself. Some devotees who were present there looked at Bhagavan with apprehension. Bhagavan, very calmly, with a slight sense of humour remarked: “See, we do not need swami, God, vision and so on. It is sufficient if the ego that rises up vehemently saying, 'I want to see God', 'I will kill myself' is erased. Then there will be peace. That itself is the truth.”

Another seeker prayed: “Swami, show me a sacred place where I can perform *tapas.*” Bhagavan replied: “*Vanda vazhiyē pō"* - 'retrace the way by which you came'. What a great teaching! In other words, if you wish to perform austerities, then seeking the source of this 'I' and merging in the heart is real *tapas*. Time and place are irrelevant here. It is purely an internal process.

yathā ghanōrkaprabhavōrkadarśitō
hyarkāmśabhūtasya cha chakṣuṣastama:
ēvam tvaham brahmaguṇastadīkṣitō
brahmāmśakasyātmana ātmabandhana:

–Srimad Bhagavatam 12-4-32

'The light of the sun touches the waters in the sea
And lo! It takes form, incarnates as the cloud.
The cloud born of the sun, illumined by the sun,
Clouds the vision and hides the sun;
So too the ego born of the Self, enlivened by the Self,
Clouds and hides the Infinite nature of the Self.'

ghanō yadārkaprabhavō vidīryatē
chakṣu: svarūpam ravimīkṣatē tadā
yadā hyahaṅkāra upādhirātmanō
jijñāsayā naśyati tarhyanusmarēt

– Srimad Bhagavatam 12-4-33

'When the clouds move away, the eyes behold the sun
When the ego which confines and covers the Self
Subsides by the inquiry, the knowledge of the Self dawns
In the horizon of the heart, like the splendorous sun.

yadaivamētēna vivēkahētinā
māyāmayāhaṅkaraṇātmabandhanam
chhitvāchyutātmānubhavō avatiṣṭhatē
tamāhurātyantikamaṅga sampḷavam

–Srimad Bhagavatam 12-4-34

'O dear child! When, by the sword of enquiry
The bondage of the ego created by illusion is cut off
And one is firmly established
In the eternal blemishless divine beingness
Then that is said to be the ultimate dissolution -
mahāpraḷayā!'

VERSE TWENTY-EIGHT

...munnar
ezhumbu mahan-tai yezhu-miḍattai nīril
vizhunda poruḷkāṇa vēṇḍi—muzhugudalpōṟ
kūrnda-mati yāṟ-pēcchu mūccha-ḍakkik koṇ-ḍuḷḷē
yāzhn-daṟiya vēṇ-ḍu maṟi

nīril vizhunda poruḷ kāṇa vēṇḍi	In order to recover an article that has fallen into the water (of a well or a pond)
muzhugudal pōl	like diving deep inside, holding the breath
(munnar) ezhumbum ahantai	that which rises as the primal thought-'I', the ego
ezhum iḍattai	The source from where it springs
pēcchu mūcchu aḍakki koṇḍu	with speech and breath (prāṇā) restrained
uḷḷē āzhndu	diving deep into the heart
kūrnda matiyāl	with a sharp single-pointed intellect
aṟiya vēṇḍum aṟi	one should realize it (the source from where the ego emerges and the spot where it merges) Be convinced thus

Paraphrase:

As one would dive deep into a well or a pond, holding one's breath in order to recover an article, one should plunge into one's heart holding speech and breath and with a keen intellect find the source from where the ego 'I' emerges. This is the only way to extinguish the ego; know this.

Commentary

"If one watches whence this notion 'I' springs, the mind is absorbed into that. That is *tapas*." This is the foremost of the teachings that Bhagavan Ramana gave to Kavyakanta Ganapathi Muni in 1904 itself. This unique, all-powerful teaching inspired the Muni to name the then Brahmana Swami as 'Bhagavan Ramana Maharshi'. 'Maharshi' means the great seer who reveals a new stream of practice to unlock the portal of liberation. '*Kōttam illādu kulavum semporuḷ pūṭṭai viḍuttanan'* - 'He simply unlocked the secret of beholding the blemishless 'whole' and all the sages sang his glory!' sings Muruganar in his Ramana Sannidhimurai. In the Upanishads, several practices that prepare the mind for the experience of Brahman are indicated by the term *vidyā*. In the same way, the instruction in this verse is called by terms like *ramaṇa vidyā*, *hṛdaya vidyā* and *dahara vidyā*.

Verses twenty-seven to thirty of this text may be called its *upāsanā hṛdayam*. They are the heart of the practice. *Upāsana* is that which is meant to be practised. Upanishad is to be known, recognised, here and now. *Mahāvākyās* such as, 'You are That' and 'I am That' are for knowing i.e. instantaneous recognition. The thirty-second verse is an instance of such instantaneous knowledge, an Upanishad. The quest for the source of the 'I'-thought is an *upāsana* that glides into the realm of an Upanishad. Hence Bhagavan remarks "the *sādhana* of the *sādhaka* is the *sahaja* of the *siddha*". Practice is for preparing the mind. By *upāsana,* the mind becomes introverted and by *mahāvākya* - spiritual instruction - *pratyabhijña* or recognition occurs. While practising Self-enquiry, the attention is on the movement of the ego; in *pratyabhijña,* the attention is arrested in the Self here and now. The 'I-I', which is the substratum for all experiences reveals itself. Unless the illusory superimposition of the snake is removed, the substratum or the rope will never be seen. In the same way, only when the illusion of the ego disappears, does the *pratyabhijña* of the Self occur.

It has already been stated that unless investigated, the individual-'I' will continue to appear to be real. This verse reveals the process of Self-enquiry. The *ahamgraha vidyā* prescribed here was taught by ancient rishis to their disciples in confidence. They believed, the more secret it is, the more sacred it proves. But in course of time, this *vidyā* was lost. It was in order to revive this hidden knowledge that Arunachala, the fire of *jnana* incarnated in the form of Sri Ramana. 'His was a re-discovery of a lost technique in divine awareness' writes Swami Rajeswarananda.

Ahamgraha Vidyā

The term, 'I' represents the ego as well as the Self.

It also stands for the extremely subtle pulsation in-between the two. This subtle pulsation is variously called *aham sphūrti, chit-śakti, spandana* and so on. It is this *chit-śakti* which reveals the Self. The same *chit-śakti* by its contact with gross objects gets transformed into the mind. In the *Lalita Sahasranāma,* this is indicated by the expression - *chit-śakti: chētanārūpā.* Its transformation as the mind is also mentioned there itself - *jaḍa-śakti: jaḍātmikā*. The same *śakti* manifests first as the feeling 'I'. It then expands itself as its various expressions: as emotions, moods, as *prāṇa*, as intellect, and as sleep. Although this *śakti* manifests in various forms, its root is the 'I'-thought. Therefore we have to depend on this *aham vṛtti* in order to dissolve this *śakti* completely in *Śivam. Śaktiyoḍuṅgiḍa ōṅgum aruṇāchalam* - when *śakti* subsides in this motionless form, Arunachala Siva, or the Atman will reveal Himself says Bhagavan in Arunachala Navamanimalai.

Mūlānvēṣaṇam (Seeking the Source)

If something valuable falls deep into water, he who resolves to retrieve it, first restrains speech and breath (holds the nose and mouth tight) and only then dives in. In the booklet, 'Who Am I?' Bhagavan cites the same analogy. He says: "Just as the pearl-diver ties a stone around his waist, and then dives deep into the ocean to retrieve the pearl which lies there, each one must dive deep within himself with *vairāgya*, and obtain the priceless pearl of the Self". These are words of grace bestowed upon us. Only after tying the stone of *vairāgya* around the waist can we dive deep into the heart. Sri Bhagavan defines *vairāgya* in these words: "As thoughts arise, destroying them utterly without any residue in the very place of their origin is *vairāgya*". If the attention has to remain in the Self without getting scattered onto sense-objects, *vairāgya* is essential and inevitable. The *vivēka* or discrimination that in indulgence in sense-objects lies the root of all misery, is the immediate cause of *vairāgya*. The main motivating factor for developing *vairāgya* is *ātmadidṛkṣā* (the intense thirst to know the Self). When one turns inward with the thirst for Self-realization, then *itararāga vismāraṇa* (forgetfulness of the desire for other objects) will naturally happen. The dispassionate mind effortlessly plunges deep into the heart.

Now let us go on to describe the process. Although Bhagavan has not mentioned or advocated living in solitude, neither has he denied its immense benefit for a practitioner. He has personally guided many of his direct devotees to live alone and diligently practise. Self-enquiry could be practised in a secluded spot. Pure, *sātvik* food in moderation will be conducive to Self-enquiry. Excess of sleep, sleeplessness and gossip must be avoided. One must be careful not to let the mind wander into the affairs of others or into indulgence in sense-objects. These are the minimum rules that a spiritual seeker must carefully follow. If we scatter the life-force that naturally flows within us, we will not obtain the introverted strength *(antarmukhi śakti)* required for *vichāra sādhana*. He who conserves and uses the energy in the right way is indeed efficient. Such an intelligent seeker will be able to do the *sādhana* with great ease.

One who is convinced and determined that Self-realization alone is the goal of life will spontaneously conserve his energy. "I have had enough of this world, now I must be free." This single-pointed determination or resolve is very important. This is called *vyavasāyātmikā buddhi* in the Bhagavad Gita. In fact, it is with this *vyavasāyātmikā buddhi* that a *sādhaka* attains Self-realization; and not exactly by dint of *sādhana*. *Sādhana* or practice is only an external factor. The internal cause that illuminates the truth is this resolve. This resolve-mantra will indeed invoke the grace of the Self. If the mind has to become continually introverted, the energy obtained from this single, fixed, determination is essential.

ōyādē uḷguvār; uḷḷirukkum uḷḷānē

–Manikkavachakar, *Tiruvachakam*

'Siva is that existence-consciousness which glows brilliantly in the heart of those who are always and incessantly inward-turned.'

Sri Sankara maintains that *brahmavidyā* has to begin only after the completion of *prāṇōpāsanā* (in his Commentary on the Kenopanishad). *Prāṇopāsanā* is conservation of energy. Energy gets dissipated by disorder in food, sleep and entertainment. So such activities must be controlled by suitable methods and energy must be conserved. Through anxiety, fear, conflict, depression and boredom also one gets drained out. First of all lack of right understanding and guidance is the chief cause for this disorder. Clarity born of contact with realized souls will clear the clogged streams of insights from within and one will discover life's rhythm or order. This order is *dharma,* so called because it 'sustains' (*dhāraṇāt*). Through *dharma, śraddha* is born. If the *prāṇa* is transformed into *śraddhāśakti,* it is swiftly absorbed in the source.

Sri Bhagavan used to speak about *pratyavēkṣaṇam,* a simple and natural technique of *prāṇāyāma*. Anyone can practise this method before getting into Self-enquiry. Remain seated in a quiet place on an empty stomach and observe your breath. Observe the breath going inward. Observe the outgoing breath. That is all - mere observation *(avēkṣaṇam)* of breath. There is no need to control the breath or watch the mind. Observe very carefully the incoming and the outgoing breath. With this attention, the breath becomes orderly and the mind also becomes silent. The *prāṇa* also will begin to move slowly and rhythmically. This is a very simple technique. It is attention that is important here. If this much is achieved, we are ready to get into the next step, which is *majjanam* (diving).

Ezhumbum ahantai ezhumiḍattai - The 'I' is the first throb of thought in the stillness of the Self. This is an experience which can be grasped internally with a subtle intellect. As a man sitting in a dark room slowly begins to see clearly, if one internally goes on repeating 'I-I,' the mind will slowly learn to hold to that pulsation. When emotions such as anger, joy, fear and sorrow arise, it is the opportune moment to grasp this pulsation. If someone insults us, a series of feelings which revolve around 'I' and 'me' will be felt inside, such as, 'he insulted me', 'I am humiliated', and so on and so forth.

Only if one is very alert and vigilant can one notice this centralised feeling of 'I' in the womb of those whirlpools of thoughts *(asmitā)*.

This rising ego *(ezhumbum ahantai)* is the heart-knot (*hṛdaya granthi*) which is the cause of all misery. By standing apart from one's thoughts without getting identified with them alone, can one make the 'I'-thought - the source of all mind-modifications - subside at its source. Be still, observe the 'I'-thought very carefully. To stay in the state where the 'I' is not and one is 'That' is indeed the greatest *tapas.* This was the first *upadēśa* given by Sri Ramana Maharshi. This same teaching was repeated both verbally and in writing throughout Bhagavan's life. The Kashmiri yogi Acharya Lakshman Joo called this as the master's *nistaranga upadēśa* - the *upadēśa* which can lead the listener's mind to a 'waveless state'.

In order to observe the pulsation of the 'I'-thought with the inward eye, some practice is necessary. Let the thoughts come forth naturally. When each thought arises, ask: 'To whom does this thought arise?' The feeling that sprouts up will be: 'To me'. Examine this. Who is this 'I'? What is this 'I'? Observe inwardly and grasp the continuous pulsation 'I''I''I'. Then the mind will dissolve in the heart and remain still. Stillness, in which there are no thoughts or sleep. Do not initiate any thought. Abide in that stillness firmly. Bhagavan calls this Maha Yoga. If this practice of dissolving the ego at its source becomes habitual even during day-to-day activities and in all its relationships nothing will poke the ego out of its source. If the ego is restrained at the time of worldly interactions also, then there will be natural peace - *sahaja nirvikalpa anubhava.* The 'I'-thought can be seen arising from the heart forcefully due to former habit when the tides of praise and insult, loss and gain, victory and defeat hit the mind from outside. At all such times, its source must be sought by the enquiry: 'Who am I?'. Instantly the ego will disappear in the source and the awareness of the Self will dawn - *amṛtānubhava*.

Āzhndu aṛidal - Thus, if the attention is focussed on the 'I'-thought, speech and breath will subside by themselves. It is the 'I'-thought that manifests as the body and the mind. The 'I'-thought pervades all the nerves in a subtle form as a psychic stream. So if one holds on to this 'I'-thought firmly, the current of the force will run through the entire nervous system. Bhagavan calls this the 'churning of the nerves' - *nāḍīmathana*. It is this 'I' - current that controls all our emotions and even our very lives. What will happen if this is subsumed by the centre? Sri Bhagavan sings in Atmavidya Keertanam that annihilation of the ego (*ahavināśam*) will become the cause for *aruḷvilāsam* - dance of grace.

In Self-enquiry, the 'I' or the centre of experience unfolds in three planes. At the starting point of the enquiry, it is the *aham-vṛtti*, the 'I'-thought or the ego that is grasped. This alone is common to all. Then when the *aham vṛtti* begins to get more and more disentangled from the body-mind limitation, it slowly sheds its material vestures and transfigures itself as the 'I'-current, the *aham-sphūrti.* Yogis describe this *sphūrti* variously as *chit-śakti, kuṇḍalini*, Siva's *śakti, dēvatā*, and so on, corresponding to their *samskārās,* as this is the connecting link between the finite and the boundless. When this *sphūrti* completely dissolves in the heart, the pure *aham-bōdha,* the seamless awareness, reveals itself - *ellai aṛa tān oḷirum,* says Bhagavan. This is known as *prajñānam,* or Brahman.

THE FINAL DISSOLUTION

Tethered to the pillar of dispassion, dive deep into the Heart
And Listen with the ear of attention to the pulsation 'I-I'
See with the eye of attention to the throbbing 'I-I'
Hold on to the feeling 'I am', stay without a stir in the centre
The 'centering' will unleash tremendous force to the surface
The entire thought-currents in the body feel a churning
The turbulent waves of the mind are all subsumed by the centre
Earth merges in water, water merges in fire
Fire dissolves in air, wind moves and is absorbed in space
Space vanishes when the mind subsides
The mind arises only when the 'I'-thought arises
The 'I'-thought merges into consciousness
Ātmānubhūti, the pure and absolute experience!

VERSE TWENTY-NINE

...piṇam pōṛ—tṛīrnduḍalam

nā-nenḍṛu vāyā navilā-duḷ ḷāzhmanattā

nā-nenḍṛeṅ gundu-mena nāḍu-dalē—jñāna-neṛi

yāman-ḍṛi yanḍṛi-dunā nāmadu-ven ḍṛunna-tṛuṇai

yāmaduvi chāra-mā mā

piṇam-pōl	like a corpse
tīrnduḍalam	ignoring and having nothing to do with the body
nān enḍṛu	without uttering 'I'
vāyāl navilādu	with the mouth
uḷ āzhmanattāl	with the mind completely sunk within
nān enḍṛu	the individuality or the ego-sense as 'I'
eṅgu undum ena	'Where does it spring from?', thus
nāḍu-dalē	to seek and know,
jñānaneṛi ām	is the path of jnana
anḍṛi	instead,
anḍṛu idu nān	'I am not this body'
adu ām enḍṛu	'I am that Brahman', thus
unnal tuṇai ām	to meditate in the mind is only an aid to sādhana in jñāna-mārga
adu vichāram āmā?	but (that meditation itself) can it become ātma-vichāra (Self-enquiry), the direct path?

Paraphrase:

Not uttering aloud 'I', 'I' but with the mind diving deep within, to enquire, seek and know, whence this 'I' arises is the *sādhana* in the path of *jnana* (supreme wisdom). Instead, to meditate with an imagined attitude of 'I am not this body; I am That (Brahman)' is a helpful aid, but can it suffice by itself as a direct *sādhana* of *ātma vichāra* or Self-enquiry?

Commentary

To negate 'I am not the body or mind and affirm 'I am Brahman', or 'I am Atman' is the commonly known meditation in Vedanta. This is the '*nēti, nēti*' path. Here Bhagavan says that eliminating the *upādhīs* like body, mind, *prāṇa,* and affirming the truth that remains as the real Self, although helpful in the enquiry, is not itself the 'enquiry', the direct path. Then what is 'enquiry'? Be still, still like a corpse and without allowing the individual-sense to express itself verbally as the word 'I' go deep within and focus the entire attention on the 'I'-thought. Negations and assertions are of the mind. But in *vichāra* attention is directly on the source. All spiritual practices *(sādhanās)* other than Self-enquiry are done by the mind, by retaining the mind. Self-enquiry shuts the *chittanāḍi dvāram* (mind-nerve opening) at the very first step. *Nān enḍru eṅgu undum?* If attention is focussed on the rising ego, the individual-'I' will dissolve at its very source. In this manner, repeatedly dissolving the ego at its source is Self-enquiry, the path of *jnana*. Where the 'I' does not rise, there, the truth or the real Self will reveal itself. When the 'I' arises, it clouds the real, the wholeness of being. Bhagavan says that any spiritual practice done while retaining the individual-'I' is like a thief searching for the thief in the guise of a policeman. The ego will evade our grasp and will continue to remain hidden behind various forms and pretensions. Hence, in the first step itself, one must investigate where this 'I' arises from. 'Ignoring the body like a corpse' means completely transcending the body idea. This is an aid to focus the attention on the pulsation 'I'. With the conviction that the body is not me, keep the body absolutely still and vigilantly look at the 'I' throbbing within. This is the process.

This method was revealed to Sri Ramana during the 'death experience' that he had in his seventeenth year. Letting the inert body lie like a corpse is an external *sādhana* which is very helpful in Self-enquiry. As the thought of the body is totally rejected, the effect of the path of negation, '*nēti, nēti*' is already attained here. *Uḍalam piṇam pōl tīrndu* - The word *tīrndu,* as used by Bhagavan, indicates the conviction that the inert body is not me. The method of practising Self-enquiry is clearly stated in this verse. Sitting still in a solitary place, and with an introverted mind, one must carefully observe within. One is not to utter the word 'I'. Without mentally articulating the word 'I', one must, with single-pointed attention, closely observe the 'I'-thought which arises and pulsates. It is not meditation that is required here. One must find out the meditator. This is not meditation which depends on imagination. Find the one who is the source of all imagination. What happens when one observes in this manner is discussed in the next verse.

AWAKE IN THE INNER CHAMBER

Shut all the doors of senses, Be still
Be still like a corpse and Awake in the inner chamber
Listen to the *mantra* 'I, I' with the ear of attention
It is not your sense, it is the NAME of the inner being!
He is indeed chanting this seed WORD from eternity
Touch that throb with the ray of *śraddha*, it becomes vibrant
Hold on to that 'I' and it will take you into the stream
Glide into the inner 'I'-current and get sucked into the Heart
It is the door for the sacred to descend and expand as the seen
Through that very stream, retrace to the source and find Home

VERSE THIRTY

...adanān—mīmuṛaiyē

nānā rena-manamuṇ ṇāḍi-yuḷa naṇṇavē

nānā mavan-ṭṛalai nāṇa-muṛa—nānānāt

tōnḍṛu-monḍṛu tānā-gat tōn-ḍṛinunā nanḍṛu-poruḷ

pūnḍṛa-madu tānām poruḷ

Adanāl	therefore
mīmuṛaiyē	in the above manner
nān ār? ena manam	'Who am I?', thus, the mind
uḷ nāḍi	turned inward and enquiring
uḷam naṇṇavē	on reaching the heart
'nān' ām avan	the 'I' appearing as the individuality
talai nāṇam uṛa	put to shame, hangs its head and subsides in the heart (after dissolution of the ego)
'nān nānā' ōnḍṛu	as 'I-I', one
tānāga tōnḍṛum	unceasingly appears on its own accord as 'I' 'I'
tōnḍṛinum nān anḍṛu	(thus) though It appears, it is not the ego
adu pūnḍṛam poruḷ	that is the infinite - the whole
tān ām poruḷ	it is the Atman, the true Self.

Paraphrase:

When the mind, turned inward seeking itself, enquiring 'Who am I?', reaches the heart, the ego-'I', put to shame, hangs its head, subsides and sinks into the heart. Then one as 'I-I' appears of its own accord, unceasingly and effortlessly. But this is not the subjective 'I', the ego. It is the Atman, the infinite, the whole.

Commentary

Enquiry into the source of the 'I'-thought is *jñāna vichāra*. This is termed *antarmukha,* the method to turn the mind to its source, the heart. The heart-centre is mentioned as the centre of spiritual experience in the *śāstrās*. The word *hṛt* means 'centre' and *ayam* means 'He', or 'this one'. The centre where 'this one' or the Self is experienced as 'I am' is *hṛdayam*. How can one locate the heart? The only way to locate the heart, which is called *uḷḷam* in Tamil, is to trace the source of the 'I'-thought. On enquiry, the 'I'-thought will dissolve into its source; and when the mind disappears, something else will be experienced in that place which is self-luminous. This is the heart. The subsidence of the ego has been described figuratively as 'hanging its head in shame'. When the ego-'I' thus disappears, what will happen? Will there be an experience of emptiness? No. The limited-'I' will disappear and in its place the absolute Self will shine as 'I-I'. This is the fullness of experience, and not the individual ego.

If water is filled in a pot, the blueness of the sky will be reflected therein. Is that reflection really the sky? If one watches the sky inside the pot, one sees only the reflection, not the real sky. Likewise, the one who sees the limited individual ego - which is only a reflection within the body - does not see the real Self. If the water is emptied from the pot and the reflection disappears, one who says that there is no sky *(ākāśam)* in the pot, does not know what sky is! It is in space that the pot, water, and the image in it, are all seen! Even if the pot breaks, nothing will happen to the infinite space within it. One who knows this space also knows that even when the pot is there, what appears within as 'pot-space' is really the infinite space that appears to be confined within the pot. He knows very well that the sky which is reflected in the water inside is only an illusory reflection. He throws out the water and the reflection, and sees the pure open space. Similarly, the ego-'I' is only a reflection. It arises, subsists and is dissolved in consciousness. If it is erased through enquiry, the *chit* or infinite consciousness will shine in its place. The experience 'I exist', appearing as though it is within the body, is actually not within the body. It is the infinite *chidākāśa*. In this infinite *chidākāśa*, even the body is a mere illusion. If one has to know 'I am That', the ego-'I' must subside at its source. The sense of individuality will disappear on enquiry. But the disappearance of individuality will not create a feeling of cessation of oneself; on the other hand, there will be the experience of another 'I''I' in its place. This is the pure consciousness, mere existence. It is the Self.

(In general usage, the words *'nān'* and *'tān'* are used to denote 'I'. Bhagavan Sri Maharshi generally uses *'nān'* to denote the *ahaṅkāra* or ego and *tān* to denote the Atman.)

THE LIGHT OF ENQUIRY

The divine being came and turned my senses inward
All the five became one light of enquiry, 'Who am I?'
The quest was an incessant intense stream of intelligence
The searchlight of attention was probing the 'I' sense
And the fellow, embarrassed, went deep, and deep
To the core, the centre where he vanished in the Whole!

VERSE THIRTY-ONE

... poṅgit—tōn-ḍṛavē

tannai yazhit-tezhunda tan-mayā nanda-ruk

kennai yuḷa-don ḍṛiyaṭṭṛu-daṛkut—tannaiyalā

danniya monḍṛu maṛiyā ravar-nilaimai

yinna-den ḍṛunna levan

poṅgi tōnḍṛavē	(As explained in the last verse) the Self surges up and manifests itself as 'I', 'I'
tannai azhittu ezhunda	to the one who emerges from the experience of the Atman after the ego, the jīvā-sense being destroyed,
tanmaya ānandarukku	to that jīvanmukta who revels in the bliss of the Self
iyaṭṭṛudaṛku ennai onḍṛu uḷadu	what else remains to be accomplished through action?
tannai alādu	other than the Self
anniyam onḍṛum	anything apart from him,
aṛiyār	he is not aware
avar nilaimai innadu	as to his profound inner state
enḍṛu unnal evan	who can conceive of it through the mind?

Paraphrase:

A *jīvanmukta* who has been reborn as his true Self, having rooted out his ego-self, rejoices in the bliss of the Self. What else remains for him to accomplish? He is unaware of anything as 'the other' apart from his own Atman. Who can conceive or comprehend by the mind such a supremely exalted state?

Commentary

Self-realization will not happen until the ego is entirely rooted out. When the individual ego merges in the source, the Self, the 'I-I' reveals itself. Once ignorance in the form of separate individuality is erased, all actions and doubts disappear and Brahman, the eternal, pure and ever-free being shines forth. For the liberated soul *(muktapuruṣa)* who has experienced the revelation of the Self *(sattā sphūrti),* and who is free from doership and enjoyership there remains nothing to be achieved. For him there is no accumulation of *puṇya* by doing good deeds or *pāpa* by not doing them. There are no dos and don'ts for such a *paramahamsa* who is ever-free, and remains unaffected by the three *guṇās.*

Who can infer the state of such a *jnani,* who does not see anything apart from the Self? Those who identify themselves with their bodies cannot even remotely imagine the bliss of Self-experience. For the *ātmajñāni* who has realized his own nature, there exists absolutely nothing other than his own Self. It is with the mind and the senses that names and forms are cognized. Mind is transcended by the knowledge of the Self. In Self-awareness, the illusion of duality is completely wiped out. How can those trapped in duality be able to comprehend the *jnani* who is ever established in the uninterrupted peace of 'aloneness' by the power of his realization - *ēkamēva advitīyam nēha nānāsti kiñchana* - 'there is one and only one non-dual reality; there is nothing other than that'. The *jīvanmukta,* even while being apparently with the body, knows well that he is bodiless – '*dēhasthōpi na dēhastha:'*. The *jnani* who is established in the bodiless being is untouched by likes and dislikes – '*aśarīram vāvasantam na priyāpriyē spṛśata:'*. This is perfect *kaivalya* or *nirvāṇa*. Here *janma-mṛtyu-jarā-vyādhi* (birth, death, old age and disease) all these have completely vanished. One who considers himself as having a body and takes pride in his class or status can never guess the inner state of the *jnani* who is perpetually established in the experience of the truth, 'I am That' *(aham brahmāsmi)*. This non-dual state transcending the realm of doership automatically dismisses all worldly and scriptural associations. Such a *jīvanmukta* who is ever immersed in the bliss of his own Self is the 'sovereign monarch' of the kingdom of the Self. Even the Vedas do not attempt to lay down any dos and don'ts for him.

Tannai azhittezhunda - The individual ego arises as 'I am so and so', imputes the factors associated with the body such as caste, creed, status, profession, gender, and the like on the ever-pure, eternal, free consciousness and limits itself. Vedantins call this imputation or superimposition as *adhyāsa*. It is by rejecting these superimpositions that the *jnani* gets centered in the Self. Worldly or religious dealings can never take place without these superimpositions. Therefore when these super-impositions are removed, *sanyāsa,* or the renunciation of all worldly and religious transactions, happens spontaneously. The superimposition is totally removed by enquiry into the nature of the ego. The tree of superimposition is upheld by the root of the ego. With the ego rooted out, the tree of *samsāra* disappears. *Jnātē tattvē ka: samsāra: -*

'Where is *samsāra* when the truth is known?' asks Sankara. This is not the *sanyāsa* that is generally known by the outer appearance. It is the internal *sanyāsa* or abidance in the Self. This alone is renunciation or *tyāga*. The blissful Self is revealed only by *tyāga.* 'To renounce the world means to see it as Brahman. This renunciation instantaneously liberates a person. This renunciation is indeed adorable' says Sankaracharya in Aparokshanubhuti.

Ennai uḷadu iyaṭṭṛudarku - There is no duty remaining for a *jnani* who abides in the fullness of the Self. For him there is no *puṇya* acquired by doing good deeds or *pāpa* in not doing them. Nevertheless actions for the welfare of the world happen through that body. The Vedas regard such *brahmaniṣṭhās* as a great marvel.

THE MUSK DEER

The fragrance of the divine was wafting around
And I was seeking frantically like the musk deer
Death, the hunter hunts the deer for the musk
The deer is me and I am the fragrance, I am the musk
The hunter I am and I never stop hunting myself
The search outside was an illusion as the source is within
I have to dive within and probe into the darkness of the heart
Yes, I have to seek the light which illumines everything
The 'self-luminous being' in the womb of darkness!

VERSE THIRTY-TWO

... paramāp—pannum

adu-nīyen ḍṛam-maṛaiga ḷārtti-ḍavun tannai

yedu-venḍṛu tānṛērn dirāa—dadu-nā

niduvanḍṛen ḍṛeṇṇalura ninmaiyinā lenḍṛu

maduvētā nāyamarva dālē

paramā pannum	Known as the supreme truth
'adu-nī' enḍṛu am	though the Upanishads
maṛaigaḷ ārttiḍavum	resoundingly proclaim in delight, 'That you are' - tat tvam asi
aduvē tānāi enḍṛum amarva-dālē	since that Brahman alone is ever shining as the Atman (the Self)
tannai edu enḍṛu tān tērndu irādu	instead of investigating, knowing and abiding as Brahman
'adu nān' 'idu anḍṛu'	'That (Brahman) I am', this body I am not'
enḍṛu eṇṇal	to incessantly think or meditate thus
uran inmaiyināl	is due to lack of purity of intellect and faith in the Guru and scriptures.

Paraphrase:

The glorious Upanishads have proclaimed that Brahman, the supreme truth is you - *Tat Tvam Asi*. Having received that *upadēśa* , instead of seeking within the heart with the enquiry, 'What is my real nature?' and abiding as Brahman, thinking or meditating 'I am that, I am not this', is due to lack of faith in Guru and firmness of conviction in the *śāstrās*.

Commentary

The teaching 'That you are' even casually uttered by the Guru should be taken as the greatest blessing. Bhagavan has ensconced this *mahāvākya* in this verse. Hence this verse could also be considered as the *upadēśa* verse. Once, a visitor devotee sitting in front of Sri Bhagavan was weeping recounting all his miseries. For a long time he went on relating his sorrows and weeping over them. Sri Bhagavan remained unmoved, sitting majestic and serene as ever. After some time, as usual Bhagavan said, "If you enquire 'Who is this 'me' who is affected?', the 'I' which suffers will vanish and you will realize that all these sorrows are unreal. Self-knowledge alone is the remedy." Hearing this, the devotee said, "I don't see any Self; I can only see misery." Muruganar Swami who was sitting nearby remarked, "Sitting in the presence of Bhagavan and complaining about your sorrows is like sitting on the banks of the Ganga and yearning for water. Even practising spiritual disciplines in the presence of a *jnani* is like digging a well on the banks of Ganga." Another devotee added, "You are standing neck-deep in water and weeping that you're thirsty". Bhagavan added with a smile: *"Gaṅgayē chollaradu enakku dāham enḍṛu!* - Ganga herself is saying, 'I am thirsty." These words were by way of indirectly initiating the listener. Here Bhagavan is telling the seeker, "You are the solution for your problem. You yourself being water you still weep with thirst! Stop seeking; own yourself. You are the truth. There is not even the space for an atom between you and God! Recognise yourself as the infinite reality."

Unaware of the truth that he is himself pure consciousness-bliss, and mistaking himself to be a limited individual, the seeker is searching for peace! In order to find peace, he practises various spiritual disciplines, and becomes exhausted after ceaseless efforts. Thus, when the act of seeking itself turns painful, the *antaryāmi* Himself appears before him as the satguru and gives the teaching: "You are not a *jīva*; you are Brahman." At that very instant, liberation is attained. The seeker has to invoke, compel the inner being to manifest as Guru; then one word from the Master will put the seeker in the limitless being instantly. That one word is *mahāvākya.*

The *mahāvākya, 'tat tvam asi'* occurs in the Chandogya Upanishad. Sage Uddhalaka gives the instruction, '*tat tvam asi Śwētakētō*!' nine times with various similes to his son Swetaketu. This *mahāvākya* is called '*upadēśa mahāvākya'*. Its literal meaning is, *tat* (That) *tvam* (you) *asi* (are). Its experiential meaning will be revealed within the heart of the mature listener when a competent teacher transmits it. The limited person in one snap crosses the border of all limitations and finds himself as the boundless being. When the intended meaning of this *mahāvākya* becomes clear, the listener experiences it directly as *aham brahmāsmi* (I am Brahman). The *jnani* or the liberated man knows his real existence as self-luminous intelligence *(prajñānam brahma).* He realizes that this so-called *jīva* is only a misapprehension like mistaking a rope for a snake, and in truth, he is Brahman the limitless: *ayam ātmā brahma* - this Self is Brahman. Thus, by means of all these four *mahāvākyās*, the *śruti* makes us aware of our real Self. This is what

Bhagavan means by saying: *adu nī enḍṛu am maṛaigaḷ ārttiḍavum.*

A devotee who came from Lahore asked Bhagavan "Can you show me God?" Bhagavan replied: "No, but I can make you God or rather I can show you that you are already 'That' which you are frantically seeking." The Self or 'I' which wants to see or realize God, when it knows its own real nature, finds fulfilment. Liberation is not to reach somewhere or to attain some state; it is to know that you are not what you consider yourself to be. You are realization. You are freedom. God is your own name.

Sri Kunjuswami, at the age of twenty, met Bhagavan at Skandasramam. He had decided to accept Bhagavan's very first words as *upadēśa*. He saw Bhagavan heating some rice gruel on the stove. After a while Sri Bhagavan opened a basket kept nearby. Four little puppies came out of it. Bhagavan told Sri Kunjuswami, "Hold all the four and leave them one by one." Kunjuswami considered these words as his Guru's *upadēśa*. He was certain that the essential meaning of the *upadēśa* was: "Grasp all the four *mahāvākyās*; leave the desire for sense objects one by one."

If we carefully read Bhagavan's talks, it will be clear that their underlying essence is *tat tvam asi*. Sri Bhagavan's attention was not in answering the questions of the devotees, but in helping the questioner go beyond his individual-sense, and see the truth which is eternal, pure, and ever-free consciousness. When people harped on 'I', 'me' and 'mine', without caring to turn within, Sri Bhagavan used the *brahmāstra,* by asking, 'Who is this 'I'?' This would often arrest the attention of the questioner and make it stay in the 'I AM'. Often fortunate souls have crossed the realm of darkness in a single leap with the grace of Bhagavan. It is the pure, eternal Brahman which is experienced in the heart constantly as 'I-I'. By the enquiry, 'Who am I?' if one traces the 'I'-thought to its source, the ego will vanish, and consciousness which is pure existence, will shine forth in its place. Very existence is Brahman. Veiling it, the ego arises as a subtle mental image. It projects the three states of waking, dream and deep sleep. In the waking state itself, it further creates worldly and *yōgic* states. If this limited individuality does not subside at its source, the infinite awareness will not be known.

Fortunate ones wake up to the truth at the moment they listen to the Master's words. They are the rare beings who have very little dust in their vision. They were only waiting to hear the words and instantly the *pratyabhijñā* - the recognition that 'I am that infinite Self' occurs. At that very instant, the illusion of the individual, separate from the whole disappears just as the snake vanishes from the rope in light. Without experiencing this, merely engaging in the mental repetition, 'I am Brahman' will not dissolve misery. Instantaneous realization shows the power of intense, undivided devotion. Mere repetition of 'I am that, I am not this' indicates lack of determination or *śraddhābala*. Bhagavan says *uran inmaiyināl*, lack of firmness (of faith). See Sri Sankara's words:

adyāṣṭamīti navamīti chaturdaśīti
jyōtiṣkavāchē upavasanti bhaktyā

śrutēstvahō tattvamasītivākyam
na viśvasantyadbhutamētadēva – Mahavakyadarpanam

'Today is *aṣṭami*, sacred for wish-fulfilling worship
Morrow is *navami,* do fasting; do the rite for *chaturdaśi'*
Thus the soothsayer says and you obey religiously
'**That You Are**' is the constant song of Mother *śruti*
If you listen for once, redeemed you would be here and now
But alas, you never heed these words of compassion
Astounding indeed is this power of delusion!

Aduvē tānāy enḍrum amarvadāl - There is no moment when you are not Brahman. The experience of 'I' itself is Brahman. It is the *svayamprakāśa vastu* - the self-effulgent being. Here and now you are 'That'. Be convinced of this now. *Sādhana* does not refer to 'doing' something, but to be still as you are. In other words, it is being aware of, being conscious of one's existence. As the dark clouds of thoughts and doubts overshadow this consciousness, it becomes difficult to have the eternal uninterrupted experience of the Self. Like the sky that is visible between the clouds, the stillness between successive thoughts is nothing but the Self. That is our real nature. Becoming convinced that, that is our real nature, one must abide in the Self. Even when thoughts arise, one must not forget the silence behind them. Abiding is knowing. Sri Bhagavan sings in Aksharamanamalai - *'tānē tānē tattuvam'* -The 'I AM' is the truth.

When the Guru gives the instruction, *tat tvam asi*, it is not an intellectual idea that a mature disciple receives, it is direct, immediate, realization. This is *pratyabhijñā samādhi.* This recognition of the Self happens in the quietude of the mind. Ideas such as 'I am a man', 'I am a woman', 'I am learned', 'I am ignorant' are mere thoughts, superimposition. The consciousness-I, behind these perceptions, is not a thought. It is pure experience, existence, awareness. The experience of 'I' purged of limitations is not the individual. It is the whole, the Brahman. The *mahāvākya* rejects the superimposition and makes us recognise the consciousness devoid of the ego, as the Brahman.

jāti nīti kulagōtra dūragam nāmarūpa guṇa dōṣa varjjitam
dēśakāla viṣayādi varttiyad brahmatattvamasi bhāvayātmani
–Vivekachudamani 254

'Meditate in the heart that, 'You are That Brahman' *(tat tvam asi)* untouched by the identification with caste, family, group or clan; shining forth nameless, formless and attributeless, and not limited by time and space.'

yatparam sakala vākagōcharam
gōcharam vimala bōdha chakṣūṣa:
śuddha chidghanamanādi vastuyad
brahmatattvamasi bhāvayātmani –Vivekachudamani 257

'With complete conviction and decisiveness, meditate that you yourself are Brahman - *tat tvam asi.* You are the beginningless reality, the immaculate mass of awareness which is beyond all sense organs, that which is experienced as 'I' or as pure consciousness. This has to be beheld through the eye of consciousness.'

The real import of the *mahāvākya, tat tvam asi* cannot be grasped by mere verbal understanding. Hence the term '*sakala vāk agōcharam'* (beyond the reach of all speech) is used. At the same time it is available to all as consciousness or existence and as the import of the 'I'. Therefore, in the next line it is said, '*gōcharam vimala bōdha chakṣuṣa:'* perceptible to the eye of pure awareness. The *śruti* also declares the same thing: '*asti ityēva upalabdhavya:'*. That is, 'Brahman can be grasped only as the experience of 'is-ness', that is, as mere existence. It is also stated that truth will be clearly experienced by those who have understood the Self as 'existence'.

astītyēvōpalabdhasya tattva bhāva: prasīdati –Kathopanishad

The Self-realised Master, abiding in the state of *sat-chit-ānanda* (Existence-Awareness-Bliss) voices 'That you are!' and his words (voice) carry the power of *chit-śakti*. This unfathomable power conveys the *upadēśa* directly to the 'inner listener' (heart-ears) in the disciple. If the disciple has intense dispassion and *mumukṣutva*, his mind will not obstruct the transmitting power of the Master. Purified by *śravaṇa*, the mind turns inward and the *śraddhā śakti* (single-pointed dedication) will make the seeker fully grasp and directly experience the Self. This is the sacred mystery behind the *guru-śiṣya* relationship.

THOU ART THAT

When we look without, its plurality; within is diversity,
Alas! Where is that joy of oneness, *advaita*?
The whirlpool of misery was about to subsume me;
On came my Master, breathed into my being His power
And whispered, 'Dear child, weep not, wake up, THOU ART THAT'
Anon flashed that blessed state of infinite being, the *pūrṇa*
Inside and outside fused together as one mass of consciousness!
Within is God, without is God; dream and waking is God
God alone is, not as a person but the only Reality in all forms

VERSE THIRTY-THREE

...aduvumalā(du)
ennai yaṛiyēnā nennai yaṛindēnā
nenna nagaippuk kiḍanāgu—mennai
tanai-viḍaya mākkaviru tānuṇḍō vonḍṛā
yanai-varanu bhūtiyuṇmai yāl

aduvum-alādu	in addition to that
'nān ennai aṛiyēn'	'I do not know myself'
'nān ennai aṛindēn'	'I have known myself'
ennal nagaippukku	if one says so, ridicule
iḍan āgum	it invites
ennai? *tanai viḍayam ākka*	why is it so? To know and to be known
iru tān uṇḍō	can the awareness 'I am' be dual?
onḍṛāi anaivar *anubhūti uṇmaiyāl*	as the Self and the awareness of it are but one, it is the essence of the experience of all

Paraphrase:

Both the statements, 'I do not know myself' and 'I know myself' invite ridicule. Why is it so? Are there two selves, one to be known by the other? Can the awareness 'I am' be dual? Indeed, the awareness of the Self shines forth as one in the experience of all.

Commentary

'There are no *jnanis*; only *jnanam* exists' is a well-known saying of Bhagavan Ramana. We have already made it clear that Self-knowledge is the complete dissolution of the ego. It is impossible to know the Self as an object. The *śruti* asks, *vijñātāram arē kēna vijānīyāt?* - 'How could the knower who knows everything be known?'

nāham manyē suvēdēti; nōnavēdēti vēda cha –Kenopanishad 2-2

'I do not feel that I know the Self perfectly. Nor do I feel that I do not know the Self.' Thus the rishi expresses his experience of the Self. The Kenopanishad further adds that the same statement has been made by rishis down the ages.

yō nas tadvēda tadvēda nōnavēdēti vēda cha –Kenopanishad 2-2

'We cannot say that we do not know' are the words of those who transmitted that knowledge to us. They have known it as an awareness in which the knower, known and knowledge are one. Even to say that I do not know the Self, there must be consciousness. Inert objects cannot declare that they do not know. Therefore, in order to say 'I do not know', the light of the Self must be present. For instance, for us to make the observation that the clouds hide the sun, the light of the sun must be present. This is so because the clouds that hide the sun are themselves made visible by the light of the sun. Similarly, while declaring that I am ignorant, the light of consciousness, the 'I' that illumines the ignorance, does exist. That light itself is *jnana*.

Iru tān uṇḍo? - Is there two 'I' in us, knower and the other to be known? Even in a dark room one clearly experiences, 'I exist'. This experience may be called *aparōkṣam* or direct experience. This direct or immediate experience is absolute. There is not even a semblance of duality in it. The 'Is-ness' of existence is unique and beyond the senses. Then, who is the one experiencing existence? There is no need for another to experience 'existence'! The nature of existence itself is *anubhava* - 'experience'. Otherwise that which experiences it, will remain above and beyond it, and this proposition progressively can stretch indefinitely and cause *anavasthā*[2] (an unsettled condition or endless series of concepts). To see a lamp another lamp is not needed. In the same way, 'experience' too is self-luminous. See what Bhagavan says in Upadesa Saram: - *satvabhāsikā chit kvavētarā* – 'Is there another awareness, to illumine existence?' *Sattayā hi chit chittayā hi aham* - 'Awareness makes itself felt as existence and the 'I' shines as awareness.' So awareness, existence, experience and 'I am' are all synonymous.

Vijñātāram arē kēna vijānīyāt - 'By whom, is the knower known?' asks the Brihadaranyaka Upanishad. The knower knows the Self by the Self. Nothing other than the Self exists there; it is of the nature of self-effulgence - *swayam prakāśa*. Here the knower, the known and the knowledge becomes one effulgent mass of intelligence. In the second verse of Arunachala Ashtakam, Bhagavan Sri Ramana expresses the same idea in his uniquely effective and clear way while revealing his Self-experience: *kaṇḍavan evan ena karuttinuḷ nāḍa kaṇḍavan inḍriḍa ninḍradu kaṇḍēn...* – 'On deeply

[2]An endless series of questions and answers is termed *anavastha* by the Vedas

enquiring, 'Who is the one that saw.' the ego did not arise to declare, 'I am the one who saw'. There was no individuality left to say 'I saw', or 'I did not see'. Only the absolute consciousness, the 'boundless ocean of self-effulgent grace' - *aruḷ oḷi kaḍal* - reigned supreme. It was through such profound egoless silence - *mounam* - that Lord Dakshinamurti taught the highest truth. *Chit-śakti* flows uninterruptedly from this state of *mouna*.

A doubt arises here. We have heard this declaration since Vedic times: '*vēdāhamētam puruṣam mahāntam āditya varṇam tamasa: parastāt*' which means: 'I know the supreme *puruṣa* who is effulgent like the sun, beyond darkness.' How could such an assertion be made? Bhagavan Ramana Maharshi himself declares, '*tan padam enakku tandanan'*. This means: 'Arunachala Siva has bestowed upon me His own state.' Sri Maharshi has also remarked in several contexts that Self-realization had dawned upon Him in all its brilliance when he was in Madurai. Here the contradiction between 'I have known' and the statement that 'one cannot say I have known' occurring in the *śruti* is merely apparent, not real. Actually, there is absolutely no contradiction between them. The words of Bhagavan, and the *śruti* quoted above, *vēdāhamētam,* are not egoistic remarks but factual statements. It only means that one cannot egoistically claim *ātma jñāna* as an individual achievement. The current of *chit* has the power to transmit Self-knowledge without the use of words. This power of knowledge is an adversary of ego. For the same reason the *jnani* cannot claim, 'I have known the Self.' As long as there is even a trace of the ego, one cannot be regarded as liberated (a *mukta).*

There is a story about a monk whom Yama, the god of death wanted to capture. The monk was egoless, had no image about himself and hence the lasso of death could not locate the person. The lasso could not find a centre to trap him with. So, Yama sent some sycophants to earth, to praise the monk incessantly. They did it so cleverly that slowly an image appeared in the monk's mind. The praise made the monk's head turn and at that precise moment Yama's noose could catch the person!

As the burnt rope appears to retain its form but is only mere ash and cannot bind, the ego destroyed by *jnana* may continue to appear the same, but it can never confuse or deceive the *jnani*. Hence the *jnani* does not regard him alone as liberated and others as worldly. For the *jnani,* everyone is the Atman. For him there is no *jnani* at all; all are Atman.

yasmin sarvāṇi bhūtāni ātmaivābhūt vijānata:
tatra ko mōha: ka: śōka: ekatvamanupaśyata:

– Isavasyopanishad - 7

'What delusion, what sorrow is there for one in whose heart, all beings have become the very Self? Such a *jnani* is a perpetual seer of oneness.'

In the words of Acharya Sankara: *Dvaitādvaita vivarjitē samarasē mounam param sammatam* (Proudanubhuti 11) - 'When the all-inclusive reality, the state that is beyond dvaita and advaita is realized, the enlightened one finds silence as the most efficient means of communication'. The *muni* who has realized the truth does not act as if he has seen or not seen the truth; as if he is a *jnani* or an *ajnani*. A *mukta puruṣa* is one who has realized that the individual-'I' does not exist at all. He has no tussle with his ego as he has seen its non-reality. He is verily Brahman himself. *Brāhmi sthiti* refers to the absolute peace that remains when the movement of the ego is stopped entirely. Sri Bhagavan Ramana Maharshi remained unaffected by praise or blame, reverence or humiliation, in Arunachala for fifty-four years as a personification of this state. Sri Bhagavan Himself is the perfect illustration for this *śloka.*

Anaivar anubūti - 'It is the experience of all' is a profound statement of this verse. That the Atman is experienced by all is a foregone conclusion in Vedanta. The very experience of 'I' is nothing but the Atman. Stay still in the 'I AM'. Budge not from that centre and you will come to know God. Experience is already there. Indeed the spark that is felt by you now as 'I am', is the same primordial fire that baffled all the gods of yore. (Reference is to the story in Arunachala Purana about the column of fire that appeared before gods). This knowledge that, the self within me is the Self in all, has not happened. For that to happen alone one has to do *vichāra.*

See what Bhagavan says in his conversation with Swami Madhavatirtha: "For the Atman there is nothing to know or to be known. It is the one who has no knowledge who has to make an effort to gain knowledge. This is what takes place in the waking state. *Anātman,* which is the non-self, which can also be called *chidābhāsa,* the reflected consciousness, has the ignorance, so this reflected consciousness has to make an effort for *jnana,* or knowledge. Knowing and not knowing happen in the non-self. The Self does not have to obtain knowledge, for it is knowledge itself. When the knower, the reflected consciousness, is felt, at that time *ajnana* or ignorance is present. The one who feels this ignorance then makes an effort to attain *jnana,* which is knowledge. When the reflected consciousness gets the knowledge, it no longer remains. This is because the reflected consciousness always remains with ignorance or *mithyājñāna.* During sleep there is no reflected consciousness. So, (at that time) the false knowledge is not to be obtained. This is only from the point of view of the current conversation. In reality, there is only the Atman. Because this is so, there is nothing to know and nothing to be known." (The Power of the Presence, p-262)

'I AM THAT'

There is an invaluable treasure within you.
Having it you have everything, 'the whole'.
You can never lose it as it is eternal, ever attained.
Your fear of losing it is founded on mere delusion.
It is self-luminous and its light is reflected outside.
Seeking outside is seeking a mirage as it is only reflection.
As your attention is on the seen you see your light there
All seeking outside is to jump in the pond to catch the moon.
The reflection of the moon is not real, see the sky.
Turn within and look at the inner effulgence;
You are the moon; you are the light, wander no more,
Own it by abiding in it, identify with it as '**I am That**'.

VERSE THIRTY-FOUR

...ōr—ninai-vaṛavē

enḍṛu mevarkku miyalbā yuḷa-poru-ḷai

yonḍṛu muḷattu ḷuṇarndu-nilai—ninḍṛiḍā

duṇḍin ḍṛuru-varuven ḍṛon-ḍṛiraṇ ḍan-ḍṛenḍṛē

saṇḍai-yiḍan māyai chazhakk-ozhiga

enḍṛum evark-kum	always and to all
iyal-bāi uḷa-poruḷai	that reality which is ever attained as their very nature
ōr ninaivu aṛavē	devoid of a single thought
onḍṛum uḷattūḷ	by merging the mind in the heart,
uṇarndu nilai ninḍṛiḍādu	instead of thus knowing by experience and abiding as That
uṇḍu inḍṛu uru aru enḍṛu	'It is', and 'It is not'; 'It has form'; 'no, it has no form'
onḍṛu iraṇḍu anḍṛu enḍṛē	'It is one'; 'no, it is two'; 'It is neither' – thus
saṇḍai iḍal	to dispute and quarrel
māyai chazhakku	is due to the delusion of māyā
ozhiga	be free of it.

Paraphrase:

The Self is ever-attained and experienced by all as their very nature. One has to make the mind abide in it with rigorous refusal to harbour any thought. Instead of abiding in the heart, by recollecting one's real nature and gaining perfect identity with that, to dispute and quarrel 'That (reality) exists'; 'no, it exists not'; 'It is with form'; 'no, it is without form'; 'It is one'; 'no, two'; is nothing but the deluding power of *māyā.* Shun it.

Commentary

Atman is the ever-attained reality. *Iyalbu* means 'spontaneous' or natural - *sahaja*. The experience of 'I' *(aham)* is available to all. In fact 'I exist' is the only experience that is constant for all. This experience of 'I AM' must be held in the ambit of inner vision. One should not ignore this or take it casually. One should learn to adore this experience with reverential attention and soulful meditation. With constant reflection one must learn to stay in that state of simple 'existence', the 'I AM'. This constitutes *jñānatapas*. Behind our body-identity and thoughts, this eternal, pure, free consciousness which is spontaneous *(iyalbāi uḷa)* shines like the blue space behind the clouds. That is the Self. I am That!

This self-luminous consciousness remains unchanged in all states, for all. One who has known this unchanging substratum will be established in the 'unshakeable-yoga' - *avikampayōga* - at all times and in all places. For one who has experienced this reality, distinctions like inner-outer, one-two, and truth-untruth are all meaningless. The *jnani* is not inclined towards any kind of argument. The *jnani* is like a bee that drinks the nectar of Self-experience in silence. The bee drones only till it gets honey. Once it starts sipping honey, it becomes still! So too one who is established in that uninterrupted eternal experience, will not enter into any argument. The *Swātmasukhi* - the one who is happy in Himself - remains indifferent and silent even when debates go on around him.

Sometimes even the most sincere *sādhakās* who have undertaken vows like *sanyāsa* for the purpose of gaining enlightenment, are overtaken by *śāstra vāsana*. They diligently study various doctrines such as advaita, dvaita, visishtadvaita etc. and later on forgetting their original aspiration, get involved in unending debates. Self-realization can be obtained only by the eradication of the ego, but it is obvious that debates can only lead to the fattening of the ego and distraction of the mind. Narada gives a word of warning in the Bhakti Sutra: *vādō nāvalambya:* (debate should not be resorted to). It is Siva Himself who remains in each one as 'I-I'. If we just accept this one truth, we will be able to transcend all doctrines and give up all individual opinions. This is real love. The Self alone is the truth! This truth shines within us at all times as our very essence. The Self experienced as 'am-ness' or existence must be worshipped constantly with the flowers of attention. This is the sole duty of the seeker of refined intelligence. The wealth of attention should not be dissipated in any other manner. The grace and power of the Self is awakened in the one who worships the inner-being with the sacred waters of meditation.

tamēvaikom jānatha ātmānam
anyāvācho vimuṅchata amṛutasyaiṣasētu:

– Mundakopanishad 2–2–5

'Be aware of that Self constantly. Give up all other talk and activities of the senses. This is the bridge leading to the experience of Immortality.'

Onḍṛum uḷattu uḷ uṇarndu - The Self is the ever-attained truth for everyone, 'like a gooseberry in the palm of one's hand' *(karatalāmalakam)*. Even then, the Self must be sought, with an introverted mind; and *chit-śakti,* scattered in the form of the mind should be gathered and concentrated upon the 'I'. It is for this purpose that Bhagavan has revealed this method of Self-enquiry 'Who am I?' Such an introverted flow of the mind is called *onḍṛum uḷattu.* In this manner, when one merges the 'I'-thought into the heart-cave, the experience of the pulsation or *chit* will happen. This is what is meant by *uḷ uṇarndu*. In this manner, with this *ahaṁgraha upāsana*, the false ego must be traced back to its source till the nerve centre which travels from the heart to the head - *amṛtanāḍi* - opens. It is when the *amṛtanāḍi* that is at the heart-centre is opened up, that the pulsation of the 'I-I' is felt, and then the mind gets transformed into pure *chit* and the deluding power of the mind disappears entirely. Such an illumined one can never misapprehend the Self to be an individual or the seen world as real. The body, mind, the world of objects and senses - all are nothing but the Self! The *jnani* clearly sees that the entire world is a wave in the ocean of the Self. In such a state of Bliss what is there to discuss, what doctrine to be established? It is the same Self that argues for or argues against any proposition. There is absolutely nothing apart from the Self.

Māyai chazhakku (māyāmōham) - Anything that diverts our attention from the Self, causes delay and obstructs the flow of the mind towards the Self, is *māyā.* Some among those who came to the ashram for Bhagavan's *darśan*, would go round the ashram and make comments about the administration. Some of them even made certain propositions in Bhagavan's presence, to reform the existing system. Hearing this, Sri Bhagavan once remarked: “Oh! So you have come to reform the ashram! Alright, what to do? One forgets the purpose of his visit, and becomes involved with setting right other things!” He then, laughed and added: *“vanda vēlayai pāru ōy!* – 'Attend to the purpose for which you have come'. The very purpose of your birth is to realize yourself; why not be vigilant about that?”

The purpose of life is to know the Self. Until the veil of ignorance is removed, one will have to go through births and deaths again and again. *Āvaraṇa* is nothing but layers of *vāsanās*. Remaining in the intellect, this dark cloud of inadvertence makes one disinterested in the Self, and interested only in the world. There is no way other than *jñāna vichāra* or the enquiry 'Who am I?' to destroy this. The necessity and importance of doing so will dawn upon the *jīva* only after it gets worn down by experiencing much sorrow and suffering. Till then, the individual continues to remain extroverted. Even some serious seekers who have renounced their worldly life and dedicated their life to attain Self-realization, are seen to forget their goal and start building hospitals, schools and so on in the name of service to mankind. The way they get involved in such activities is really nothing but the delusion caused by *māyā (māyai chazhakku)*. This is not a criticism of social service. In fact, it is obligatory on the part of service-minded family men to perform acts of service for the welfare of society and for acquiring mental purity. But how immensely greater is the peace that Self-knowledge brings to a suffering soul! The very presence of a Self-realized person will bring peace and tranquillity to those who approach him. There is no greater service than this. So focussing attention on liberation, one must remain vigilant at all times. After attaining that which has to be attained, there is nothing to gain or lose; whatever the body does thereafter is according to its *prārabdha.* But till the goal is reached, be ever vigilant! Be alert! Be awake!

BE STILL

'Is it dual or non-dual, this or that?' - thus to dispute is delusion
In the inexpressible beyond, one or two, who is there to speak?
If there is no two, then how to speak about the One?
So the wise remain silent without allowing the mind to rise.
Do not allow the thoughts to take form as this or that
Any volition stirs the pool of the mind and thoughts arise
Be the Self here and now and forget clean all that is not the Self.
Mere thought of the non-self disturbs the pristine purity of silence
Neither deny nor accept but abide in the Self naturally
With all the gentleness of a bubble that falls back to the ocean

VERSE THIRTY-FIVE

...oṇḍiyuḷam

siddhamā yuḷporu-ḷait tērn-diruttal siddhi-piṛa

siddhi-yelāñ soppa-namār siddhigaḷē—niddirai-viṭ

ṭōrndā lavai-meiyō vuṇmai-nilai ninḍṛupoimmai

tīrn-dār tiyaṅgu-varō tērn-dirunī

siddhamāi uḷ poruḷai	The reality, the Self, which is ever attained
uḷam oṇḍi tērndu iruttal siddhi	making the mind to enter and subside in the heart and to recognise the true state is perfect siddhi (attainment of the highest power)
piṛa siddhi elām	all the other attainments of eight-fold siddhīs, like aṇima etc.,
soppanam ār siddhigaḷē	are dreamlike gains that appear to be real
niddirai viṭṭu ōrndāl	on waking up from sleep, if one recollects it
avai-meiyō	are they (that which was seen and enjoyed in dreams) real
uṇmai nilai ninḍṛu	abiding firmly in one's own true and natural state
poimai tīrndār	those jīvanmuktas for whom the illusion is no more
tiyaṅguvarō tērndiru nī	will they ever be deluded again? Be convinced of this and abide

Paraphrase:

With the deep 'innering' to know the Self, that forever shines as the 'ever-attained reality', and to be established as 'I am That' alone is truly the perfect siddhi (attainment). All other *siddhīs* (attainments of supernatural or occult powers) are as unreal as the attainments seen in dreams. Will they be real on waking up from sleep? No. Will those *jīvanmuktas* (the liberated ones) who are firmly poised in the Self, having woken up from the sleep of delusion, ever be deluded by the lure of *siddhīs?* Be convinced of this and abide.

Commentary

'The Brahman which is *sat-chit-ānanda* - existence, awareness, peace - is ever attained as our own being; it is the import of 'I am'. This profound truth alone should be known from the Upanishads. Often, many of us who wear spectacles, at times ridiculously search for them even while we are wearing them! We search for the spectacles through the very glasses! Similarly the Self is within us as existence, as the pure consciousness, as the essence of the awareness-'I'. Being illumined by this consciousness all our sensory perceptions appear to be real. The Atman is ever-attained behind the mind, intellect and ego as the self-effulgent, pure awareness that gives reality to the visible world of the senses. To recognise 'That' is the true *siddhi.* It will then be clearly experienced that the ego and the world are all just waves and bubbles in the ocean of the Self. The *jīvanmukta*, who has realized Brahman as the ever-attained *(nityasiddham)* Self through instantaneous intuition (*pratyabhijñā*) and abides in the uninterrupted bliss of the Self, does not give any importance to the *siddhīs*. Sri Sankara mentions in the Dakshinamurti Stotra that to a knower of truth not only the eightfold *siddhīs*, but even Godhood *(īśvaratvam)* is available. But, does the *muni* immersed in the bliss of *nirvāṇa*, ever care for these trivial powers?

'Self or the Atman is not something which has to be produced *(utpādyam);* it is not something to be experienced after bringing about changes in the body or mind *(vikāryam);* it is not something that happens by purifying the body or mind through rituals *(samskāryam);* it is not something which is to be newly attained *(āpyam)*. Doership and enjoyership do not operate in this process. The bodiless, infinite nature of the Atman is known when a seeker listens and absorbs the words of the *śruti.* It is ever-attained. But because of ignorance it appears unattained' says, Sankaracharya in his commentary on Isa-Upanishad.

At the very instant when attention is focussed on the Self by the grace of the Guru, it shines as if newly gained. Thereafter the profound peace of *ātmānubhūti* becomes an abiding experience. The knower of truth realizes that his very individuality, its virtues and vices are all a mere dream. How then will *siddhīs*, paraded by the individual ego, be of any worth to him?

palavidhamām siddhikaḷum pādāḷam munbāi
ilagumi rasāyanamum enba-ulagil
pratyakṣamāgavē peṭṭṛālum paṭṭṛal
oruvugavē sādhaganuḷ – Sri Devikalottaram 66

'Even if he truly attains *siddhīs* like *aṇima* and *mahima*, and *rasāyanavidyā* like *anjanam* which enables one to see objects buried in *pātāḷam,* deep under the earth, the seeker who longs for peace must vigilantly stay away from them.'

All these *siddhīs* are to be attained and can be manifested only with the help of the mind. There is not even a trace of the happiness of realization in them. In the Anubandham also Bhagavan says - *chittattin śāntiyē siddhamām mukti* – 'peace of mind alone is the sign of liberation or *mukti.'* As all the astonishing achievements of modern science and technology have been achieved by the activities of the mind, they have to be entirely ignored by the seekers as illusion. While *siddhīs* can be obtained by intense concentration of the extroverted mind, Self-realization is attained by directing the mind inwards and merging it at its source. The former is *avidyā* and the latter is *vidyā*. *Dūramētē viparītē* - these two are mutually contradictory says the Kathopanishad.

One person dreams that he is flying in the sky and walking on the waters. In the dream he feels that he has attained *dēvalōka-gamanam,* (entry into the world of the gods), *indrapadavi* (rank of the king of the gods) and so on, which is impossible for him in the waking state. But, the moment he wakes up from his dream, everything vanishes. He realizes that whatever he had experienced in his dream was an illusion. He realizes this only when he comes back to the waking state and in the waking state he doesn't regard them as achievements at all. Similarly, it is only when one is in the sleep of ignorance, or when one forgets his real Self that he regards the waking state which is but a dream, as his real life. Imagining that *siddhi* means developing unique and astonishing skills impossible for others, he practises *yoga* and other such methods and accomplishes them. He takes pride in them and assumes that he is a *siddha*. Forgetting himself in the praise and admiration shown by others, he considers himself an *avatāra puruṣa*. His happiness lies in this praise from others, not in the Self. If there are no flatterers around him, he has no happiness. What is the ultimate gain from these *siddhīs* that exist only in the realm of *avidyā?*

Sant Jnaneswar was a great *jnani* born in Maharashtra whose devotion and knowledge had a revolutionary impact on people. The three brothers, Nivruttinath, Jnanadeva, Sopanadeva and their sister Muktabai - the four child-saints - went on foot throughout Maharashtra propagating spiritual knowledge. At that time in Maharashtra, there was a *siddha* called Changdev who was a *haṭhayōgi* who possessed innumerable *siddhīs*. With the help of rejuvenation techniques he was believed to have lived for about thousand five-hundred years. But he was not satisfied with his *yōgic siddhīs.* He wished to meet Jnanadeva and one day set out to do so. But his devotees said: "It is not proper for such a great *jnani* like you to go and visit a child. Please write a note and give it to us. We will bring Jnaneswar to you." Accordingly, Changdev sat down to write the letter. But he did not know how to address Jnaneswar. Should he call him 'Mahatma' or 'Dear child', he wondered. Unable to decide, he sent a blank sheet of paper to Jnaneswar. The brothers smiled when they saw the letter. The four-year old Muktabai remarked: "This letter is proof that the one thousand five-hundred-year old *haṭhayōgi* is merely a blank sheet!" Jnanadeva replied to the letter by writing forty *ślokas* on the same sheet. These *ślokas* named *Chāngdēv Paśaṣṭi* dealt with disapproval of *siddhīs* and imparting of *jnana*. After reading the *ślokas,* Changdev set out to meet Jnanadeva. He sat on a tiger which was bound by a snake, and accompanied by thousands of disciples he approached Jnanadeva. Seeing Changdev, Jnanadeva, who was sitting on a wall with his brothers and sister, straight away commanded the wall to move towards Changdev. The lifeless wall began to fly!! Seeing this, the great old *yogi* Changdev got down and repeatedly prostrated before the boy-saint saying, "Please show me the way towards peace." The little sister of Jnaneswar, Muktabai, was the one who gave him *Jñānōpadēśa*. "It is not possible to attain the infinite through action. All your *siddhīs* are obtained through actions. They will not give you peace. BE STILL, give up the thought, 'I am the doer; I am the enjoyer'. Stillness is the Self. Stillness is peace. Stillness is liberation. Learn the language of silence and embrace the silent being with the spaceless-body and meditate on the infinite with the timeless-mind." Instantly, Changdev became liberated.

Kavyakanta Ganapati Muni was a *yogi* with many *siddhīs.* Still not at peace, he surrendered himself to Bhagavan unconditionally. Having *siddhīs* does not make a person a *jnani* and *jnanīs* need not display *siddhīs* either. What does a *jnani,* enjoying the bliss of the Self, gain by the *siddhīs*? *Siddhamāi uḷ poruḷai tērndiruttal* - *Siddhi* means achievement. Whatever is achieved anew will be lost. The Self, on the other hand, is not something to be achieved; it is ever-attained. Then one may ask, 'Why is it that the bliss of liberation is not experienced? What causes the fear of death?' It shall be explained. The following explanation is the most important part of this text. It is to be read and contemplated again and again.

The bliss of *nirvāṇa* or experience of immortality or absence of sorrow is present in everyone as the very nature of the Self. The experience of the Self is present in everyone as the consciousness-'I'. The simple experience of 'I AM' is realization. But this 'reality', *uḷḷadu,* is not recognised because of attachment and identification with the body and undue importance given to the waking state. A mysterious phenomenon that takes place is that although everyone knows that we will all die one day, no one seems to be conscious of it. All of us live as if we are here forever. Could it be because of the inherent awareness of eternity hidden within that we generally do not believe that we too will die one day? In the Mahabharata there is a story of Yama, the god of death appearing before Yudhishtira and asking him "What is the greatest wonder in the world?" Yudhishtira replies, "Lord! Every day men see creatures die and still they long for eternal life. This, O Lord, I feel is the greatest mystery!" Even when one witnesses the death of a beloved one, one fails to ponder over the nature of death. Instead, after grieving for a while we tend to forget it completely. If death is a fact how do we forget such a terrible thing? This indeed is an intimation of the imperishable that lies within us.

The Self is immortal and the heart knows this truth; hence the thought of death could never reach and stay in the heart. The fear of death is merely mind-deep and mind itself is an illusion appearing in the substratum. The very nature of the substratum is deathlessness and this is the essence of 'I'. This must be understood by deep contemplation. The fear of death does not obscure the experience of the immortal being. The cloud does not hide the sun. It only veils our vision. In the same way, the fear of death is located in the intellect, whereas the experience of eternity is in us, in the 'is-ness'. Misery is only a thought whereas bliss of the Self is not a thought; it is existence. While suffering comes and goes, the bliss of the Self remains as the substratum.

In deep sleep, when the body and mind are absent, no one experiences fear, sorrow, desire or ego. There is only the substratum, the experience of pure happiness; an experience that cannot be taken away from anyone. Cognition of this undeniable experience will instantaneously put one in realization. The intelligence inherent within, the *buddhi*, has the ability to point to that Self which lies beyond the intellect and which is never touched by sorrow or fear, which is eternal and ever-attained. As we indicate the moon by pointing at the nearby branch of a tree, the Self is indicated by the phenomenon appearing in it. Often the words of an enlightened Master have the power to take the intellect of the disciple beyond its periphery in a trice to the Reality. By clear and intense *vichāra*, the bliss of the ever-attained Self will become an abiding experience.

In deep sleep, the body, mind, intellect, senses, ego and identification with a particular individuality - all these disappear but the Self continues. From this it is obvious that they are only illusions that appear like magic in the waking state and disappear during sleep. Even in their absence in deep sleep, the essence continues to remain. This essence alone is the ever-attained Self. This truth is not something that comes and goes. Sleep is always in the past, a memory; but this realization is here and now, immediate experience. This is clearly explained by Bhagavan thus: "'I' is not known in sleep. On waking 'I' is perceived with the body, the world and non-self in general. Such associated 'I' is *ahamvṛtti.* When *aham* represents the Self only, it is *ahamsphuraṇa.* This is natural to the *jnani* and is called *jnana*. Though ever-present, including in sleep, it is not perceived. It cannot be known in sleep all at once. It must first be realised in the waking state, for it is our true nature underlying all the three states. Efforts must be made only in the *jāgrat* state and the Self realised here and now. It will afterwards be understood and realised to be the continuous Self, uninterrupted by *jāgrat, swapna* and *suṣupti.* Thus it is *akhaṇḍākāravṛtti. Ahamvṛtti* is broken, *aham-sphuraṇa* is unbroken, continuous." (Talks-307) Gaining such a clear vision is the import of the term, *tērndiruttal.*

Abiding in the Self after recognising it, is not a separate process. The very recognition is instantaneous abidance. Abiding in it is natural. This instant-recognition is *pratyabhijña* which makes one a 'seer', a rishi. Once this sun of recognition - *pratyabhijña* - arises in the inner horizon, it never sets again.

This indeed is Self-realization. Once this happens, the seer abides in the bodiless inner being, even though the body continues to be seen till the end of its *prārabdha.* The body, *prāṇa* and mind have no more existence in the Self. Self-knowledge is the experiential knowledge of the ever-attained reality - *nityōpa-labdha nijalābha*. The very news that this experience is here and now and is timeless could often make the inner-being remove the veil from within. In order to experience it, one must have *jijñāsa*, the intense yearning for the experience. Empowered by that yearning or hunger, attention will cut through all irrelevant imaginations and focus itself on the 'I AM' here and now.

Uṇmai nilai ninḍṛu poimai tīrndār - When light comes darkness vanishes. In the same way, the moment one experiences the truth and abides in it, illusion vanishes. The water in the mirage appears to be there. One who goes near the mirage and knows that there is no water will never ever be deluded again, even though the water continues to appear from a distance. That is, he overcomes the illusion and gets himself established in the truth. Illusion is overcome by knowledge. For the object of illusion to vanish externally, destiny will take its own time. The illusory water in the mirage continues to appear to the knower also, but he is not deceived by it. When the rays of the sun become dim, the mirage does disappear. When it becomes bright again, the phenomenon reappears. It is the knowledge that the water in the mirage does not really exist, and not its external disappearance that is the cause for removing the illusion. Similarly, the universe, the 'I' that sees the universe, the adjuncts like the ego, mind, intellect, and body vanish temporarily in deep sleep; and death. Enquiring how and why this illusion appears now, is as meaning-less as casting the horoscope of an unborn son. The universe, and the *jīva* who sees the universe, are both mere appearances. The reality, which is their substratum, is never affected by them. One who tries to explore the mysteries of creation will get trapped in *māyā.* This is because the extroverted intellect itself lies within the realm of this deluding force.

karaṇam kāraṇam kartā vikartā gahanō guha:
'The Lord Himself is the instrument, the cause, the master and the destroyer of the universe. His ways are inscrutable. The 'guha' who glows in the heart-cave can be known only through internal worship' states the Vishnu Sahasranama. In the Brahma Sutra, sage Vyasa explains the creation of the universe in the words, *lōkavattu līlākaivalyam*. That is, 'what appears as the universe is only a *līla,* a sport of the Lord'. How can we ascribe motive or reason for the non-dual one, the one without a second? He sports purely out of His joy. Children, when they lose in a game, leave it crying, and rush to their mother. In the same way when there is sorrow in the game of life, one becomes dispassionate, introverted and starts enquiring, "Who is the 'I' that is suffering?" If the ego 'I' is traced back to its source, truth or absolute consciousness will be revealed in the centre of the heart-cave. There the triad of the seer, the objects seen and the act of seeing will all end and supreme bliss will prevail.

THE INVALUABLE TREASURE

Vain was my search in the world, mere useless toil
Absurdity is another name for involvement with the fleeting
Life was fast ebbing while seeking the unsurpassable
And all the experiences were found only mind-deep, mere illusions!
There came a Being, whose body was Light; He whispered
"Dear, why seek outside what is within, immediate and obvious?
Stay in your Existence, still as the simple awareness 'I am' "
Mighty words that instantly put me in the Timeless
What I sought was a mere shell in the sea shore of scriptures
Gained was the invaluable treasure, the fruit of boundless grace
Attainment of the ever attained, revelation of the ever revealed!

VERSE THIRTY-SIX

...kūrndu mayal
nām-uḍalen ḍṛeṇṇi-nala nāmadu-ven ḍṛeṇṇu-madu
nām-aduvā niṛpa-daṛku naṭṭṛu-ṇaiyē—yāmen-ḍṛu
nām-aduven ḍreṇ-ṇuvaḍē nān-manida nenḍṛe-ṇumō
nām-aduvā niṛku-mada nāl

mayal- kūrndu	Affected by deep ignorance
nām uḍal enḍṛu eṇṇin	as long as we think we are the body
ala nām 'adu' enḍṛu	this body we are not; we are That, the Brahman
eṇṇum adu	this bhāvanā, or attitude, in meditation
nām aduvāi niṛpa-daṛku	for us to abide as that Atman
naltuṇaiyē ām	is indeed a great aid (but)
nām aduvāi niṛkum	we remain always as that form of Brahman
adanāl	Therefore
enḍṛum adu nām enḍṛu	always as 'we are that Brahman'
eṇṇuvadu ēn?	why contemplate ceaselessly?
nān manidan enḍṛu eṇumō ?	Does one have to keep thinking, 'I am a man'?

Paraphrase:

So long as we think 'we are this body', the meditation with the attitude of 'this body we are not, that Brahman we are', will be a help and support to destroy that thought. Since we ever abide as Brahman, why should we ceaselessly think 'we are Brahman'? Will a man ever keep thinking, 'I am a man'?

Commentary

nāham dēhō nendriyāṇyantaraṅgō;
sākṣī nitya: pratyagātmā śivōham – Advaita Pancharatnam 1

'I am not the body, or the mind or the senses. I am that pure *Śivam,* the witness, eternal, which is the innermost Self of all.'

Several such *ślokas* have been written by many *jnanis* from the time of Sri Sankaracharya. Some *ślokas* such as Dasasloki and Nirvanashatkam are considered as the essence of Vedanta. The Upanishads, too, point out the reallty which is pure consciousness that remains after everything else is rejected or given up as '*nēti, nēti*'. Bhagavan Ramana also, at the very beginning of his first text of spiritual instruction, 'Who am I?' gives the same teaching. It is not possible to touch the Self with the mind. The mind that negates the non-Self dissolves and the Self alone remains as the substratum. This process of negation *(nēti, nēti)* is an external aid. To reject the non-self and realize 'I am that which remains as consciousness' and to abide in it as the Self, is *pratyabhijñā*. Once arisen, it never sets.

Instead of realizing the Self in this manner, thinking repeatedly that 'I am not the body', 'I am Brahman', 'I am the

Self' and so on, is an obstacle to stillness, and for the same reason does not lead to realization. As thought itself is finite, it has no way of directly revealing the infinite. Thought is an aid which helps with the negation 'I am not the body' to negate the 'I am the body' idea. That is all. The mind too is to be similarly negated like the body and the senses. So thoughts must also go. The remaining awareness, *jñapti* is self-effulgent and so it does not require the mind to illumine it. It knows it by itself.

Thoughts always arise by holding on to name and form. Only when the thinker 'I' arises on one side, do the objects of thought arise on the other side. Thoughts are always related to 'you' and 'me' *(yuṣmad-asmad vṛtti)*. Thoughts can only indicate those things that are not me (the Self); they cannot abide in the 'I' (the Self). So after analyzing and rejecting the non-Self (as *nēti, nēti),* and being firmly convinced that 'I am the Self', and giving up all thoughts, one must abide in stillness. Removing the veil of the illusory non- Self through knowledge and giving up all the activities of the intellect, one must remain still. The 'thought-free state' that occurs when the veiling is removed from the intellect is *samādhi*. This stillness that accompanies the dawn of wisdom is assuredly *ātma svarūpa* (the Self). The experience of 'I' is itself Brahman. Beyond the thoughts of the mind, the experience of 'I' remains self-luminous. Imaginations of the mind cannot even touch this 'I'. If one thinks 'I am Brahman', even this will stay in the intellect as a pleasant thought veiling the substratum, the Self. The thought 'I am Brahman' might help in giving up other thoughts; but in the end since this is also just a thought, it too must disappear. When this also thus disappears, the resplendent, eternal existence-consciousness will be revealed.

DOOR TO INFINITY

To think 'I am the body' is the only fault,
'Body I am not' is also a thought,
To think is to invite 'what is not'
Neither think this nor think that, be quiet.
Quietude is the door to infinity, the nameless Being.
Be silent, still all the thoughts, rest in Self.

VERSE THIRTY-SEVEN

...aṛiyā—dēmuyalum
sādha-katti lē-duvitañ sāddhi-yatti laddu-vida
mōdu-kinḍṛa vāda-madu muṇmai-yala—vādara-vāi
tān-ṭṛēḍuṅ kālum tanai-yaḍainda kālat-tuṅ
tān-ḍṛaśama nanḍṛi-yār tān

aṛiyādē muyalum	The efforts of a seeker before attaining
sādhakattilē duvitam	in the sādhana phase the duality of sādhaka and sādhya exists
sāddhiyattil adduvidam	once attained advaita results
ōdukinḍṛa vādam adum	the above argument
uṇmai ala	is not true
ādaravāi tān tēḍum	while seeking with
kālum	devotion and
tanai-aḍainda kālattum	after attainment of the Self
tān daśaman anḍṛi tān yār?	who else is he but the 'tenth man'? (refer to the parable of the ten fools)

Paraphrase:

'In the phase of spiritual practice, the duality as *jīva* and *īśwara* or *sādhana* and *sādhya* is real. Once realization is attained, *advaita* is the result' - this argument is not true. Who else is he but the tenth man (of the parable), both when he anxiously searched for himself, thinking he was lost (as he forgot to count himself), and at the time he found himself to be the tenth man?

Commentary

Advaita is not a concept or philosophy; it is experience - *anubhūti*. It is not a state to be attained at some later time in the future. It is also not an experience that comes as a result of any *sādhana*. Advaita is the eternal nature of the Self. The one who mistakes a rope for a snake when it is dark is ignorant. There is not even a trace of the snake in the rope. The appearance of the snake is only an illusion. Similarly duality exists only in the mind. The mind is a synonym for duality. The mind itself appears due to duality. The mind creates a series of illusory dualities. In this way the mind and the duality are mutually dependent. The 'I' that shines beyond the mind is the pure, absolute Self without any illusion of duality.

One common understanding is that at the time of spiritual practice, the triad - the seeker, that which is sought and the act of seeking - prevails, and that later in the realized state, duality disappears. Bhagavan says this distinction does not really hold good. When the snake was superimposed on the rope, and also when the snake disappeared, the rope existed only as the rope. Even in the state of ignorance what appears as *jīva* is nothing but Brahman. Guru or scriptures only remove the misapprehension. When the individual 'I' arises, the Self is perceived as a limited entity. Bhagavan used to say that accepting that this individual 'I' really exists, and seeking to find Brahman as an object to be attained, is as devious a method as a thief disguised as a policeman attempting to find the thief!

Daśama: tvamasi - Ten fools set out on a pilgrimage. On the way, they had to swim across a river. On reaching the other shore, each one counted to check whether all the ten had reached safely. But as each of them counted only the others leaving himself out, each one counted only nine. Imagining that one of them had been drowned they began to weep and wail aloud. A passer-by took pity on them and asked for the reason for their grief. He found out the folly in their method of counting and in order to drive it home to them, he tapped each one of them on the head with his walking stick and began to count - *prathama: tvamasi* (you are number one), *dvitīya: tvamasi* (you are number two) and so on, till he reached the last one and pronounced *daśama*: *tvamasi* (you are the tenth). At once the tenth man began prancing about crying, "Aha! I had lost myself! Now I've been found. You are a great being who made me rediscover this!" It is in the same way that a *dēśika* (Guru) gives the *upadēśa, tat tvam asi* (You are That). The tenth man had been present all along, even when assumed to be missing, and also later when they seemed to have found him. Any one of the ten men could, in fact, be termed the 'tenth man'. Due to ignorance alone, one of them was assumed to be missing, and it was as if he was newly regained when someone pointed him out, that was all!

The science that seeks truth in the external world while ignoring the seeker is somewhat like these ten foolish men. For the same reason this sort of enquiry remains incomplete. The Self is ever-attained as the enquirer, in the one who enquires and as the practitioner, in the one who practises *sādhanās*. Without realizing this and considering oneself as an individual apart from the Self is the *mūla avidyā* (the primal ignorance). In removing this primal ignorance, the Guru is the external factor, and earnestness (*śraddhā*) the internal factor.

When one believes there is *dvaita* (duality) and later when one feels one has realized *advaita* (oneness), there is no duality. Only the Self exists. There is nothing apart from the Self. Three dimensions of truth are accepted from the seeker's stand point - *vyāvahārika* (related to the affairs of the world), *prātibhāsika* (related to the world of imagination) and *pāramārthika* (the ultimate truth). But, from the point of view of reality, the first two are merely dreams resulting from ignorance. The one who has awakened from the dream can never agree with the point of view of the dreamer, however logically presented, that the dream is real. If the dreamer has faith in the words of the one who has woken up, he too can wake up. On enquiring 'Who is this 'I' that sees duality?' the ego simply vanishes without trace and the non-dual, absolute truth shines forth.

PURNA

Wander not, in the world of chaos and confusion
Stay centered in you, the Self; make not a move
You are the fulcrum and all whirls around you
You are the pivot of the wheel of *karma* and *dharma.*
Stay there and you have clarity, peace and virtue,
Leave that centre and lo, you are out for trouble!
Do not seek yourself like the ten fools of the parable
Every seeking brings a space between you and Truth
There is not even a space for an atom, to bring in a second
The 'one-whole' fills here, there, everywhere - *pūrṇa*
Trust this saving knowledge here and now, Be silent

VERSE THIRTY-EIGHT

...vittu—pōnḍṛa
vinai-muda nāmā-yin viḷai-payan ḍṛuip-pōm
vinai-mudalā ren-ḍṛu vinavit—tanai-yaṛiyak
kart-tat tuvam-pōik karuma-mūn ḍṛuṅ kazhalu
nit-tamā mutti nilai-yīdē

vittu-pōnḍṛa	like the seed which is the cause for a tree
vinai-mudal nām āyin	if we consider ourselves as the cause for doing these actions
viḷai payan tuyppōm	we will be the enjoyers of the results of those actions
'vinai-mudal ār?' enḍṛu vinavi	on investigating 'Who is the doer?'
tanai aṛiya	once the real nature of the 'I' is known
karttattuvam pōi	the sense of doership, as 'I am the doer', having disappeared
karumam mūnḍṛum kazhalum	along with that, the three types of karma (sañchita, āgāmi and prārabdha) will drop off
nittam ām mukti nilai īdē	this, indeed, is the state of eternal release

Paraphrase:

If we consider that we are the doers of actions, the fruit of these actions will have to be experienced by us. When by enquiring, 'Who am I, the doer of deeds?' we know the real nature of the 'I', the sense of doership along with the three karmas - *sañchita, prārabdha* and *āgāmi* - will drop off. This state, devoid of *karma* of any kind, is liberation indeed.

Commentary

Just as the seed is the cause for the tree, the ego is the prime cause for the pleasures and pains of the body. The primal ignorance that one is a specific individual gives rise to the twin branches of doership and enjoyership. It is with this sense of doership that we have performed all actions in the past; this also begets present action and the desire to perform more actions in the future. This ego-seed is thus the cause for the poisonous tree of *samsāra*. Here is what the sage Vasishta says in Yoga Vasishtam-

rāma: svātma vichārōyam kōham syāmitirūpaka:
chitta durdrumabījasya dahanē dahana: smṛta:

'Dear Rama! The enquiry 'Who am I?' is found to be the fire that could burn the very seed of the vicious tree called mind.'

Until we undertake the enquiry, 'Who am I?' the individual ego will appear to be real and will bring about bondage. If we diligently enquire, 'Who is this individual that appears as 'I'?' 'Where does this ego *(aham vṛtti)* arise from?', and merge the 'I'-thought in the heart, the pure absolute existence or consciousness or supreme peace *(parama praśānti)* will shine forth. This is itself liberation. In villages often people say that someone has seen a ghost. But mostly when investigated in light what they have misapprehended to be a ghost will turn out to be a mere post or a wooden stump. The idea that one is a separate individual, a person, is similarly just an illusory appearance in the pure Self. If one boldly and alertly observes with the inward-enquiring eye: 'Who is it that remains within the body as the doer of all actions and the enjoyer of all pleasures?' the 'I'-thought will merge at its source in the heart-hole *(hṛdaya suśiram)*. There the ever-free Self will be revealed. Action and the fruit of action are based upon and supported only by the 'I'-thought.

na kartṛtvam na karmāṇi lōkasya sṛjati prabhu:
na karmaphalasamyōgam svabhāvastu pravartatē
nādattē kasyachit pāpam na chaiva sukṛtam vibhu:
ajñānēnāvṛtam jñānam tēna muhyanti jantava:

– Srimad Bhagavad Gita 5 - 14, 15

'The Lord creates neither actions nor doership. Nor does He create *karmaphala-samyōga* (the relation between action and its fruit). It is the ego born of ignorance that converts itself into natural tendencies - *vāsanās* - which then prevail upon individuals to perform action; it further grants them the fruit of their action in the form of joy and sorrow. Mistaking the individual ego for their real Self, living beings get trapped due to attachment and aversion, and fall into delusion.' Bhagavan describes the child of this delusion, the ego, as the *vinai mudal*.

Karmam mūnḍṛum kazhalum - Karma is categorized into three types: *āgāmi, sañchita and prārabdha*. They may be elucidated by means of the following example. An archer has a stock of arrows in his quiver. He has the option to destroy them without using any and this is *sañchita*. He may withdraw an arrow at the last moment, just before it is released *(āgāmi)*. In this manner, it is commonly acknowledged that *āgāmi* and *sañchita* are two types of action that are destroyed by *jnana*. On the other hand, can anyone recall an arrow that has already been released? *Prārabdha karma* is somewhat like this; therefore it has to be experienced and exhausted. This is the general understanding from the standpoint of the seeker. However, the knower's experience is at variance with this. Should there not be a target for the arrow to strike? If that target itself has been removed, then what will the arrow hit? Destiny might affect the body; yet the *jnani* never feels that he is experiencing sorrow due to his *prārabdha,* as the ignorance that he is the body is not for him. It follows therefore, that the *jnani* becomes freed from *prārabdha karma* also. For instance, if a man who has three wives dies, all the three wives become widows, not just one or two. Similarly, if the ego in the form of doership and enjoyership is annihilated, undoubtedly all the three *karmas* too get extinguished.

jñānāgni sarvakarmāṇi bhasmasāt kurutē

–Srimad Bhagavad Gita 4- 37

'The fire of *jnana* burns down all the three actions to ashes' says Bhagavad Gita. Bhagavan Ramana Maharshi was himself an example for this. In his old age, Bhagavan's body was affected by sarcoma (cancer). Even when the wound had to be cut open and stitched up several times, Bhagavan lived as though he had no disease whatsoever. Even when the body seemed to undergo immense suffering due to this fatal illness, Bhagavan, the majestic seer of truth remarked with a smile: "Who is affected? To whom is the suffering? I am not the body. I do not have a body. I have neither *prārabdha* nor happiness nor sorrow." This is the absolute freedom enjoyed by a *jīvanmukta!* The fatal disease was the cause for the greatest revelation of the power of Self-knowledge.

Freedom from the grip of the gross body is the destruction of *prārabdha*. Freedom from the grip of the subtle body is the destruction of *sañchita karma*. Freedom from the grip of the causal body is the destruction of *āgāmi karma*. These three bodies are not 'I'. A *jīvanmukta* is one who is ever-established in the awareness: 'I am the ever-free consciousness.' The Upanishads authoritatively proclaim 'when the individual ego or the *hṛdaya granthi* gets cut, instantly all doubts are resolved, all *karmas* are demolished, and the eternal, pure, free consciousness reveals itself.'

bhidyatē hṛdaya granthi: cchidyantē sarvasamśayā:
kṣīyantē chāsya karmāṇi tasmindṛṣṭē parāvarē!

– (Mundakopanishad 2–2–8)

Here too the plural term *karmāṇi* indicates all three types of *karma*.

THE ENQUIRY

Desires bind, actions bind, knowledge and ignorance too bind
The quest 'Who am I?' alone releases one from the prison of illusion
When sought, the doer and enjoyer vanish like the snake in a rope
The ego is the knot of ignorance that binds the shadow with the sun!
When one enters the Heart with the laser beam of 'Who am I?'
This chain made of shadow disappears into nothingness
And there, Self, the ever free, reigns Supreme
That indeed is Realization!

VERSE THIRTY-NINE

...mattanāi
baddhanā nennu-maṭṭē bandha-mutti chin-tanaigaḷ
baddhanā renḍṛutan-naip pārk-kuṅkāṛ—siddha-māi
nitta-muttan tṛāniṛka niṛkādēr bandha-chintai
mutti-chintai mun-niṛku mō

Mattanāi	Like a man intoxicated (ignorance)
baddhan nān ennum maṭṭē	so long as one thinks 'I am bound'
bandha mukti chintanaigaḷ	thoughts about bondage and release will keep arising
baddhan ār enḍṛu tannaip parkkuṅkāl	when one seeks 'Who is this 'I' who assumes bondage?' and knows oneself
nitta muktan tān siddhamāi niṛka	the eternally free being is revealed as the ever-attained Self
bandha chintai niṛkādēl	the delusion that 'I am bound' will disappear without a foot-hold. When that is the case,
mukti chintai mun niṛkumo?	will the thought, 'I have to gain release from samsāra' be active? Even the thoughts about finding ways for liberation will vanish.

Paraphrase:

So long as the thought, 'I am bound' remains, thoughts about either bondage or *mukti* will also be present. 'Who am I so bound?' For whom, is the bondage?' — When one enquires thus, seeking the Self, the direct experience of 'being' shines as the eternally free, ever-attained Atman. In such a state, if thoughts of bondage cannot rise, how then can thoughts about attaining *mukti* stand their ground?

Commentary

To the question: 'How can one attain freedom from bondage?' Bhagavan replies: "For whom is the bondage? Who is the one that feels he is bound? If one carefully enquires in this manner, this small 'i' will vanish. In its place, the ever-free consciousness alone will shine forth." Self-enquiry is attention-oriented. If the attention moves away from the Self, the individual-'I' will resurface and create innumerable projections in the form of bondage, freedom, *samsāra* and *sanyāsa*. Till the veiling is completely removed the practice of Self-enquiry 'Who am I?' has to be pursued moment-by-moment like the repeated chanting of a *mantra*. In the example of the rope and the snake, once one sees the rope, the snake will totally disappear, never to emerge again. But here that example will not serve us fully. When attention is directed to the ego, it disappears and consciousness reveals itself. If attention wavers, however, the ego will resurface and the reality will get veiled again. Therefore until the superimposition *(adhyāsa)* that one is a separate individual is completely and finally removed, the enquiry 'Who am I?' must be constantly practised (one must redirect attention to the heart and remain as the Self moment by moment).

Baddhan ār enḍṛu tannai pārkkum kāl - When the enquiry 'Who is bound?' is done with subtle and one-pointed attention the individual-'I' will shine forth as the absolute reality. *Siddhamāy nitta muktan* - the Self will radiate as ever-free and ever-attained. With this, all thoughts will subside naturally. Fire burns only so long as there is fuel. How can the fire survive when the fuel is exhausted? The mind cannot survive without the illusion of individuality. How then can there arise any thought about attaining Self-realization as the Self alone shines as real?

The illusion or error that 'I am a particular individual' is nourished by all the *vāsanās*, and it multiplies as the causal and subtle bodies; also as the extremely fine nervous system that carries the flow of emotions and thoughts; further also as *kapha-vāta-pitta* (phlegm, rheum, and bile). It turns into gross matter as blood vessels, bones, flesh and blood, and turning into the gross body, further creates the illusion that consciousness is inseparable from the gross body!

bandha vīḍaṭṭṛa parasukham uṭṭravār
inda nilai niṭṭṛal undīpaṛa
iṛaipaṇi niṭṭṛalām undīpaṛa – Upadesa Undiyar 29

'The greatest service to the Lord is abidance in this state of supreme bliss transcending both bondage and freedom.'

OWN ETERNITY

When delved deep into one's inner being
With the quest 'Who am I?' the 'I' reveals itself
As the self-effulgent, ever-free light of awareness
Could bondage or ignorance stay in the Atman?
How could darkness ever inhabit the sun?
The Self is never bound and is ever attained
Freedom or *nirvāṇa* is the very nature of the Self
Own eternity by knowing your oneness with 'That'

VERSE FORTY

...manattuk-kottāṅgu
uruva maruva muruvaruva mūndṛā
uṛu-mutti yenni luraip-pa—nuruva
maruva muruvaruva māyu mahantai
uru-vazhitan mutti yuṇar

manattukku ottāṅgu	According to the mental maturity of each individual
uṛum mukti mūnḍṛu ām	mukti gained is of three kinds
uruvam aruvam uruvaruvam	with form, without form, and both with form and formless
ennil uraippan	if one were to debate so, what is its truth? Listen now to what is said
uruvam aruvam uruvaruvam āyum ahantai uru azhidal mukti	annihilation of the ego which discriminates mukti as with form or without form or as both, is true liberation
uṇar	know thus and realize

Paraphrase:

If one opines that the kind of *mukti* which a *jnani* attains on release may be threefold - *mukti* with form, *mukti* without form, and *mukti* with and without form - know for certain the truth. The form of the ego that investigates whether *mukti* is with form, or without form, or with and without form, totally extinguished, the state which remains is real deliverance. Know it thus and realize.

Commentary

There will surely come a time when the *jīva,* exhausted with all sorts of pleasure and pain, and the maladies that inevitably follow doership and enjoyership, at last thirsts for real peace or complete repose. At this juncture, the words: 'Seek liberation; that is the supreme state of rest and peace', either from the *śāstrās* or from a Guru reaches his ears. This message about *mukti* awakens the inner-being, the ancient one, the primordial poet (*kavi).* His power sets to movement, ecstatic reveries about that state of *nirvāṇa.* All the *purāṇās*, mythologies and theologies are the progeny of this yearning for the 'transcendental-other' that has awakened in the human soul. This thirst for freedom and the descriptions about this state in the scriptures have led to various assumptions regarding the nature of liberation such as 'liberation while still in the body' - *jīvanmukti*, 'liberation after the body is given up' - *vidēhamukti* and so on.

Freedom is the very nature of the Self and will be revealed only through *jnana*. It is not a state of body or mind. However lofty these 'states' might be, they are only temporary. Our real nature is not a state but is existence, awareness and bliss. Liberation, I, consciousness and existence are synonyms. Due to the veiling of the ego, this ever-attained truth somehow remains hidden. It is when the ego subsides at its source that the ever-attained Self reveals itself. This is verily liberation or *mukti*. Sri Bhagavan refers to this as '*ahantai uru azhidal*' - the dissolution of the ego. This is the most clear indication of the goal to be reached.

When one enquire into the real nature of the 'I' it is revealed as the pure Self. This natural state of one's self-awareness which makes itself felt as the *sphūrti* 'I-I' is called *jñāna samādhi*. That revelation of the non-dual beingness is *nirvikalpa*. It is that ever-present experience which is here and now. Anyone who has experienced this can never again take the body and world to be real. The body-world appearance henceforth appears to the *chittvadarśi* like a movie that is played on the screen of consciousness. This is *tattva darśanam* - the vision of reality. In Upadesa Saram Sri Bhagavan declares: *chittvadarśanam tattvadarśanam*. When this is the truth, why should one identify oneself with the body-mind complex which has no existence in the light of authentic vision *(prāmāṇika jñāna)?* The text concludes with the word *uṇar* which means 'be aware' or 'be awake'. If we combine the first and the last words of thls text, we get the message *uḷḷadu uṇar* - 'Be aware of the truth that IS'. The Kathopanishad says: 'Be awake and be aware. Approach the sages and know the Atman.' This indeed is the eternal message of the awakened ones and the Vedas.

...īdu—aruḷramaṇan
uḷḷadu nāṟpadum onḍṛu kali veṇbāvām
uḷḷadu kāṭṭum oḷi

'These forty *ślokas* revealing the truth have been strung together as *kaliveṇbā* by Sri Ramana satguru, the embodiment of compassion and grace. This is the light that illumines the ultimate truth.'

THE BUBBLE SWALLOWS THE OCEAN

When exhausted with pleasures and pains
And the maladies of doership and enjoyership
One thirsts for real peace or complete repose
There, the words: 'seek liberation' reverberates in the ether
This message of *mukti* awakens the inner being
The power of the Ancient one, the Primordial poet (*kavi)*
Unlocks streams of ecstatic reveries about *nirvāṇa*
This yearning for the 'transcendental-other' kindled in the soul
Fascinates the infinite to manifest in flesh and Word
His message makes the finite see the infinite in its own womb
The grace of Him makes the bubble swallow the ocean!